Managing People at Work

Managing People at Work

Leadership Styles and Influence Strategies

MAHFOOZ A. ANSARI

SAGE PUBLICATIONS
New Delhi / Newbury Park / London

First published in 1990 by
Sage Publications India Pvt. Ltd.
M 32 Greater Kailash Market I
New Delhi 110 048

Sage Publications Inc.   **Sage Publications Ltd.**
2111 Hillcrest Drive   28 Banner Street
Newbury Park, California 91320   London EC1Y 8QE

Published by Tejeshwar Singh for Sage Publications India Pvt Ltd.,
phototypeset at Jayigee Enterprises and printed at Chaman Offset Printers, Delhi.

ISBN 0-8039-9650-0 (US-hb.)   81-7036-194-X (India-hb.)
     0-8039-9651-9 (US-pb.)   81-7036-195-8 (India-pb.)

Contents

List of Tables

List of Figures

Acknowledgments

Many people have contributed to the development of this volume—some indirectly by shaping my interest and world-views, and some more directly by assisting with data collection, analysis and literature review. Among those who first kindled my interest in leadership and power relationships were Jai B.P. Sinha and Howard J. Baumgartel. The expressed personal concerns and involvement they exemplified greatly influenced my views. Their constructive comments and advice on the research proposal proved to be of immense value to this project. Much of what I learned from them remains with me and my dialogues with them continue to be intellectually and attitudinally meaningful.

This volume is the product of a team of persons. I am particularly indebted to Rashmi Shukla and Reeta Kool for their assistance with data collection and coding. Rashmi Shukla also helped with data analysis and assembling the manuscript. My special thanks are due to Alka Kapoor who assisted with the literature review, to Kanika Tandon and Uma Lakhtakia who helped with data analysis and proof-reading the manuscript, to Arti Shankar and Seema Saxena for assembling the final manuscript, to V.N. Katiyar for meticulously typing the manuscript, and to Sudama Prasad for his painstaking cyclostyling. This project would not have been possible without their assistance.

I feel impelled to record my warm appreciation to innumerable friends who helped and encouraged me during this research. The names of Lila Krishnan, B.N. Patnaik, A.K. Sharma and N.K. Sharma come to my mind most readily, but the list is definitely much longer.

Funding for this research was provided by the Indian Council of Social Science Research, New Delhi. My warmest appreciation is expressed to this institution and to the many public and private sector organizations as well as the various individual managers who took time off from their working day to participate in this study.

Finally, I must acknowledge the contribution of my wife and children who gave me the time I needed to accomplish this undertaking. They indeed continue to be a source of encouragement for my writing.

Preface

Seeking to understand and predict human behavior is one of the most challenging tasks for anyone who has ever interacted with another individual. Business organizations are no exception. They are usually in some stage of planning for management succession. They try to identify executives and managers who have the greatest potential for task accomplishment and good leadership. In essence, they try to *predict* which managers will achieve organizational objectives. With few exceptions, 'prediction' ends in 'best guess'. Nevertheless, we predict events even though we cannot influence outcomes.

The central theme of this volume is leadership as a power phenomenon in our society of organizations. In essence, it deals with the leader's exercise of power over subordinates and superiors. It blends a theoretical foundation and particular application so that it is relevant to the tempo of our worklife today.

Over the past several years, social psychologists have touched upon two of the most difficult problems of human behavior at work—leadership and power. We have learned far more about the nature of these concepts than could have been stated with any confidence even a few years ago. This includes information layered upon information; a mixture of the truly important and the utterly useless; and endless complexity. The magnitude of the puzzle now becomes somewhat apparent. Thus, Chapter 1 of this volume presents a review of what has been learned, and where the discoveries might lead. Chapter 2 deals with the objectives and strategy of the main survey. Several research questions are posed, followed by a note on the research site and sample, and instruments and procedures. Finally, analytical strategies are highlighted.

Chapters 3 and 4 present the main survey data along with a discussion and conclusion—the former comprising data on managing subordinates and the latter on managing immediate superiors.

An attempt to integrate the findings on downward and upward influence processes is made in Chapter 5. Finally, Chapter 6 deals with a summary of the main findings, potential limitations of the survey, implications of the findings for those in leadership roles, and directions for future research. I hope that the intellectual flavor of this volume will help to open the reader's eyes to organizational life.

January 1990   M.A. ANSARI

1   Introduction

Leadership as an Influence Process

This book provides empirical evidence to support the concept of 'leadership' as a particular type of power relationship. In essence, it deals with reciprocal influence processes in leadership—that is, leader power over subordinates and that of subordinates over leader. Five key elements are considered in this volume—leadership style, bases of power, leader behavior, perceived climate and organizational characteristics. These elements are examined in relation to the actual use of power tactics by leaders and subordinates. While examining the relationships between the first three key elements and influence tactics, the role of objective organizational climate is treated as a moderator.

The fundamental aim of this chapter is to present leadership as a particular type of power relationship. Rather than provide a comprehensive review of an endless or exhaustive series of individual studies, it mainly highlights the approaches to and findings on leadership and power. The first section of this chapter reviews what we know about leadership effectiveness. The second deals exclusively with the exercise of power. Finally, the third section is devoted to the main task of considering leadership as a power phenomenon.

The Background

What makes an organization successful? Some management analysts believe that the basic difference between a successful and unsuccessful organization is its leadership. Evidence (Schultz, 1982) exists that half of all new businesses fail within the first two years and only a third survive five years. In most cases the failures are caused by poor leadership. Therefore, an organization's leaders are a major determinant of its success or failure (Katz and Kahn, 1978). In other words, 'the successful organizations consistently differ from ineffective organizations in one respect—the former are characterised by dynamic and effective leadership' (Hersey and Blanchard, 1977, p. 83). Such generalisation is a significant element underlying the vast amount of investigations into the area of leadership. Hence, leadership abilities are crucial skills which must be learned and practised to achieve organizational goals. They are the focus of activity for managers through which organizational objectives are accomplished as they constitute an important element of the managerial process. Controlling, planning, organizing and innovating constitute the balance of a manager's job. It should, however, be noted that people not having official sanction from organization can also use leadership in organizational settings.

'Most leaders are despised, some leaders are feared, few leaders are praised, and the rare good leader is never noticed' (Tao Te King, 600 BC as quoted in Andriessen and Drenth, 1984, p. 481). This statement implies that, even in the very distant past, leadership was controversial and today it has become more complicated than ever before. It has come under pressure in all types of social institutions (for instance, the family, school, church and club), labor organizations, and in politics. Notions such as authority, responsibility and centralized decision-making power have been replaced by new ideas like the primacy of the group, the disposability of the leader, one-man–one-vote, and the role of a diligent leader. Similarly, in various modern organizations, the rewards and punishments controlled by the leader have, in the 1980s, been replaced by expert, informational and referent power.

The term leadership has no single and clearly agreed upon definition. In fact, it means different things to different people. As a result, different researchers have defined leadership differently depending on their individual perspective and research purposes.

Thus Bennis (1959, p. 259) comments: '. . . we have invented an endless proliferation of terms to deal with it [leadership] . . . and still the concept is not sufficiently defined.' Similarly, after a comprehensive review of leadership research, Stogdill (1974, p. 259) states that 'there are almost as many definitions of leadership as there are persons who have attempted to define the concept'. In this section, I do not intend to resolve the controversy over the definition, nor will I attempt to provide the single-best definition. I am simply trying to make the readers aware of the problem of leadership definition. However, for the present purpose, leadership will be viewed as *the process of influencing people in efforts toward the achievement of some particular goal(s)*. A leadership style will be viewed as *the characteristic manner in which a leader exercises influence over the subordinates*.

Approaches

Although the literature on leadership is voluminous, much of it is still confusing and contradictory. In order to make our way through this thick forest, I shall consider the various approaches that explain leadership effectiveness. In the study of leadership, the early trait and behavior theories and the current situational and contingency theories have generally focused on the *same* goal — that of identifying the factors which affect leadership effectiveness.

The trait approach sought to identify some universal psychological and physical characteristics which leaders possessed to a greater degree than non-leaders. It examined leadership by posing such questions as: What traits do leaders have in common that other people do not? The behavior approach tried to explain leadership in terms of behavior that a person is engaged in. The main question asked was: Is one leadership style more effective than any other leadership styles? Thus attention shifted from a concern of 'who the leader is' to 'what the leader does'. Contemporary theorists developed situational approaches of leadership to explain the inadequacies of previous approaches in reconciling and bringing together the diversity of research findings. The basic tenet of contingency-determined leadership theories was: how important is it for a leader to analyze each situation and 'then play it by ear'? Taken together, these approaches viewed leadership as a complex process which would involve the leader, the subordinates, and the situation. Thus, the modern approach led the leadership theorists to believe that 'effective leadership is a function of the characteristics of the leader, style of leadership, the characteristics of the subordinates, and the situation surrounding the leadership environment' (Szilagyi and Wallace, 1980, p. 278).

Trait Approach

Prior to the fifties, interest in the personal traits of leaders clearly waned, notably because a set of identifiable characteristics could be found that differentiated leaders from non-leaders or successful leaders from unsuccessful leaders. An exhaustive search was made to identify the biographical, personal, emotional, physical and intellectual traits of leaders. For example, leaders were found to be taller and heavier (Gowin, 1915), healthier (Bellingrath, 1930), and physically smarter (Patridge, 1934) than non-leaders. In a review of dozens of studies dealing with leadership traits, Stogdill (1948) indicated that intelligence, physical traits, social background, personality, and task-related characteristics were traits on the basis of which a distinction could be made between leaders and non-leaders. He concluded that leadership is not a personal property, but certain fixed personal characteristics seem to play a crucial role in leadership. Stogdill, however, asserted that the search for leadership in physical characteristics and personality traits was a misdirected one.

Though the results of studies identified certain salient traits of leaders, understanding or predicting leadership effectiveness received little attention. The list of traits is endless, and aspects like personality are only a few of the many factors which play a vital role in leadership effectiveness. Byrd (1940) analyzed this category of research up to 1940 and reported that only 5 per cent of the traits identified in any one study were common to four or more investigations. So, one cannot differentiate successful leaders from unsuccessful leaders simply on the basis of a finite set of traits. Gibb (1954, p. 227) concluded that 'the numerous studies of personalities of leaders have failed to find any consistent patterns of traits which characterize leaders'. Such negative results are partly due to separating leadership studies from different situations, as the effectiveness of leadership depends to a large extent on the environment which surrounds the influence process. A particular leadership pattern may work effectively and successfully in one situation but may be totally ineffective and unsuccessful in another situation. Also, trait differences between highly successful leaders and less successful leaders do not hold up well from one research to another. It is possible that replication of the investigation would not show the same results. In his synthesis of all known empirical leadership investigations, Stogdill (1974) concluded that only one leadership quality — letting subordinates know what to expect and what is expected of them — encouraged both productivity and job satisfaction. Thus, uniformity of traits across all levels is questioned. Additionally,

> focusing on individual traits does not show what the individual *actually does* in a leadership situation. Traits identify who the leader is, not the behavioral patterns he or she will exhibit in attempting to *influence* subordinate actions. The trait approach has ignored the subordinate and his or her effect on leadership... therefore, focusing on one part only of the influence relationship provides an incomplete view of the leadership process (Szilagyi and Wallace, 1980, pp. 282-83, emphasis added).

Behavior Approach

During the 1950s, the unsuccessful efforts to strike 'gold' in the trait approach 'mines' directed investigators to turn their attention toward the specific behavior of leaders to check if there was something different in the behavior of successful and effective leaders. According to this point of view, successful leaders with a particular style were expected to lead persons and groups for the attainment of specific goals, which would result in high productivity and morale. Investigations and researches on leadership in formal organizations and in small informal groups resulted in the identification of a restricted number of leadership styles. In brief, some view authoritarian or task-oriented and participative or people-oriented styles as discrete dichotomies (for instance, Lewin, Lippitt and White, 1939); others (such as Likert, 1961, 1967; Vroom and Yetton, 1973) conceptualize them as the two extremes of a broad continuum which can be further divided into a number of categories; still others treat them as two orthogonal dimensions (for instance, Halpin and Winer, 1952; Blake and Mouton, 1964). Some of the representative approaches to the dimensions of leader behavior are described below.

1. *The Lewin, Lippitt and White Study*: One of the earliest and probably the most influential attempts to delineate the dimensions of leadership behavior was made by Lewin *et al*. (1939). They distinguished two non-overlapping types—authoritarian and democratic (in addition to laissez-faire style). Their study can be summarized as follows: The experimenters organized groups of 10-year old boys into clubs. Each club was exposed to three different leadership styles—authoritarian, democratic or laissez-faire. The leaders of these groups were adults trained by the experimenters to exercise the three styles. During each meeting, the behavior of the boys was observed and interviews were conducted with them as well as their parents. The clubs met once a week for several months. Some general conclusions emerged. (*i*) Groups with democratic leaders were the most effective and efficient. The members seemed to be group-minded. They pronounced 'we' rather than 'I'. (*ii*) Groups with authoritarian leaders tended to display hostility and aggression toward either the leader or a scapegoat for the leader, and the atmosphere of the group was strained and tense. (*iii*) The least productive was the laissez-faire style. Obviously, the democratic style was considered to be the most effective.

2. *The Ohio State Leadership Studies*: Among the various research efforts that developed after World War II, the most comprehensive and replicated of behavioral theories resulted from research conducted by the Ohio State University (Columbus, US) researchers. The main objective of these researches was to identify the independent (orthogonal) dimensions of leader behavior and to determine the effects of these dimensions on work group performance and satisfaction. The Ohio State researchers began their studies with 1,800 observationally derived statements which could be grouped into ten broad categories of leader behavior (such as, communication, domination and evaluation). By employing a factor analysis approach, they ended up with two dimensions: consideration and initiating structure. Taken together, the two dimensions accounted for about 83 per cent of the variance in the matrix (Halpin and Winer, 1952). 'Initiating structure' refers to the extent to which the leader defines and structures the various tasks and roles of group members for the attainment of goals. 'Consideration' is

viewed as the extent to which the leader has a supportive work relationship characterized by warmth and mutual trust, developing good relations, and a respect for the feelings and suggestions of group members.

Some of the major conclusions about the Ohio State Studies, according to Vroom (1976), are as follows:

1. Leaders who are high on consideration tend to have subordinates who are more satisfied with them than those who are low on this leadership dimension. This is by far the most consistent finding in the literature.
2. Leaders who are high on consideration tend to have subordinates who are likely to have fewer absences.
3. Consideration and initiating structure interact significantly in determining both grievances and turnover rates.
4. The relationship between consideration and rated leader effectiveness varies with the population. For example, a negative correlation has been reported for air-crew commanders in combat while a positive correlation has been found for managers and office staff in an industrial organization.
5. Effects of high and low scores on these dimensions may be mediated by such situational factors as subordinates' characteristics, superior's characteristics, and task characteristics.

The main difficulty with the Ohio State formulation is that of causal ambiguity (Yukl, 1981). Studies are based on the 'static correlational' approach (Korman, 1966). They employ questionnaire measures and examine the relationship between leader behavior and criterion measures (such as, group performance and subordinate satisfaction). Yukl, (1981) states that whenever a positive correlation is found, there is no way of determining causality. In fact, there can be several interpretations. For example, one common assumption may be that a positive correlation between consideration and subordinate performance means that consideration causes subordinate performance. Another possible interpretation may be that consideration is caused by subordinate performance. That is, leaders will act in a more considerate manner toward subordinates who perform effectively.

However, while making criticisms, we should not forget the other side of the coin, i.e., the contributions of the Ohio State efforts to distinguish and interpret the exhibited behaviors of leaders in a fully designed and descriptive manner. The contribution of the Ohio State Studies in giving basic knowledge to leadership literature is immeasurable. Also, they have laid the foundation stone on which the contemporary approach is built.

3. *The Michigan Leadership Studies:* Leadership studies were in progress at the University of Michigan's Survey Research Center at about the same time the Ohio State research was being conducted. The basic aim of almost all researchers emerging from the University of Michigan was to identify the styles of leadership which were related to the measures of performance and satisfaction. Like the Ohio State Studies, the Michigan group also developed two distinct dimensions of leadership behavior from their studies which they labelled job-centered leadership and employee-centered leadership styles. Like the Ohio State dimension of initiating structure, the job-centered leadership emphasized the broad technical and work-related aspects of the job. The employee-centered leader, on the other hand, tended to emphasize on interpersonal relations and the delegation of responsibilities. This factor was similar to the Ohio State dimension of consideration.

The criticisms against the Michigan studies focused on two aspects. First, evidence (Hill, 1973) exists that leadership style/behavior changes according to situations. Secondly, the cohesiveness of the group, the nature of the subordinate's personal traits, or the task factors were not included in the Michigan studies while investigating the effectiveness of a particular leader behavior.

Probably the most popularly known among the Michigan contributions is that of the participative style of leadership which grew out of the hard and massive data collected by Rensis Likert (1961, 1967). This style was proposed with the assumption that it is people-oriented and productive irrespective of organizational variations. Likert isolated three variables which were representative of the System IV model (or participative management): (*i*) the use by managers of supportive relationships, (*ii*) the use of group decision-making and group methods of supervision, and (*iii*) high performance goals.

The first variable (i.e., the principle of supportive relationships) is exemplified by such factors as the degree to which the superior exhibits confidence and trust; interest in the subordinates' future; understanding of, and desire to, help overcome problems; training and developing the subordinates to find better ways of doing the work; giving help in solving problems as opposed to always giving the answer; giving support by making available the required physical resources; communicating the information in such a way that subordinates must know how to do their jobs as well as those things they would like to know and to be able to identify more closely with the operations; the degree to which the superior seeks out and attempts to use the subordinates' ideas and opinion; approachableness; and the extent to which credit and recognition for accomplishment is given (Likert, 1961, 1967).

The second variable (i.e., group decision-making and group methods of supervision) requires that the whole organization be turned into overlapping groups with individuals having multiple group-membership; that they (subordinates) help and facilitate the process of communication across hierarchies; and that all subordinates of a particular group make joint decisions and arrange for group supervision. Thus,

> communication is clear and adequately understood. Important issues are recognized and dealt with. The atmosphere is one of 'no-nonsense' with emphasis on high productivity, high quality and low costs. Decisions are reached promptly, clear-cut responsibilities are established and tasks are performed rapidly and productively. Confidence and trust pervade all aspects of the relationship. The group's capacity for effective problem solving is maintained by examining and dealing with group processes when necessary (Likert, 1967, pp. 50-51).

The third variable (i.e., high performance goals) follows from the fore-mentioned two principles—supportive relationships and overlapping groups (i.e., linking-pins in Likert's terminology). This variable suggests that the leader should guide the group in setting performance goals that are high *but* realistic.

The importance of a participative leadership approach in certain situations has been recognized as an applied value of the formal study of leadership. Even in those organizations where real employee participation is scarce, the term 'participative management' can be heard. In fact, this phrase is over-used and applied even where it does not exist. In any event, this shows the popularity of the participative approach.

Generally speaking, employees' active participation in the decision-making process is the basic feature of participative leadership. Because of employees' participation in the decision-making process, the manager will be free from less important tasks and thus he or she will have the time to pay greater attention to more important matters. Besides, employees have opportunities to train themselves for further promotions within the hierarchy. Out of sheer interest the employees will do their best to carry out the decision in the best possible manner and feel self-worthy.

But the effects of participative leadership are situational, though positive. Various factors affect the relationship between participation and organizational productivity. Like knowledge and ability of the group leaders, the nature of task (i.e., routine or complex, structured or unstructured) has been seen to play an important role. For example, the findings of House and Baetz (1979) indicate that unlike the complex tasks, little participation is needed for simple routine tasks, since generally no relationship exists between participation and performance. It has also been found that task complexity affects both the knowledge and experience factors simultaneously. House and Baetz state that participation as a moderator variable is crucial for relatively dull tasks as people willingly participate in interesting tasks.

In reality, the use of participative management is limited. Stogdill (1974) examined the relationship between participative management and cohesiveness and productivity in twenty-six organizations. He found that out of 26, 22 correlations were negative while 10 of them were statistically significant. A similar view was expressed by Yukl (1971, p. 432): 'research on the relation between consideration and productivity does not yield consistent results'. Baumgartel (1974) also states that the participative system within the university is seldom justified due to its effectiveness. Rather, the rationale is based on the 'right' to participate and on the inherent value of self-rule. Two recent reviews (Stogdill, 1974; Locke and Schweiger, 1979) with respect to the relationship between participative styles and the measures of organizational productivity are summarized in Table 1.1. These reviews suggest that participative leadership is more closely related to job satisfaction and group cohesiveness than to productivity. Stogdill's review categorically points out that essentially there is no difference between participative and task-oriented leadership so far as productivity is concerned.

Table 1.1 *Relationships of Participative Leadership with Outcome Variables Reported in Published Literature (Percentages)*

Variables	Stogdill (1974)			Locke & Schweiger (1979)		
	+	0	−	+	0	1
Productivity	30	57	13	22	56	22
Satisfaction	67	25	8	60	30	10
Cohesiveness	56	25	19	NA	NA	NA

Note: NA: information not available. +, 0 and − indicate positive, zero and negative correlations, respectively.

Does this mean that participative leadership (or management) is a complete failure and should not be practised? This is not the case. Locke and Schweiger (1979) feel that such a failure may partially be attributed to the fact that surveys have paid very little attention to the psychometric properties of the scales measuring participative leadership. In fact, researchers have used different scales in different studies. It may, therefore, be reasoned that because the researchers have used psychometrically weak instruments, the results are obscure. The presence of factors like managerial philosophy, organizational climate, time and money, separately or in combination, limit the extent to which a participative technique can be successfully implemented. To overcome these barriers, first of all, limitations must be minimized. Besides, the establishment of a favorable (benign) organizational climate is necessary (Likert, 1967).

Contingency / Situational Approach

In view of the complexity of findings with respect to trait and behavioral approaches, modern behavioral scientists propose that in the prediction of leadership success, the consideration of situational factors like the traits of the leader and subordinates, nature of the task, stage of group development, group structure and several organizational factors is a must. The basic tenet of the contingency approach is that for the evaluation of leadership effectiveness, not only leader behavior but some other variables should also be considered, because a particular style cannot be equally effective or successful in all situations. There are various approaches to isolate or distinguish crucial elements deemed to be more effective or successful than the other ones. This is the reason why the contingency approach has gained wider recognition in modern times. Some of the major contingency or situational approaches are described below.

1. *Fiedler's Contingency Model*: One of the earliest and perhaps most important contributions to the theory of leadership effectiveness which included situational factors in its framework is the model set forth by Fiedler (1967). According to this model, the tasks for the model builders are to discover which leader characteristics are important; which situational factors potentially condition leader behavior; and how these two sets of variables *interact* in determining leadership effectiveness. Fiedler proposes that the need structure of the leader and the favorableness of the situation play a vital role in the effectiveness of the leader. Instead of measuring leadership behavior, Fiedler measures a personal property— leader's attitude towards the least preferred co-worker (*LPC*)— through a semantic-differential scale. The scale consists of 13 bipolar words rated on an 8-point scale. Low *LPC* means that a leader is basically more concerned with task activity than with interpersonal relations. High *LPC* means that a leader is more concerned with interpersonal relations than with task activity. Initially, Fiedler investigated the relationship between the *LPC* scores and the objective measures of group performance. The results were confusing: sometimes the relationship was found to be negative and sometimes positive. He conceptualized these differences in results in terms of the following three situational factors:

Leader-member relations: This is the degree to which group members like and trust the leader and, therefore, are willing to follow him or her.

Task structure: This is the extent to which the group task can be spelled out step-by-step and performed according to standard or well-defined procedure.

Position power: This is the power inherent in the leader's position, including the freedom to hire, fire, promote or demote.

The model predicts that the low *LPC* leader (task-oriented) will be more effective in situations that are either very favorable or very unfavorable to the leader than in situations of intermediate favorability. High *LPC* leaders (relationship-oriented) will be more effective in situations of moderate favorability than in situations of either extreme. On the basis of various researches, Fiedler concluded that the better the leader-member relations, the more structured the task, and the stronger the leader's power, the more favorable the situation is to the leader. Some major conclusions from Fiedler's contingency model are as follows: (*a*) Persons who are unsuccessful in one leadership situation may be quite successful in another. (*b*) No one set of personality traits or leadership characteristics will determine an effective leader for every situation. Both the situation and the leader's personality must be evaluated in order to select a successful leader. (*c*) There is no such thing as an ideal leader. (*d*) Task-motivated as well as relationship-motivated leaders excel in some situations and not in others. (*e*) The model offers some guidelines to help management to predict the appropriate situation for a specific leadership style. (*f*) The model suggests some possibilities for changing the behavior of leaders to *fit* situational requirements. If this is not possible, then perhaps the situation can be changed to *fit* the behavior of the existing leaders.

A stream of research has appeared for almost two decades to determine the validity of the model. The studies (for instance, Graen *et al.*, 1970; Schriesheim and Kerr, 1977) have identified some serious shortcomings. The important issue is that of the unidimensionality of the *LPC* variable and its low test-retest reliability. The three aspects of the situation are conceptually obscure and predictions of the situational cell are not completely supported by empirical data. Another point is that the relationship between the leader and the situational variables is not included in the model. Besides, the critics say that Fiedler has involved non-significant and small correlations in the model. Except for task structure, the other two situational factors appear to be a part of individual characteristics.

Despite its limitations, this model has stimulated much theorizing for over twenty years and has exerted a powerful impact on organizational behavior literature. Being one of the first contingency approaches to leadership, it is a crucial source of new ideas related to situational leadership. The model provides the subtle but crucial information that a particular leadership style may be effective in one situation but not in another. Most importantly, the effectiveness or success of leadership style is dependent on the motivational bases of the leader and their interaction with situational factors, and by modifying either of them, the effectiveness of a particular work environment can be improved.

2. *Hersey-Blanchard's Situational Model*: The situational model (Hersey and Blanchard, 1977) was proposed to combine the Fiedler studies with previous studies of the Ohio State University to construct a tri-dimensional model of leadership effectiveness. It was originally called the life cycle theory of leadership. The first two dimensions are 'task behavior' and 'relationship behavior' which correspond approximately to initiating structure and consideration respectively. The third dimension in the model deals explicitly with one single situational moderator, called 'follower maturity'.

According to the situational model, leadership effectiveness is defined as the *matching* of the appropriate leadership style with the appropriate situation. Follower maturity is defined as 'the capacity to set high but attainable goals (achievement motivation), willingness to take responsibility, and education and/or experience' (Hersey and Blanchard, 1977, p. 161). Maturity has two related components: 'job maturity' and 'psychological maturity'. The former refers to the subordinate's task-relevant skills and technical knowledge while the latter refers to a feeling of self-confidence and self-respect.

The model suggests that the manager should check the maturity level of the work group being dealt with and then apply the appropriate leadership style which fits that maturity level. Imagine a task force which has well-motivated and competent members who are working for the first time on a project. At the early stage of this project, the group needs considerable structure, so that the group understands its purposes and limitations, but little consideration (relationship) is needed. At the next stage of group development, more attention can be paid to building a good emotional relationship with the subordinates, although much structure is still needed. By the time the group reaches the third stage in its maturity cycle, less task behavior is needed, but considerable emotional support is still important. At the final stage, the group is functioning as independent professionals who require a minimum of structure or consideration. Thus, the group proceeds about its tasks with a minimum of supervision.

Critics feel that the conceptual basis of the theory is weak because the theory does not provide a coherent, explicit rationale for hypothesized relationships (see Yukl, 1981). In addition, Hersey and Blanchard have provided no validation studies testing their theory. Nevertheless, one contribution of this model is noteworthy—there is adaptability and flexibility of leader behavior. That is, the model holds that different subordinates be treated differently, and that the same subordinate be treated differently depending upon circumstances, i.e., maturity level. In a nutshell, the model predicts the possibility of a regression in subordinate maturity, which again calls for a flexible adjustment of the leader's behavior (Yukl, 1981). In any event, full-proof studies are needed to test the applicability of this model.

3. House's Path-Goal Model: Robert House (1971) developed the path-goal model of leadership by integrating the expectancy model of motivation with the Ohio State University research. The model has gone through much refinement and extension in recent years (e.g., House and Dessler, 1974; Stinson and Johnson, 1975). The model assumes that the leader is responsible for 'increasing personal payoffs to subordinates for work-goal attainment, and making the path to these payoffs easier to travel by clarifying it, reducing roadblocks and pitfalls, and increasing the opportunities for personal satisfaction en route' (House, 1971, p. 324). In accomplishing these activities, initiating structure acts to 'clarify the path', and consideration makes the path 'easier to travel'.

According to this model, the 'best style' of leadership is seen as a function of the individual and the task. The model holds that subordinates will view the behavior of leaders as acceptable to the extent that they see such behavior either as an immediate source of satisfaction or as instrumental to future satisfaction. Thus, specific dimensions of the style are important. For example, some people respond best to leaders who are friendly and approachable while others respond to leaders who tell them what is expected of them. With regard to task as a situational variable, the model predicts that the extent to which leaders help clarify path-goal relationships determines the acceptability of their behavior. For example, when tasks and goals are readily evident and the work is basically of a routine nature, any attempt to further explain the job is seen as unnecessarily close control. In such a setting, a supportive leader is more likely to have satisfied subordinates than a directive leader. On the other hand, when the task is highly unstructured, a directive leader is more likely to have satisfied subordinates.

In the initial version of the model (House, 1971), only two leader behavior were included: initiating structure and consideration. The latest version of the model (House and Mitchell, 1974) includes a total of four categories of leader behavior: supportive, directive, participative and achievement-oriented. Causal relationships for the effects of each leadership behavior on subordinate effort have been advanced and tested (see, for instance, Yukl, 1981, for an extended discussion). Yet, critics say that the major hypotheses of the model are valid only in some cases. For example, the findings are stronger for the consideration hypotheses than for the structuring hypotheses. Similarly, they are stronger for satisfaction than for subordinate performance. To date there has been little validation research testing the model. So it is too early to make any substantive assessment. Nevertheless, much of what has been done is encouraging and the direction the model is taking holds promise.

Conclusions

As mentioned at the outset, this section does not aim to provide a comprehensive review of the field of leadership. Instead, our main task is to highlight the representative models in each approach. We have not touched upon a number of other models such as the managerial grid (Blake and Mouton, 1964), the leader-participation model (Vroom and Yetton, 1973), the leadership-continuum approach (Tannenbaum and Schmidt, 1958), and the vertical dyadic linkage model of leadership (Dansereau, Graen and Haga, 1975). This certainly does not mean that they are unimportant. Had these been included, I would have been forced to cut out those which have been included because of space constraints.

Finally, if we take an overall perspective there is every reason to conclude that 'substantial progress has been made in developing an understanding of the leadership processes and identifying the determinants of leadership effectiveness', (Yukl, 1981, p. 269).

Leadership Studies in India

D. Sinha reviewed over 500 studies in industrial psychology which were carried out during the period 1926–70. Of these, about 25 studies were concerned with leadership and supervision. While summing up these studies, Sinha (1972, p. 210) made the following comments:

Researches on leadership and supervision in industry and government organizations have been significant, and the primary question has been whether Indian researchers on the pattern of effective supervision and its impact on worker behavior yield similar or different findings from those obtained elsewhere. While the reports show some conflicting results, there is ample evidence that they generally support the Western studies on the behavioral characteristics of effective supervisors.

Jai B. P. Sinha (1981) updated and expanded a part of the survey reviewed by D. Sinha (1972). He reviewed 39 studies on organizational leadership which appeared between 1971 and 1976. In his review, some of the studies were related to the emergence of leadership (for instance, Jain, 1971; Singh and Misra, 1973) and leadership functions (such as, Dayal, 1975; Sheth, 1972). But a bulk of studies were counted on the styles of effective leadership. This trend continues even now. In a recent volume entitled *Psychology in India*, Khandwalla (1988, p. 190) concludes that 'the linkage of leadership to macro-organizational phenomena such as the organization's operating context, its goals, strategies, structure and systems, its technology, etc., has not been studied.' The more recent studies also indicate that, with some exceptions (Prakasam, 1980; Sayeed and Mathur, 1981; Singh, 1983), the organizational leadership using the current situational approaches is relatively few.

Literature is witness that the issue of effective styles of leadership is crucial yet controversial. In general, the growing trend of democratization of the workplace in the West highlights the importance of participative leadership which has been shown to be effective as well as satisfying in the long run; the reverse holds true for autocratic leadership. The authoritarian-democratic dichotomy of leadership styles has attracted the attention of Indian researchers too. Early researchers such as Meade (1967), Meade and Whittaker (1967), and Murphy (1953) asserted that because Indian culture, by and large, is authoritarian, it is authoritarian leadership which would promote organizational productivity in the Indian set-up. But this assertion has lost ground in recent years. Indeed, many Indian investigators have tried to prove that people-oriented leadership (democratic, considerate or participative) is universally effective (e.g., Daftuar and Krishna, 1971; Kakar, 1971; Pandey, 1976; Pestonjee, 1973; Sarveswara Rao, 1973; Singh and Pestonjee, 1974; Venkoba Rao, 1970)—that is, if it is effective in the West, it can also be effective in a developing country like India.

However, some evidence is available which seems to be inconsistent with the participative approach but somewhat congruent with the autocratic approach. For example, Sharma (1973) states that the headmasters of open-climate type schools were high on 'initiating structure'. Another piece of evidence comes from a systematic study by Saiyadain (1974). He has reported that employees high on social competence felt more satisfied with autocratic supervisors. Although autocratic supervisors were less rewarding than the democratic ones, they could be more satisfying to those who were predisposed to establish meaningful and mutually supportive relationships. Furthermore, Sinha (1974) postulates that a participative style of management may experience a reversal if the surrounding cultural influences are not actively checked.

These conflicting results, thus, emphasize the need to draw upon familial values in India to set up organizations just as the Japanese have been doing (Ray, 1970). Sinha and Sinha (1974), for the first time, expressed doubts about the appropriateness of the authoritarian (F) style in Indian culture. They identified a few sociocultural values—such as, preference for *aram* (rest or relaxation without being tired), dependence proneness, lack of commitment, showing-off, personalized relationships, and lack of team-orientation—some of which, of course, seem to share the rubric of authoritarianism. Given the presence of such values, Sinha (1980) wondered whether a task-oriented (with a blend of nurturance), discipline-minded, tough leadership with a personalized approach would be more successful in the Indian setting. Such a leadership style was named 'nurturant task' (NT).

Not that participative (P) management is not conducive; rather, it is considered to be trans-cultural and, hence, applicable to Indian organizations, too. However, when this system was introduced into public sector enterprises, the net result was found to be far from satisfactory (Sinha, 1973). So it was postulated that unless an organization passes through a phase of preparation in which employees understand and accept the normative structure and goals of the organization and thereby develop a fair amount of commitment to the organization, any attempt to introduce participative management is likely to be misunderstood (Sinha, 1973). The employees tend to take undue advantage causing indiscipline and loss of productivity

e P style of leadership.
action effect of success.
< 0.01). The analysis
electricity company
as more nurturant
the contrary, the
eived the climate
ess technology,
cessful execu-
also perceived
the salient
tulates in
e valida-
port of
ratory
ship

his, Sinha (1980)
d to the Indian

...inates have
...end to depend
on their superior
...ed (De, 1974; Sinha
ork relationship. They
perior (Kakar, 1971) and
valu... ...lf. Yet, the sub-
...tra hard as a par.. of their efforts
...onship with the superior. Under
Sinha (1980, p.55), a nurturant task
NT leader 'cares for his subordinates,
...ersonal interest in their well-being and,
...d to their growth'. He, however, makes his
...ent on the subordinate's task accomplishment.
...ader is effective for those subordinates who want
...dependency, a personalized relationship and a status
...erential. He or she helps his or her subordinates grow up, mature
and assume greater responsibility. Once the subordinates reach a
reasonable level of maturity, they generate pressure on the leader
to shift to the participative (P) style. From this perspective, the NT
style is considered to be a *forerunner* of the P style in the reciprocal
influence processes between a leader and his or her subordinates.
The only uniqueness of this model is the priority attached to productivity over job satisfaction. It assumes that meaningful and
lasting job satisfaction has a precondition, i.e., the productivity of
an organization.

The NT style receives meaningful support from later findings,
too. For example, a survey (Ansari, 1981) was conducted to examine
the leadership styles and organizational climate for successful and
unsuccessful executives in three contrasting business organizations.
The success of an executive was determined through a salary pro-
gression/length of service ratio and validated by peers', superiors',
and subordinates' ratings. The results disclosed that while the
organizational differences had a significant ($p < 0.01$) effect on the
NT and P styles of the executives, neither success nor its interaction
with organizations had any significant effect on any of the three
styles. In two of the organizations, a majority of the executives

reported employing the NT and, in one, th

An interesting finding was the significant inte

and the NT climate of the organization (*p*

indicated that the successful executives in an

and in a steel company perceived the climate

task-oriented than the unsuccessful ones. On

unsuccessful executives in a fertilizer company perc

as more nurturant task-oriented. Probably, proc

which is considered to be more advanced, led the su

tives to perceive the climate as less NT-oriented. They

the climate as less authoritarian but more participative

In sum, Sinha (1980) and his associates unfolded

features of the NT model and tested some of the pos

around fifteen studies. Furthermore, in a review of twelv

tion studies Sinha (1983) presented additional evidence in su

the model. These studies accumulated data from several labo

and survey investigations employing variables such as, owne

organization size, functions of the organizations and geograp

location. Samples ranged from students and department head

company executives and bureaucrats. Recently, some empiri

evidence was provided by Ansari (1986) in support of the NT

model. His survey was based on a sample of 189 executives in

middle positions representing about fifteen organizations. He con-

cluded that (*i*) the NT style was perceived as distinctly different

from other styles, and that (*ii*) it had a positive impact on several

indicators of effectiveness—commitment, facets of job satisfaction

and perceived effectiveness. Evidence (Ansari, 1987; Ansari and

Shukla, 1987) also exists that NT leaders earn more favorable ratings

on the evaluation of the leader and attributions of leadership than

the autocratic ones. Interestingly, on some occasions, they were

rated even higher than the participative leaders.

Though researchers have provided sufficient data with regard to

the usefulness of the NT model, Khandwalla (1988, p. 190) feels

that 'exhortations to leaders to be NT or participative in disregard

of macro-organizational realities would be nonsensical'. Thus,

there remain many questions to be answered, many quests to be

undertaken, and many webs to be unravelled. For example, we

do not have any solid evidence regarding the shift in leadership

style from NT to P. Nor do we have any data to show how a leader varies his style from subordinate to subordinate. And we have yet to examine the leader's power relationship with his subordinates, peers and superiors which may have an important bearing on organizational effectiveness (Ansari, 1986, p. 34).

This volume addresses some of these unexplored issues. Specifically, it proposes to examine how influence strategies are related to different forms of leader behavior or leadership styles. In other words, how actual influence takes place in superior-subordinate or leader-follower relationships, that is, how influence strategies are affected by bases or possession of power and leadership styles.

Power as a Means of Influence

The Background

Power is perhaps humankind's most pervasive social phenomenon. The consequences of power are experienced at every level of social organization but are most extensively experienced in formal organizations at all levels of the hierarchy. Because power is such a pervasive part of organizational life, researchers have attempted to explain organizational events and the outcome of these events in terms of power relationships that exist between organizations (Kochan, 1975; Pfeffer and Leong, 1977), between organizational subunits (Hinings *et al.*, 1974; Salancik and Pfeffer, 1974), between organizational levels (Bacharach and Aiken, 1976; Blau and Schoenherr, 1971), and among organization members (Bachman, *et al.*, 1968; Patchen, 1974).

Power has been characterized as 'the fundamental concept in social science... in the same sense energy is the fundamental concept in physics' (Russell, 1938, p. 18). A large number of social theorists—from Plato and Aristotle through Machiavelli and Hobbes to Pareto and Weber, to name a few—have paid a fair amount of attention to power and associated phenomena. Social power is one of the most significant determinants of social interaction, but it is also one of the most inadequately articulated concepts in the social sciences. It continues to hold great promise for those who wish to understand the role it plays in social relationships (Mintzberg, 1984). At the same time, it presents an equally great problem. 'In the entire lexicon of sociological concepts none is more troublesome than the concept of power. We all know perfectly well what it is— until someone asks us', (Bierstedt, 1950, p. 730).

In his 1953 presidential address to the Society for the Psychological Study of Social Issues, Dorwin Cartwright exhorted social psychologists not to neglect the variable of power. It was his contention that any social psychological theory was incomplete without this construct and that 'a concerted attack on the problem of power should produce a major advance in the field of social psychology', (Cartwright, 1959a, p. 13). In 1959, two theoretical frameworks of power were independently articulated—the field theoretical framework elaborated by Cartwright (1959b) and the social exchange model proposed by Thibaut and Kelley (1959). Both dealt largely with power in dyads. Power at the group level received much less attention, as Sherif (1962) observed that the power dimension was the most neglected topic in small group research (see Ng, 1980, for an extended discussion of the historical perspective on power).

Growing evidence attests that in the 1960s, most of the works on power were largely theoretical (see, Dahl, 1957; Emerson, 1962; Janda, 1960; Schopler, 1965). The field theoretical and social exchange systems dominated the studies. Two reviews (Collins and Raven, 1969; Schopler, 1965) contained literature that was within the conventional theoretical systems. With the studies of coalition formation (Wilke and Mulder, 1971), some light was thrown on power in general. In the early 1970s, the emphasis was still more on the conceptualization of power (see Minton, 1967). However, some experimental works on the bases of power were made available. In trying to account for differential effectiveness in the ability to influence decisions, researchers examined the bases and distribution of power in organizations (French and Raven, 1959; Hickson *et al.*, 1971; Hinings *et al.*, 1974; Martin and Sims, 1956; Mechanic, 1962; Salancik and Pfeffer, 1974, 1977; Tannenbaum, 1968). Questions, such as 'what are the bases of individual power', were addressed. Despite the fact that the French and Raven (1959) taxonomy of power bases dominated power literature for about three decades, their efforts provided only implicit answers to such questions as 'how does an individual amass power initially' or 'how does an individual add to current levels of power?' Another approach to the study of power shifted the level of analysis from the individual to the organizational sub-unit. One of the earliest conceptualizations on the power of organizational sub-units was made by Hickson *et al.*, (1971). Their model was later supported by empirical works (Hinings *et al.*, 1974; Salancik and Pfeffer, 1974).

Approaches

There are three main approaches to defining the concept of power: the field approach, the decision-making approach and the interaction approach.

Field Approach

The most prevalent definition of power in social-psychological literature has its roots in Lewinian field theory and has been comprehensively articulated by Cartwright (1959b). Power has been defined as the maximum 'resultant' force A can bring to bear on B with respect to a particular region of B's lifespace. Even French and Raven's (1959) taxonomy of power bases is consistent with the field-force framework. Cartwright's aim was to place power in a network of variables that was grounded in a general theory of behavior and only incidentally to develop hypotheses about the determinants and consequences of power. Because of this orientation, the emphasis of his work falls 'more on the vocabulary of power than on its syntax' (Jones, 1960, p. 68).

Decision-Making Approach

March (1955) maintained that a large portion of human behavior can be treated as an example of a decision-making process. He placed the concept of power, or influence, in a decision-making context. Influence was viewed by him as the inducement of change in an organization. The influence of a particular behavior could be ascertained by determining its consequences, regardless of the role player enacting it. Accepting March's general definition of power, Dahl (1957) modified its referents. That is, A's power over B was defined as the net increase in the probability of B enacting a behavior after A has made an intervention, compared to the probability of B enacting the behavior in the absence of A's intervention.

Interaction Approach

The Thibaut-Kelly (1959) conceptualization of power was based on the analysis of the way individuals interact. Power was defined by them as A's ability to affect the quality of B's outcomes. Specifically, the amount of power A has over B is determined by the range of outcomes through which he or she could potentially move B in the course of their interaction. The larger the range of outcomes that B could experience, the greater is A's power. For them, power was a potential for exercising influence, which is activated under specific conditions of mutual control and is affected by the outcome matrix characterizing a relationship. The power A has to induce behavior changes in B is mediated through learning mechanisms. Somewhat parallel treatments can be found in Blau (1964) and Homans (1958) in which interaction was viewed as an 'exchange' process.

Other Approaches

In addition to these frameworks of power, some other views are worth noting. As early as 1938, Russell talked about power while focusing on its intentional characteristics. He viewed power as 'the production of intended effects' (p. 35). Heider (1958) conceptualized power as a function of intentions and abilities. Bierstedt (1950) regarded power as a social phenomenon *par excellence*; it is a latent force and force is mainfest power. Lippitt, Polansky, and Rosen (1952) conceived of social power as the potential to induce forces in other persons to act or change in a given direction. Minton (1967) presented power as a personality construct. Psychoanalytic theorists such as Adler and Horney assumed that each individual has an inherent feeling of powerlessness which instigates compensatory strivings toward power goals. Kaplan (1964) showed that power marks the ability of one person or a group of persons to influence the behavior of others—that is, to change the probabilities that others will respond in certain ways to specified stimuli. When the weight of power is maximal or nearly so, we may speak not of power or influence but of 'control'.

In the preceding paragraphs, power as conceptualized by the early thinkers in the social sciences has been briefly touched upon. Before going deeper into more recent conceptualizations, I would like to briefly discuss the different aspects and dimensions of power. Only then will one be in a position to understand the precise meaning of power.

Definitions and Distinctions

Social power is a wide-ranging concept with a broad spectrum of definitions (see, for instance, Bacharach and Lawler, 1980; Pfeffer, 1981). Although power was considered to be one of the most thoroughly analyzed and debated concepts in the social sciences during the last two decades, it still remains ambiguous—that is, no general definition has been agreed upon. In reviewing some major definitions of power, a number of different aspects of power can be identified.

1. Power is often seen as a function of *sources* of power. French and Raven (1959) viewed power as a 'potential influence' that one actor could exert on another.

2. Power is often seen as *control*. Dahl (1957, p. 203) defined power as 'the ability of one individual or group to prompt another unit to do what it would not have otherwise done.'

3. Power has been regarded as a *general capacity*, that is, the distributive aspect of power. Weber (1947, p. 152) defined power as 'the probability that an actor within a social relationship will be in a position to carry out his own will despite resistance.' Khandwalla (1977, pp. 52-53) viewed power as 'the ability to secure one's goals through the explicit or implicit use of force.'

4. Power has been looked upon as a function of *dependence*. According to Emerson (1962, p. 32), 'the dependence of actor *A* on *B* is (*i*) directly proportional to *A*'s *motivational investment* in goals mediated by *B*, and (*ii*) inversely proportional to the availability of these goals to *A* outside of the *A-B* relation.' Similarly, Mechanic (1962) suggested that a person becomes subject to another's power when he or she is dependent on another's control of access to information, persons and instrumentalities.

5. Power has been viewed as a *structural* concept as expressed in organization theory. According to Hickson *et al.* (1971), the power of a sub-unit is related to its ability to cope with uncertainty, its substitutability and its centrality through the control of strategic contingencies upon which other activities are dependent.

6. A distinciton should be made between *potential* and *realized* power. The possession of power does not necessarily mean that

power is used or exercised. The major difference between potential and actual power, as defined by Wrong (1968), is whether or not an observable attempt to influence someone is made. For both types of power, behavior is influenced (implicitly or explicitly) by and leads to immediate outcomes. In both cases, power is enacted. Exchange theorists also imply that power has both potential and enacted components (Blau, 1964; Emerson, 1962). According to Minton (1967), the production and implementation of power—as exemplified by effectiveness, influence, power strategies and attempts to gain or use power—are at the level of manifest power. On the other hand, expressed feelings of individual power and the readiness to apply manifest power represent latent power. Thus potential power, essentially, is the capacity of one social actor to influence another.

While discussing power one must distinguish power from other related concepts. Through common usage, the term power has become synonymous with several other concepts, such as, influence, authority and control.

For organizational theorists like Dahl (1957), Heller (1971), and Katz and Kahn (1966), there exist certain differences in the conceptual meaning of these terms. For example, Katz and Kahn made a clear distinction between the two terms *influence* and *power*. They defined influence as a transaction in which one person (or group) acts in such a way as to change the behavior of another individual (or group) in some intended fashion. Power is the capacity to exert influence. Power does not have to be enacted for it to exist whereas influence does. Influence is the demonstrated use of power, and it is viewed as the process of producing behavioral or psychological (for instance, values, beliefs, and attitudes) effects in a target person.

Power is different from *control*. One definition that Lawler (1976, p. 1248) suggests to describe control is 'to direct, to influence, or to determine the behavior of someone else'. Tannenbaum (1962, p. 239), in a similar fashion, defines control as 'any process in which a person or group of persons or organization of persons determines, i.e., intentionally affects, what another person or group or organization will do.' Whereas power is described as the ability or potential to influence others, control is viewed as the actual process of exercising influence over others. Control refers to an extreme form of influence. Power can exist without any control, but control cannot take place without the use of power.

Power and *authority* are inter-related concepts. Power may involve force or coercion, whereas authority is a form of power that does not carry the force implication—rather, it involves a 'suspension of judgment', on the part of its recipients (Weber, 1947). Thus, power is defined as the capacity to exert influence while authority represents only a single type of power, that is, a power associated with position (i.e., *kursi* or chair).

Power has most often been confused with *power motive*, which is the desire to feel powerful (McClelland, 1975) or striving to be powerful (Winter, 1973). A person may have the capacity to influence the behavior of others but he may not feel like using it. On the contrary, 'a person may have such a strong power motive that he manipulates, cuts corners, climbs on others' shoulders to push the limit of his authority up, and eventually jumps up the hierarchy in the rush to actualize his propelling power need' (Sinha, 1982, p. 342).

Despite the various nuances of meanings ascribed to the terms associated with power, there appears to be a substantial agreement among the researchers that power is a process of interpersonal influence where one individual, group or organization induces another person, group or organization to produce the intended behaviors. This study would view power simply as *the ability to exercise influence over others* (Etzioni, 1969; Khandwalla, 1977; Raven, 1974; Sinha, 1982). Conclusively, it may be stated that power involves a transaction between persons, groups and organizations in which individuals interact, that is, a reciprocal power—the power of *A* over *B* and that of *B* over *A*. At this point in time, it is very important to develop a better understanding of how a given base of power is translated into effective influence in organizational decision-making. That is, how do individuals exercise the power they have to influence others.

Bases of Power

What are the various sources or bases of power that give a manager the ability to influence and change the behavior of others? A power base is a source of influence in a social relationship. Etzioni (1975), French and Raven (1959), Mechanic (1962), Mulder (1971), Peabody (1962), and Weber (1947) are but a few of the many social scientists who have analyzed the sources of power. Some of the bases as given by these writers will now be discussed.

French and Raven (1959) distinguished five bases of power that to them 'seem especially common and important'. These were reward power, coercive power, legitimate power, referent power and expert power. Etzioni (1975) enumerated three types of power along with three types of congruent involvement on the part of the lower participants in organizations—coercive, remunerative and normative. Similarly, Peabody (1962) described three sources of power—position power, competence and personal power. According to Kelman (1958), influence may be understood in terms of its consequences for the recipient—either compliance, identification or internalization. Mulder, de Jong, Koppelaar and Verhage (1977) expanded the French and Raven (1959) taxonomy and designed a measuring instrument to assess eight fundamental influence factors. Of these, four sub-scales were designed to measure four aspects of power: sanction power, formal power, referent power and expert power. Two were called non-power sub-scales—open consultation and expertise. The remaining two referred to the direction of influence—influence upward and influence outside one's own system.

Several reviews (such as, Yukl, 1981) suggest that of the various conceptualizations on the bases of power, the French and Raven (1959) classification has been widely used in organizational literature. In the beginning, French and Raven had proposed only five bases of power. Subsequently, two more bases—information and connection—were added (Hersey, Blanchard and Natemeyer, 1979; Raven 1965). These bases of power are defined below.

Reward Power: This is based on the perception by one member of the relationship that another member has the capacity to provide rewards.

Coercive Power: This is based on the perception by one person in a relationship that another person has the capacity to remove rewards or administer punishments.

Legitimate Power: This is based on the perception that one member has the right to influence and that another member in the relationship has an obligation to yield to this influence.

Referent Power: This is based on the perceived attraction of members in a relationship to one another. The source of this power may arise from friendship, identification with a successful model, or feelings of shared identity.

Expert Power: This is based on the perception by one member of the relationship that another member has special knowledge and expertise in a relevant area.

Information Power: This is based on the perception by one member of the relationship that another member possesses or has access to information that is valuable for others.

Connection Power: This is based on the perception by one member of the relationship that another member has connections with influential or important persons.

The way a manager uses one base of power may affect the value of the others. For instance, those managers who reward subordinates may well be liked and may have substantial referent power. On the other hand, those managers who use coercive methods may be liked less and may have less referent power. Research on the bases of power is complicated by the fact that several bases may be operating at the same time. Sometimes an attempt to influence can increase the operation of one power base but may decrease or even negate another. For example, coercion may lead to public compliance but cause the agent to be so disliked that there is private noncompliance (Raven and Kruglanski, 1970).

Several studies have been conducted to compare and contrast the effects of using different bases of power. The findings of these studies are well summarized in Yukl (1981, pp. 40-41). Some clear trends are apparent in the results. Two bases of influence—referent and expert—are generally associated with greater satisfaction, less absenteeism and turnover, and higher performance. The use of legitimate power and coercive power is unrelated or negatively associated with criterion measures. The use of reward power has no clear trend across studies. Recently, Raven and Rubin (1983) have demonstrated the effective use of informational power.

Summarizing the findings with regard to the bases of power, Yukl (1981) concludes that power research tells us more about the manner in which a manager influences or is influenced by subordinates than about the bases of power behind this influence. Thus, coupled with research on the power base is the need to examine the actual influence exercised by managers. Power bases alone are insufficient unless one uses them. Behavioral manifestations based on the various resources available are important for successful influence attempts. A wide range of influence tactics used by people have been reported in studies (see Goodchilds, *et al.*, 1975; Kipnis, 1976; Kipnis, Schmidt and Wilkinson, 1980). But many of these tactics do not really fit into the existing classifications of power (for instance, French and Raven, 1959; Kelman, 1958). Sometimes managers use strategies not mentioned by French and Raven, such as, coalitions, ingratiation, and deceit. Thus, a description of the existing classification of power bases does not describe fully the use of various power strategies in organizations.

Influence Strategies

Power is exercised through the use of various behavioral strategies or methods. Both superiors and subordinates exercise their power but by using different methods, in different situations, and for different reasons. Research on power strategies was accelerated with the introduction by Goodchilds *et al.* (1975) of a procedure that directly asked subjects to answer either orally or in the form of a written essay a question about the strategies they used to influence others. Since then, a number of studies in a variety of contexts have employed this procedure to assess power strategies (see, Ansari, Kapoor and Rehana, 1984; Falbo, 1977, 1982; Falbo and Peplau, 1980; Goodstein, 1981; Kipnis *et al.*, 1980). Various studies have been reported among students attempting to get their way with friends and parents (Goodchilds *et al.*, 1975), among lovers and married couples attempting to influence each other (Kipnis, 1976; Kipnis, Cohn and Schwarz, 1976), and among employees attempting to influence their bosses, co-workers, and subordinates (Ansari *et al.*, 1984; Kipnis *et al.*, 1980).

A survey of studies on power strategies indicates that a number of overlapping strategies are available in the literature. Some of the most widely reported strategies of downward, upward and lateral influence in organizations are now described.

Assertiveness: This involves demanding, telling a person to comply, expressing anger verbally, pointing out rules, or becoming a nuisance (Kipnis, 1976). Kipnis *et al.* (1980) and Mowday (1978) found a greater use of these tactics in influencing persons at all levels (superiors, co-workers and subordinates).

Coalition/Forming Alliances with Others: This involves such things as the use of steady pressure for compliance by 'obtaining the support of co-workers' and/or by 'obtaining the support of subordinates'. This technique is more often used to influence superiors than to influence subordinates or colleagues.

Exchange of Benefits: This strategy is used by managers with superiors, peers and subordinates to get their work done. It involves such things as 'offering an exchange' or 'offering to make personal sacrifices'. Kipnis *et al.* (1980) and Mowday (1978) mentioned the use of this strategy in organizations.

Ingratiation: This involves making the other person feel important, inflating the importance of a request, showing a need, asking politely, acting friendly or humbly, or pretending that the other person is really going to make the decision. It is used to get one's way with the boss as well as to persuade co-workers and subordinates to act in specific ways (Allen, *et al.*, 1979; Kipnis *et al.*, 1980; Ralston, 1985). This influence strategy has been systematically investigated by Pandey in a number of studies (Pandey, 1978, 1981; Pandey and Bohra, 1984; Pandey and Rastogi, 1979). For an extended discussion on ingratiation, see Volume 2 of *Psychology in India* (Pandey, 1988).

Manipulation: Informing or arguing in such a way that the recipient is not aware of being influenced is termed 'manipulation', (Mowday, 1978, 1979; Porter *et al.*, 1981). This is a common method of upward influence. Allen *et al.* (1979) pointed out that this category of tactics involved withholding, distorting the information (sort of outright lying), or overwhelming the target with too much information.

Reasoning/Persuasive Arguments/Rationality: Writing detailed plans, explaining the reason for a request, writing memos, and giving facts and data are all tactics involving rationality. This strategy is used most often and most effectively to influence superiors at all levels of the organization. When they are presented with documents or logical arguments, superiors appear to pay more attention to requests. Although it can be used at every level, it is used quite frequently by lower level participants (Ansari and Kapoor, 1987; Kipnis *et al.*, 1980; Mechanic, 1962).

Threats or Defiance: This strategy implies stating that negative consequences will occur if the agent's plan is not accepted. It can be used at both levels, that is, to influence superiors (defiance) and subordinates (threats). However, the person must have some power before he or she can threaten others.

Upward Appeal: This involves bringing additional pressure for conformity on the target of influence by calling a person at a higher level in the organization to help. Included in this strategy are such tactics as 'making a formal appeal to higher levels' or 'obtaining the informal support of higher-ups'.

Use of Sanctions: The use of sanctions draws upon organizational rewards and punishments. It includes both informal exchange, such as promoting interpersonal attraction by praising the superior (Kipnis and Vanderveer, 1971; Mechanic, 1962) and formal exchange, such as rewarding (Porter *et al.*, 1981). Tactics include preventing salary increases or threatening an employee's job security in the case of negative sanction and increasing the salary or promoting the person in the case of positive sanction. This strategy cannot be used unless the person actually does have the power and authority to implement the action. It is generally used by superiors to get their work done by their subordinates.

All these strategies can be used by persons at all levels depending upon the power distribution between the target and the actor and the circumstances in which the use of a particular strategy takes place. The strategies have been described by different authors in terms of different dimensions. For example, Wilkinson and Kipnis (1978) described strategies in terms of two dimensions—strong and weak. The strong dimension included such methods as withholding payment, persistence or threats. The weak dimension consisted of such methods as face-to-face negotiation, compromise or request for compliance. Similarly, Falbo (1977) reported two dimensions underlying the experts' judgments about the influence strategies—rational/non-rational and direct/indirect. Rational strategies included such methods of influence as reasoning, bargaining and compromise. The non-rational part included such emotional strategies as evasion, deceit and emotional alteration of the agent. On the other hand, direct means of influence comprised assertion, simple statement and *fait accompli*, whereas indirect means included hinting and thought manipulation.

Subsequently Falbo and Peplau (1980) presented a two dimensional model of power strategies in intimate relationships. These two dimensions concerned the extent to which the strategies were direct (ranging from direct to indirect) and interactive (ranging from bilateral to unilateral). Indirect strategies comprised such tactics as positive and negative affect, hinting and withdrawing. Direct strategies included persuasion, bargaining and reasoning. Bilateral strategies comprised such tactics as bargaining, reasoning or persistence. In unilateral strategies were included such tactics as *laissez-faire* and withdrawing.

Farrell and Petersen (1982) suggested three key dimensions of political behavior—internal-external, vertical-lateral and legitimate-illegitimate. The external dimension included such strategies as whistle-blowing, lawsuits and forming alliances with persons outside the focal organization. The internal dimension, on the other hand, employed resources already within the organization, as in the exchange of favors, trading agreements or reprisals. The vertical dimension included such political activities as complaining to a supervisor, bypassing the chain of command and apple-polishing. Lateral political behaviors included the exchange of favors, offering help, coalition and organizing. Political behaviors widely accepted as legitimate included exchanging favors, forming coalitions and seeking sponsors at the upper levels. Less legitimate behaviors included whistle-blowing and threats.

In sum, it can be said that a wide variety of influence strategies are available in organizational behavior literature and that different dimensions of influence strategies have been reported by different authors.

In recent years, several attempts have been made to relate influence strategies with personal variables—such as the need for power (McClelland, 1975; Singh, 1985; Winter, 1973), the need for approval (Falbo, 1977), self-confidence (Kanter, 1977; Raven and Kruglanski, 1970), locus of control (Kapoor, 1986), Machiavellianism (Christie and Geis, 1970; Pandey and Rastogi, 1979), and cognitions of the power-holder (Kipnis, 1976)—and contextual variables—such as organizational climate (Cheng, 1983; Madison *et al.*, 1980)—and goals of the influence attempts (Kipnis and Schmidt, 1983; Kipnis *et al.*, 1980; Madison *et al.*, 1980; Mowday, 1979; Schein, 1977).

What is evident from the foregoing discussion is that the link between leadership styles and power strategies is sorely lacking.

This aspect has been dealt with in the next section. Here, leadership has been viewed as a particular type of power phenomenon.

The Missing Link

The Background

Even a cursory glance at the foregoing sections would suggest that there is almost no overlap between the two bodies of literature—leadership and power. It appears that these studies 'have been conducted almost independently of each other'. In other words, 'those who write on leadership do not write on power and *vice versa* ... the number of cross-references between the two bodies of literature is amazingly small. Footnotes appearing in the literature on leadership *seldom* cite studies of power, and the reverse again holds true' (Janda, 1960, p. 354). Although verbal references to the other can be found in the literature of either concept, these references are clearly of a superficial nature (Janda, 1960).

Janda (1960), as an example, recommends that the reader considers the volumes of the *Annual Review of Psychology* between 1950-59. In each volume there is a separate chapter dealing with the literature on 'social psychology and group processes'. Only the first volume included a section entitled 'Leadership and Power'. However, in this volume, Bruner (1950) dealt only slightly with some general literature on 'group dynamics'. Of course, in the seventh volume French (1956) explicitly referred the reader on leadership to the other sections on influence processes. In rest of the other volumes, the literature cited in one section usually did not receive acknowledgment in the other. Janda (1960) thus remarks:

> Whenever the two concepts are considered together in the same work, one of the two clearly becomes the real subject for analysis, and the treatment accorded to the subordinated concept is usually quite sophomoric, ignoring relevant literature on the topic. In short, we have two separate, practically self-contained bodies of literature—one on leadership, the other on power (p. 354).

Cartwright (1965) also maintains that 'there is no single body of literature on influence but instead a collection of discrete and more or less independent literatures concerned with various aspects of influence' (p. 3).

This practice is being followed even now. For example, consider the available handbooks on industrial/organizational psychology (Drenth *et al.*, 1984; Dunnette, 1976; March, 1965). Of these, only one (March, 1965) contained a hand-in-hand treatment of 'Influence, Leadership, Control' by Cartwright (1965). The others, as usual, seem to treat the two topics—leadership and power—almost separately. This is also the case with the various textbooks. Only rarely have the researchers empirically investigated the two phenomena in one single study. The following discussion, which relies heavily on the review works by Janda (1960), and Kochan, Schmidt and DeCotiis (1976), relates these literature by presenting the concept of leadership in terms of power.

Leadership as a Power Phenomenon

The conceptual complexities surrounding the phenomena of leadership and power are evident (see the previous two sections). Considering these complexities, Thibaut and Kelley (1959, p. 290) comment:

> leadership research will be most fruitful when it adopts an indirect and analytical approach to its task. Rather than going directly into the complex phenomena and surplus-meaning-laden terminology encompassed by the term leadership, research must first be directed toward clarifying problems of power structures, norms and goals, task requirements, functional roles, etc., each of which is complex and challenging enough in its own right.

Yet, there seems to be a great deal of agreement among writers that both leadership and power are influence processes. Cartwright (1965, p. 4) provides a useful working definition of the concept of influence: 'when an agent (exerting influence), O, performs an act resulting in some change in another agent (subjected to influence), P, we say that O influences P.' Following Cartwright's definition of influence, leadership and power can be defined as follows: 'Leadership is an influence process whereby O's actions change P's behavior and P views the influence attempt as being legitimate and the change as being consistent with P's goals' (Kochan *et al:*, 1976, p. 285). Power, according to Cartwright (1965), is O's capability of influencing P. However, 'the formal organizational position occupied by O is not the distinguishing characteristic for the concept of power, i.e., O can be a superior, subordinate, or a peer of P' (Kochan *et al.*, 1976, p. 285).

When we view leadership and power as influence processes, it follows that the fundamental issue in leadership is power. It should be immediately noted that the conceptual formulation of power is close to some of the formulations of leadership. For example, Warriner (1955, p. 367) defines leadership as 'a form of relationship between persons [which] requires that one or several persons act in conformance with the request of another.' According to this formulation, it is rather difficult to make a distinction between the concepts of leadership and power. Janda (1960) postulates that a theoretically significant and operationally useful conception of leadership can be provided by considering leadership phenomenon as a particular subset within the larger set of power phenomenon. This statement implies that all leader-follower relationships are power-wielder–power-recipient relationships. However, leadership is not necessarily involved in all power relationships. Now, consider another definition of leadership. Tannenbaum, Weschler and Massarik (1961) view leadership as 'interpersonal influence, exercised in a situation and directed through the communication process toward the attainment of a specific goal or goals' (p. 24). In addition, they attempt to make a distinction between leadership and power. According to them, power is really an ability to, or potential for, influence. Leadership, on the other hand, can be distinguished from power by its action connotation—that is, the actual use of power by the influencing agent (leader) to achieve conformance to his or her desired goals.

Gibb (1954, 1969) opines that, like authority and power, leadership can be viewed as a process of relational concepts involving influence activities within a group. In his own words:

Leadership is but one facet though perhaps the most readily visible fact of the larger process of role differentiation. Leadership is simply this concept applied to the situation obtaining in a group when the differentiation of roles results in one or some of the parties to the interaction influencing the actions of others in a shared approach to common or compatible goals (1969, p. 270).

Although Fiedler (1967) like Likert (1961, 1967) does not provide a definition of leadership functions, he does account for leadership functions. According to him, 'leadership functions are frequently shared among group members and that one person may be most influential at one time and less influential at another...' (p. 8).

Several other definitions can be considered to view leadership as a power phenomenon. For example, Bass (1960, p. 89) states that leadership exists 'when the goal of one member, *A*, is that of changing another member, *B*; or when *B*'s change in behavior will reward *A* or reinforces *A*'s behavior. *A*'s efforts to attain the goal is leadership.' However, according to Kochan *et al*. (1976), this definition fails to distinguish between leadership and other influence attempts. This means the concepts of leadership and power are almost inseparable. This is the reason why Korman (1971) argues that the concept of social influence is central to all of them. He concludes that 'the statement "a leader tries to influence other people in a given direction" is relatively simple but it seems to capture the essence of what we mean by leadership' (p. 115). Like the definitions just discussed (Bass, 1960; Korman, 1971), the definition presented by Filley and House (1969) also fails to distinguish between leadership and other acts of influence: '*Leadership* ... is a process whereby one person exerts social influence over the members of the group. A leader, then, is a person with power over others who exercises this power for the purpose of influencing their behavior'(p. 391, emphasis in original).

There are many such definitions, but the point is already well made that both leadership and power are influence processes. The connecting link between the two is *influence*, whereas the distinguishing point between them is *action connotation*. Whereas power is the potential influence, leadership involves the actual exercise of power.

Before we go ahead in trying to integrate the 'potential influence' and 'action connotation,' let us begin by asking a topical question: *How does a leader exercise power* (or *influence*) *over his or her subordinates*? Since leadership is viewed as a reciprocal influence process (Hollander and Julian, 1969), i.e., the power of *O* over *P* and that of *P* over *O*, another question may also be put simultaneously: *How do subordinates exercise power over their leader*? This conceptualization of leadership considers the mutuality, or implicit exchange nature, of leader-follower relationships. Thus this redirection of emphasis would also involve greater attention to the behavior of the follower than is naturally given. As Katz (1951, p. 140) notes, 'Leadership is a relation involving two terms and it is impossible to study the influencing agent without also studying the people being influenced.' Gamson (1968) strongly feels that the power to attain personal, group or organizational goals should not be restricted to downward influence in organizations. An organization is composed of superiors and subordinates, both of whom can influence each other; for the proper and effective functioning of the organization, a kind of harmony and sound relationship between the two is needed. Thus, the study of both downward and upward influence processes is important for understanding the complex business organizations—that is, how does a leader influence his or her subordinates (i.e., O over P) and how is he or she influenced by his or her subordinate(s) (i.e., $P(s)$ over O).

Unfortunately, empirical research and theory relating to these questions have been sparse. Despite their importance, there is not much solid evidence that can be cited. However, there has been some research which will now be discussed.

Relationship Between Leadership and Power

Let us now review those empirical studies which show at least some connection between leadership and power. Some of the experimental researches on the power variable in leadership behavior were summarized in the eleventh volume of the *Annual Review of Psychology* (Riecken, 1960). For example, Raven and French (1958a, 1958b) conducted two fairly similar experiments. In each, they compared the response to a supervisor whose position had been legitimized by election with one who had simply taken over from the legitimate leader. They found that the elected leader was perceived as having a greater right to her office and was more attractive. However, they did not find any significant difference in the acceptance of the supervisor's instructions to slow-down the amount of work turned out. It should be noted that coercive power reduced the perceived attractiveness of the supervisor but not the agreement with her evaluations of work nor the perception of the legitimacy of her position. These findings cast some doubt on the notion of legitimacy of authority. 'Perhaps legitimacy is less important in groups in which motivations are relatively weak' (Riecken, 1960, p. 490).

One of the earliest attempts to investigate the exercise of power by a leader was made by Kipnis (1958). He compared the effectiveness of the two styles of leadership (directive and participative), coupled with reward and punishment, on both public compliance with and private acceptance of an attempt to influence a preference. Some of the major findings of Kipnis are summarized by Riecken (1960, p. 40) as follows: 'Both reward and punishment were equally effective in producing public compliance. In private acceptance, however, an interesting difference was found. Participative leadership was more effective than directive leadership in both the reward and in the control group, but less effective in a punishment group.' Kipnis (1958) interpreted these findings to mean that under participative punitive conditions members get support from each other for resisting the leader's power, but there is no such opportunity in the directive treatment.

Recently, few attempts have been made to relate the bases of power with leadership behavior. For example Lord (1977), in an experimental study, found that functional leadership behavior was significantly related to both social power and leadership perceptions. Interestingly, Lord's analysis indicated that leadership perceptions were more highly related to perceived social power than to functional leadership behavior. Such a relationship, according to Lord, was evident because of the fact that both the perception of social power and the perception of leadership were the result of similar processes. An alternative explanation was that the higher relation of social power and leadership perceptions with each other than with functional behavior probably reflected some common method variance.

Probably the most systematic attempt on this issue has been made by Mulder and his associates (Mulder *et al.*, 1977). Employing survey methods, they investigated the relationship between power and leadership in a banking concern comprising nine broad offices in west Holland. They found that, in crisis circumstances, leaders exerted more formal power, referent power, expert power, and upward influence, and less open consultations than in non-crisis situations. An interesting finding was that the relationship between type of leadership and leader's effectiveness was significantly moderated by the situation (crisis/non-crisis). That is, leaders evaluated favorably by their superiors were ascribed more formal power in crisis situations and more open consultations in non-crisis situations by their subordinates. However, for leader evaluated less favorably, no significant difference appeared between situations.

In a subsequent study, Mulder, Binkhorst and van Oers (1983) suggested that a good consultant (like any good leader) must be able to exert forceful power as well as be able to maintain personal open relationships with others when confronted with difficult requirements, some of which may involve crises. Another interesting finding was that the mild 'good chap leadership,' characterized by small power differences, was suitable for normal, non-crisis situations.

As regards the relationship between bases of power and leadership behavior, one systematic study is worth noting. In a path-analytic process model, Martin and Hunt (1980) investigated how social influence affects intent to leave. Using a cross-validation design, they tested their hypothesis in two bureaus—design and construction—in a large highway department. Social influence processes included bases of power and leadership behaviour. Four principal findings emerged. First, in both bureaus, expert power had its positive impact on initiating structure as well as on consideration—that is, employees who complied because of expert power saw their supervisors as higher on both the initiating structure and consideration leadership behaviors. Second, legitimate power had a negative impact on consideration only in the construction bureau—that is, employees who complied because of more legitimate power had less considerate supervisors. Further, referent power had a positive effect on initiating structure in the construction bureau—that is, employees who complied because of more referent power had a supervisor who initiated more structure. Finally, neither reward nor coercive power had an effect on any leader behavior in either bureau. In a nutshell, the findings of Martin and Hunt suggest that social power significantly affects leader behavior.

Another experimental study employing a path-analytic model was recently conducted by Kipnis, Schmidt, Price and Stitt (1981). The main objective of this study was to examine the extent to which employee evaluations were determined by the leaders' influence tactics and the leaders' assessments of the followers' motives rather than by the performance of the followers. The sample of Kipnis *et al.* consisted of 113 business students who were randomly assigned to act as authoritarian or democratic leaders of five-person work groups. Each group was instructed to manufacture model airplanes. Some major conclusions emerged from the study. Leaders who were expected to act autocratically or democratically used controlling or non-controlling influence tactics, respectively. The leaders who used controlling influence tactics reported that their subordinates were not self-motivated. On the other hand, the leader who used non-controlling tactics attributed their subordinates' performances to self-motivation to perform.

Finally, of interest is a field study by Singh (1985) which was conducted in a public sector fertilizer company. Among other things, Singh's major concern was to investigate how influence strategies were affected by leadership styles. He first derived factor-analytically eight dimensions of influence strategies and ten dimensions of leadership styles. Thereafter, using multiple regression analysis, he tried to relate influence strategies (criterion variables) with the leadership style dimensions (predictors). He found only four dimensions of leadership style—people-orientation, power-orientation, impersonal-orientation and suspicion and limited role—significantly contributing to the use of influence strategies. Of them, suspicion and limited role style predicted the use of such influence strategies as pseudo-nurturance, reliance and diplomacy.

If one looks back on what has been covered so far, it is evident that the picture still remains hazy regarding the relationship between the exercise of power and leadership. Hence systematic studies are needed urgently on the subject. This volume aims at understanding the reciprocal influence processes in leadership.

2 Present Investigations

While surveying briefly the constituents of influence processes in organizations, Chapter 1 highlighted the *link* between leadership and excercise of power. This chapter is mainly devoted to the objectives and strategy of present investigations.

Objectives of the Investigations

As has been mentioned in Chapter 1, superior-subordinate relationships (leader-follower relationships) in general should be treated as power-wielder–power-recipient relationships. A leader is one who exercises influence in order to meet organizational objectives. The question of how the leader *actually* influences (behavioral strategies) the behavior of the subordinates or how leader behavior is *actually* influenced by the subordinates, has received little attention in organizational research (see Chapter 1). Despite decades of systematic empirical investigations and centuries of speculation, the problem with regard to actual influence strategies used in leader-follower relationships still persists for professional experts in industrial and organizational psychology. In this volume, it is argued that an organization is composed of superiors and subordinates, that both of them can influence each other, and that both can exercise their power by using different influence strategies in different situations and perhaps for different reasons. In view of this proposition, several questions immediately come to mind:

1. In what way(s) do managers influence their immediate superior and subordinates? Do they adopt similar or different strategies in their influence attempts (downward and upward)?
2. How do bases of power affect the choice of leadership styles (or behaviors)?
3. How do influence strategies (downward and upward) vary with respect to leadership styles? That is, how does the manager with a particular style influence the behavior of the subordinates and the immediate superior?
4. How do influence strategies (downward and upward) vary with respect to leadership behavior? That is, how do superiors' leadership styles affect the subordinates' use of influence strategies?
5. How do influence strategies (downward and upward) vary with respect to perceived organizational climate?
6. How does objective organizational climate moderate the relationship between leadership style and the use of influence strategies (downward and upward)?
7. How does objective organizational climate moderate the relationship between leader behavior and the use of influence strategies (downward and upward)?
8. How does objective organizational climate moderate the relationship between bases of power and the use of influence strategies (downward and upward)?
9. How do job status (hierarchical levels) and ownership of the organization affect, independently or jointly, the use of influence strategies (downward and upward)?

A summary of the proposed relationships between the study variables is illustrated in Figure 2.1.

The prime concern of this volume is to examine the relationship between leadership styles and the exercise of power. An actor with a particular leadership style (such as, authoritarian or participative) may use different influence strategies, depending upon who the target of influence is—the subordinate or the superior. In other words, the strategy the actor uses may be guided by the status of the target person(s). The visual display in Figure 2.1 also suggests

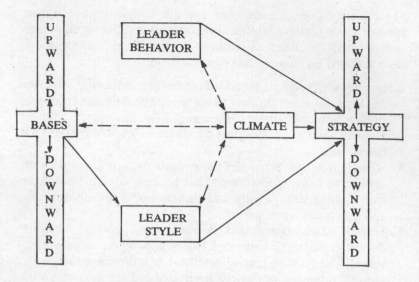

Figure 2.1 *A Dynamic Model to Study the Influence Processes in Organizations*

Note: ———— Indicates independent effects
— — — Indicates moderating effect

that the use of a particular influence strategy is a function of leadership style, leader behavior, bases of power and perceived organizational climate. It is also proposed that the relationship between these factors with influence strategies will be significantly moderated by the objective climate of the organization.

Specific hypotheses have been advanced with regard to the proposed relationships in the following chapters. The next section of this chapter deals with the strategy of the investigations.

Strategy of the Investigations

The Background

Here we shall deal with a field survey conducted to investigate the issues related to the influence processes in organizations. The survey was conducted during 1984–86. The issues and the data presented in this volume are illustrative of only a part of the on-going research activities around 'getting one's way' in work organizations.

The Research Site

The main survey was supported for a period of two years (1984-86) by a grant from the Indian Council of Social Science Research, New Delhi. The study was conducted in organizations located in northern India. Since organizations are many and they differ from one another rather radically in many respects, no attempt was made to draw the sample randomly. Rather, a few dimensions of this heterogeneous universe were taken into consideration while drawing the sample. What attracted the investigator most were the functions and ownership of organizations in the Indian economy. Keeping this end in view, around twenty organizations were approached. However, most of them were unwilling or hesitant to open their doors to investigation. A brief description of the seven organizations which agreed to participate in the study is now presented.

Organization 1

This is a large semi-manufacturing public organization established in the late forties. The headquarters are located in the state capital. Before independence, the organization was under the control of the British India government. After the formation of the Board of Control by the government of India in 1959, it was reconstituted twice during 1979-80. The aim of this organization is the production and sale of energy to all organizations as well as individual consumers within and around the city.

The organization consists of four main units and one subsidiary unit. One of the sub-units of Unit I (i.e., the Corporate Office) is the establishment department which deals with recruitments, promotions and the transfer of employees. Unit II (the Commercial Office) looks after financial matters. Unit III (the Distribution Office) supplies power. The Generation Branch (Unit IV) is responsible for generating power and Unit V takes care of the projects of the organization.

In addition to the Chairman and four full-time members, the Board is composed of two ex-officios representing the state government. The five full-time functional members and their respective functions are as follows: Chairman and Member (Administration), Member (Generation), Member (Transmission), Member (Commercial and Distribution), and Member (Finance and Accounts). The organization is headed by a General Manager (GM), who in turn is directly attached to the Member, Commercial and Distribution. The GM is assisted by four Personal Assistants—two technical and two non-technical (Legal and Accounts). Next to the GM are four Superintending Engineers (SEs): SE, Headquarter; SE, Commerce; SE, Distribution; and SE, Generation. The SEs report directly to the GM. They are assisted by a number of Executive Engineers (EEs). Below the EEs are Assistant Engineers (AEs), who in turn are assisted by Junior Engineers (JEs). Under a large chain of officers, a number of clerks, typists and workers are serving the organization. The Personnel Department is headed by a Senior Personnel Officer assisted by a Personnel Officer. The Personnel Officer is assisted by the Labour Welfare Officer.

The total capital invested in 1960 was about 600 lakh, which rose to about 21,000 lakh after twenty-five years. The various statistics available indicate that the organization is running under heavy loss. The Government of India had declared a loss of Rs 11 million in 1981. The figure of loss rose to about Rs 15 million in 1984-85. Loss of energy, low operational efficiency, over capitalization and over-staffing are responsible for annual losses which run into millions of rupees.

Several kinds of conflicts are apparent among the employees. The labor-management conflict is one of them. There are no formal restrictions; anyone can talk to the GM or the SEs directly. Strikes are a normal phenomenon and, on an average, occur four to five times in a year on different issues. During the period of the study in the organization, a strike took place. Workers were not given their due arrears which were sanctioned about five months before. When no attention was paid by the management to their problem, the employees went on strike. After thirteen days of lock-out, the management compromised with the workers by fulfilling their demands. The officers' association deals with the problems of officers and tries to solve them by negotiating with the Board. Among the workers there are a number of unions; some of them are recognized and are affiliated to and supported by different political parties. Group formation in the organization is generally on the basis of caste. Brahmans and Kayasthas dominate over the other castes. But there is no apparent conflict between the two. People are very informal in their own groups. According to the employees, promotion policies in the organization are not considered to be fair. For instance, one case is noteworthy. An engineer had suffered a lot because of differences between him and his seniors. All files related to his promotion and increments were withheld. He was not given any increment for about five years; nor was he recommended for promotion, whereas his subordinate engineers received promotions much before him. Selection procedures in the organization have been found to be so unfair that new recruitments have been completely stopped for quite some time.

The study was conducted in four main units: the Corporate Office, the Commercial Office, the Distribution Office and the Generation Office. Four levels of Engineers—JE, AE, EE and SE—and other non-technical officers participated in the study.

Organization 2

This is a medium-sized charitable hospital owned and run by a religious and philanthropic organization. Started in the early 1910s in a small way, this organization developed gradually and constructed its own premises through munificence. In the mid 1920s, the staff strength was small and included 3 doctors, 6-7 nurses and wardboys, and 2 sweepers. At present, this organisation employs about 470 persons; among them are 50 doctors, 42 nurses, staff and wardboys and 373 paramedical staff.

After independence, the accommodation and space available were found to be far from adequate for meeting public demands. With the benign help of the state government, it secured a suitable plot of land and shifted to this new site in the late sixties. To begin with, 12 well equipped Out-Patient Departments started functioning at the new building in the early 1970s which now remain open for eight hours on all working days. Three years later, the Indoor Department was opened with a provision of 100 beds. With the passage of time, the hospital continued to expand. At present, it has 20 sections functioning: Tubercular Chest Diseases, Non-Tubercular Chest Diseases, General Medicine (including Gastro-Intestinal Diseases), Paediatrics, Ear-Nose-Throat, Orthopaedics, General Surgery, Pathology including Biochemistry, Radiology, Physical Medicine (including Physiotherapy and Medical Gymnastics), Gynaecology, Maternity, Dentistry (including Dental Prosthesis), Opthalmology, Homoeopathy, Leprosy, Social Welfare and Patient Guide, Medical Records, Blood Transfusion Unit, and Ayurvedic.

The organization is headed by an Administrator subordinated by an Assistant Administrator. Both are members of the religious organization. Below the Administrator are the Superintendent and Assistant Superintendent. Next in the hierarchy are the consultants and surgeons of different units. Below them are the Senior Medical Officers/Assistant Consultants, Medical Officers, Registrars, Resident Medical Officers, House Officer, Social Welfare Incharge, Matron, Social Welfare Officers, Clerical Staffs, Pharmacists/Sister Incharge/Wardmaster, Sister, and Nurse, in that order. At the bottom are the class IV employees.

In the mid 1970s, the continued financial stringency, high level of prices, scarcity of drugs, X-ray films and chemicals coupled with the shortage of doctors, particularly in certain specialities, adversely affected the working of the hospital. However, the situation improved towards the end of the decade. During the late seventies, the hospital was recognized for the treatment of patients under the Central Government Health Scheme. During the early eighties, the local branches of the State Bank of India joined the scheme for the treatment of their employees and requested the reservation of certain number of beds. At present 25 per cent of the beds in the General Ward (20 out of 80) are free beds. In the actual working, free bed occupancy stood at around 28 in 1983. The income at present amounts to around Rs 48 lakh (against Rs 42 lakh in 1982-83). The number of outdoor-patients in 1983 was around 12.5 lakh (against 12 lakh in 1982) and the indoor-patients for special investigation were around 1,400 (against 1350 in 1982). The number of major operations performed was around 1,400 in both years and the number of deliveries was around 850 in 1982 and 800 in 1983.

The hospital is relatively large and cleaner than any other private hospital in the city. One of these is included in this study (see Organization 3). Because of the fact that the doctors are earning relatively less, they are not satisfied with their pay. This is the reason why the turnover rate is higher here compared to other hospitals. Being a private organization, the employees' jobs are not secure and the existence of any union is unthinkable. Though informal groups are based on the work area, an air of friendliness is noticeable in the organization. The educational activities of this organization are confined mainly to the maintenance of a public library and a free reading room. The library has around 18,000 books. In addition, every year sports events are organized and prizes are distributed to the winners and participants in the various events.

The sample of the study was selected from all the departments except the Blood Tranfusion Unit and the Ayurvedic Unit. The participants ranged from the Sisters to the Superintendents.

Organization 3

This is a medium-sized, private, charitable mission hospital. An awareness of the magnitude and urgency of maternal and child health care gave birth to this organization in the late 1950s. People offered their free services. At the time, there were very few staff in this organization—just 1 doctor, 2 nurses and 1 sweeper. Now it has reached a capacity of 200 beds and employs 250 persons. These include 17 doctors, 40 nurses and 12 clerical staff. The rest are sweepers, washermen, gardeners, ambulance drivers, chowkidars and wardboys. Housed in a small residential building, it had a humble beginning with an Out-patient Department and two beds for In-patients. With financial aid from some funding agencies, it became a 40-bed gynaecological and obstetrical hospital in the late sixties.

In 1969, it was entrusted to the missionary congregation. As time passed, the extension of the hospital continued. At present, it has 9 departments: General Medicine; General Surgery; Clinical Laboratory—Biochemistry, Bacteriology and Histopathology; Radiology; Gynaecology and Obstetrics; Paediatrics; Anaesthesiology; Community Health Department; and an Intensive Coronary Care Unit.

The organization is headed by an Administrator. The person below is the Superintendent cum Assistant Administrator. Following this officer are consultants and surgeons of different units. Below them are the Assistant Consultants, Registrars and Social Welfare Incharge. Next to them are Wardens, Social Workers, Clerical Staff, Sisters, Nurses and Trainee Nurses, in that order. Below them are the class IV employees. The Administrator, Assistant Administrator, and Wardens are members of the Catholic community.

Because it is an organization dealing with ailing people, its efficiency can be viewed in terms of the increase in the number of patients. The various statistics available suggest that, in the last five years, the number of out-patients and in-patients has grown to 2,650 and 13,500 from 1,900 and 10,000, respectively. Besides, 3,500 deliveries and about 1,900 major operations are performed every year. Although another private hospital (which is also dealt with here, see Organization 2), equipped with the same facilities, is available in the city, patients prefer this one.

The hospital has its own training center for Auxiliary Nurse Midwives, Nurses' Hostel and an Auditorium cum Recreation Room for patients. Besides, there are arrangements for the relatives of poor patients visiting them in the hospital to stay free of cost nearby. More than 20 per cent of the patients are treated free of cost. Though the hospital does not have sufficient doctors in relation to the workload, work never suffers. Members of the Catholic community perform their work skilfully and have the upper hand over the other staff members. They work for an honorarium and have no-promotion system or tenure for any position. Because it is a private organization and the employees are insecure, the question of a strike does not arise. There is no employees' union. An employee can talk freely about his or her problems to the management and the management, in turn, looks into his or her problem sympathetically.

There are two bases of informal groupings. One is rank and status; people of the same position move together. The other is the work area; people of the same work unit move together. But in the case of lady doctors, the situation is somewhat different. They eat their meals together. Above all there is an atmosphere of friendliness that links all the people of this organization together. As there is a great deal of pressure for performance and low pay-offs, the rate of turnover is higher at the doctors' level. Private practice is strictly prohibited except for the two senior-most persons. As far as the opportunity for advancement is concerned, the hardworking ones can rise to the top here. Their services are not limited to the boundaries of the organization. A full-fledged Community Health Department provides valuable services to the rural population, as well. Regular home visits, health education, immunization, T.B. clinics, antenatal clinics and 'well-baby' clinics are organized regularly.

In this study, all the units of the organization (except the Clinical Laboratory and Community Health Department) were involved.

Organization 4

This is a large manufacturing organization owned by the Government of India. It has seven other manufacturing divisions located in different parts of the country. The headquarters are located in Bangalore. Established in the seventies, the organization covers an area of 5,00,000 square feet set in sylvan surroundings. It has grown into a highly diversified accessories factory handling a wide spectrum of technologies. In 1974-75, it had 1,230 employees and 180 officers. It now employs over 2,500 workers and around 650 officers. At present it turns out over 550 different types of products for aircraft and helicopters, on the one hand, and armoured fighting vehicles and tractors, on the other.

The division (hereafter referred to as organization) has seven major departments.

(i) *The Personnel Department*: Its functions include the recruitment and promotion of employees, implementation of various welfare schemes, management of the canteen, provision of transport, housing and recreational facilities, and personnel policies as laid down by the head office. Besides, it is responsible for holding discussions with the local recognized unions and resolving issues/matters of a local nature.

(ii) *Accounts and Finance Departments*: These are totally responsible for the finance and accounts of the organization.

(iii) *Quality Control*: This department is approved by government authorities and renowned equipment manufacturers in the UK and France. The management aims at total quality control by integrating the development, maintenance and quality improvement efforts of the various groups in the division.

(iv) *Design and Development Department*: Backed by prototype making, performance testing, and environmental testing facilities, the department confidently approaches the increasingly complex equipment technology.

(v) *Assembly Shops*: These aim at assembling, precision setting and rigorous testings. Attached to them are facilities for testing the equipment. In addition to these major departments, two more divisions exist: the Machine Shop and Computer Center.

The organization is headed by a General Manager (GM). Under the GM is a Deputy General Manager (Dy GM). Next to him are the Chief Managers (CMs) who directly report to the GM and Dy GM. Below the CMs are the Senior Managers (SMs), Managers and Assitant/Deputy Managers. Next to the Deputy Managers are engineers of the different departments assisted by Deputy/Assistant Engineers.

One can easily categorize this organization as efficient by examining its performance. Sales of the products in 1974-75 was around Rs 433 lakh and in 1983-84 it rose to about Rs 1,170 lakh. The profit in 1974-75 was around Rs 23 lakh, which rose to Rs 144 lakh in 1983-84. Absenteeism in 1974-75 was 17 per cent, which came down to 14 per cent in 1983-84. The number of accessories was 3,817 in 1974-75 which rose to about 12,918 in 1983-84.

Strict administration is visible here. Light music can be heard in every department during the lunch break. Employees are informal with their superiors. Given any problem, they talk to their superiors without hesitation. The superiors, in turn, pay attention to their problems and help them find solutions. Group formation in the organization is based on the workplace and the nature of work. People enjoy informal meetings after office hours. A number of workers' unions exist here, but only a couple are recognized. There is an Officers' Association which takes care of the problems of officers and presents them to the higher authorities. Generally, unions do not interfere with the managerial decisions. It has been the constant endeavor of the company to establish and maintain meaningful and effective communication between the management and the employees in order to reduce and progressively eliminate any scope for conflicts and misunderstandings, achieve a better understanding of each others' point of view and, thus, facilitate the maintenance of industrial peace and morale. The organization has provided a number of facilities to its members in the form of Group Insurance, Employee Welfare Fund, Death Relief Fund, canteen facilities, transport facilities, housing facilities, educational facilities, cooperative societies, fine arts societies, sports club and a merit scholarship scheme.

The study was conducted in all departments. The participants in the study ranged from Assistant Engineers to Chief Managers.

Organization 5

This organization has nine manufacturing plants and matching service divisions located in different parts of the country. The headquarter is located in New Delhi. Our study was confined to one division only. Established in the late fifties, this division is currently one of the largest engineering and manufacturing enterprises in India. It includes two plants. This study was confined to plant 1. The construction of plant 1 commenced in the early sixties. In the late sixties, production started with a project employing 2 engineers, 4 supervisors and 1 attendant only. With the passage of time, the capacity of the plant has increased considerably. Now this plant comprises a workforce of more than 11,000 people, including 1,200 executives, 1,390 supervisors, 600 technical supporting staff, 660 clerical staff, 5,555 artisans, 1,350 unskilled workers and 60 trainees. The construction of a second generation plant of this division was started in the early seventies. It now comprises a workforce of about 1,500 people including 124 executives. This plant has an in-built level of sophistication normally associated with much larger plants. It has developed successfully various intricate castings and forgings which were hitherto imported.

This division consists of eight main units, which are further divided into many sub-units. Unit 1 deals with sub-units related to the manufacture and tooling of turbines and hydroturbines. Unit 2 deals with sub-units of industrial machines and the engineering, technology , apparatus and control gear of different types of generators. With the help of its sub-units, Unit 3 aims at total quality control by integrating quality developments, maintenance and improvement effort of the various groups in the division. Unit 4 deals with the engineering and commercial coordination of thermal and hydro motors, spares and repairs, wood working, and traffic of the division. Unit 5 has the record of loans as well as financial matters of the whole division. Unit 6 handles matters related to selection, training, publicity, security, projects, medical and vigilance, organizational development, and administration. Unit 7 deals with diversification facilities and Unit 8 deals with all the technology, methods, engineering and activities of the second generation plant. The first generation plant (where this study was conducted) is considered to be one of the most well-equipped and modern plants in the world. Some of its unique installations are the oversped balancing vacuum tunnel, blade shop, CNC machines, and TG test bed. It produces steam turbines, turbogenerators in different unit sizes, hydroturbines and matching generators of various ratings.

The General Manager In-charge is all-in-all in this division. Under him are the General Manager, Assistant General Manager, Deputy General Manager, Senior Manager, Manager, Deputy Manager, Senior Officer and Officers of different departments, in that order. Among the non-executives are different levels of artisans, supervisors, accountants, assistants, clerks, steno-typists, nurses, and so on. The skilled, semi-skilled, and unskilled workers constitute the bottom line of the hierarchy.

As per the Detailed Product Report accepted by the Government of India, the organization's original capital investment was around Rs 1,020 million. This amount has now increased to around Rs 1,650 million in the first plant and around Rs 350 million in plant 2, with the additional investment of the installation of new machine tools and additional manufacturing machines for the manufacture of thermal sets of different sized units. During the financial year 1983-84, the total output of the first plant was Rs 15,600 million while the profit was Rs 737 lakh. The average rate of absenteeism was 17 per cent and the number of non-fatal accidents per year was 24. No fatal accident had occurred in this division since its inception. This could be because the organization has enough safety measures. Also, people are taught how to take precautions and how to use the available safety devices, should an emergency occur.

The division has several employees' unions affiliated to and supported by different political parties and local people. There are two unions at the supervisory level and one at the executive level. Strikes have occurred here several times concerning issues such as, service conditions, wages and housing facilities, and against policies and new rules and regulations. For example, during the early seventies, the workers were on strike. The issues were service conditions, increase in pay and house allotment. All the unions were united in this strike. The management held several meetings with the union leaders and, after fourteen days of negotiation, it was agreed to increase wages, and the demands related to house allotment were conceded. However, some other demands were not met.

An air of friendliness is noticeable all over the plant but that friendliness is not a hurdle to the progress of work. Dedication to work and efficiency count more for promotion. The employees are entitled to a number of facilities. For example, they have loan facilities for constructing a house, buying a car and television, and the marriage and education of their children. Their children get scholarships when they obtain a good percentage or rank in class. People feel proud to be a part of this organization. They also feel secure about their jobs. This division has been instrumental in the establishment of nearly 30 ancillary industrial units. It also has the facility of houses equipped with all the modern amenities and schools. All the employees, their families and dependents, are entitled to free medical aid.

The sample for this study was drawn from the Publicity and Public Relations Department, Personnel Deparment, Finance Department, Purchase Department, Diversification Department, Machine Shop, Welding Shop, Computer Center, Training and Development, Commercial Department, Hydro-Generator Division, D/C Machine Engineering, A/C Machine Engineering, and Resource and Planning Department. Respondents from the senior supervisory level to the level of the General Manager voluntarily participated in the study.

Organization 6

This is a large manufacturing organization. It was incorporated in the early seventies as a Government of India enterprise to take over the documentation unit and machinery received from the manufacturers of a famous brand of scooters. Within a year it received an industrial licence for the manufacture of 1,00,000 two-wheeler and 30,000 three-wheeler scooters per annum. In the middle of seventies, after the overhauling, installation and commissioning of the plant and machinery, the trial production of two-wheeler scooters commenced. After a year or so, it became the first company in the public sector to float shares. The production of 150cc scooters commenced in the middle of the seventies. But this model had some serious quality problems. As a consequence, after two years, an improved version of the two-wheeler and the production of three-wheelers were introduced. In the early eighties, the production of 100cc scooters was started and, recently, it has introduced a diesel version of the three-wheeler scooter. At present, the factory employs more than 3,500 people (including 300 officers). This includes around 500 staff, 2,600 workmen and 7 casual staff.

Currently, 31 units are in operation which are engaged in the manufacture of a variety of products, such as, rubber, plastic, hardware, pressed and machined items, and a number of mechanical proprietory parts and electrical sub-assemblies. The organization consists of five main units which are headed by various General Managers. These are further divided into sub-units. Unit 1 deals with sub-units related to marketing, sales and services. Sub-units related to production, planning, materials and maintenance are dealt with by Unit 2. Unit 3 deals with sub-units of quality, production engineering, design and development, and electronic data processing. Financial matters are dealt with by Unit 4, and Unit 5 handles the sub-units of administration, personnel and medical services. Apart from this factory, the company also runs a small unit in central India, which has been obtained on lease from a public limited company presently owned by the Government of India. This unit manufactures fans and magnetos for scooters.

The Executive Director is the highest authority in this organization. Under him are the Secretary, Deputy Secretary, and General Manager of different units, in that order. Below them is a long chain of officers—Additional General Manager, Chiefs/Deputy General Manager, Senior Manager, Manager, Deputy Manager, Senior Officer/Senior Engineer, and Officers of different sub-units. The ministerial staff and workmen are at the bottom line of the hierarchy, in that order.

The production performance of two-wheeler scooters, two-wheeler power packs, and three-wheelers, respectively, were around 33,300, 12,100 and 300 in 1979-80; 35,500, 12,550 and 550 in 1980-81; and 31,800, 10,300 and 700 in 1981-82. The sales and income of this organization were around Rs 28.95, 29.68, 29.34 and 27.70 crore in 1980-81, 1981-82, 1982-83, and 1983-84, respectively. The capital employed at the time of establishment was Rs 76,50,000 (paid up capital) and Rs 1,74,40,900 (loan from the Government of India), which grew to Rs 6,56,00,000 in 1983-84. The total investment on the capital facilities of plant and machinery, civil work, and so on, was around Rs 210 million. At the time of the study, of the total issued capital of Rs 524.65 lakh, 62 per cent was held by the Government of India, 21 per cent by financial and other institutions, and the balance 17 per cent by the public. One fatal accident and 26 reportable ones were reported in 1982. In 1983, 1 fatal and 22 non-fatal accidents occurred while in 1984 only

11 non-fatal accidents were reported. The average percentage rates of absenteeism were around 16, 15, and 14 in 1982, 1983, and 1984, respectively.

The organization has been incurring losses since its inception. The cumulative loss of the company as on 31 March, 1982 was around Rs 32.50 crore. The losses sustained by the company are primarily below the break-even point due to various constraints, such as, non-availability of materials, high interest burden on the company on account of poor financial performance, extra expenditure incurred on the procurement of materials due to the lack of financial resources, break-down of machines, and marketing constraints. However, with the introduction of the 100cc scooter, there need not be any apprehension about marketing problems. With the help of a loan of Rs 200 lakh received from the Government of India in the early 1980s, it has been possible to raise the company's production. The government and financial institutions have been requested to consider charging only simple (marginal) interests up to 1985. Thus, with these financial reliefs, it is likely to shed some burden of losses and move towards a progressive and prosperous future.

As far as the existence of unions is concerned, from the company's inception till the late seventies there has been no employee union as such. Subsequently, three unions of employees came into existence, of which only one was recognized. In the early eighties, some leaders of one union resigned, thus leaving two unions functioning. But, with the emergence of a new union recently, three active unions are in existence. The organization has two associations for its officers. The company has faced strikes, tool down and lock-out problems many times. The issues were related mostly to earned leave, wage revision, bonus and housing facilities.

The sample for this study was selected from the Forge, Vigilance, Maintenance, Manufacturing, Purchase, Foundry, Dye-casting, Tool Room, Machine Shop, Process and Planning, Spare-parts, Industrial Engineering and Design, RQAD, Welding, Paint Shop, Dispensary, Time Office, Accounts, and Personnel Department. Respondents from the senior supervisory level to the deputy company secretary and general managerial level voluntarily participated in the study.

Organization 7

This is a large, renowned private organization. This organization set up the country's first synthetic fibre plant in the early 1960s. There was no infrastructure at all. Despite growing obstacles and hindrances, the company expanded its operations. The company has provided direct employment to more than 4,000 persons, while in the beginning this figure was merely 600.

A number of divisions have been established by the organization. Division 1 (the Nylon Division) produces all types of synthetic yarns, including nylon textile, texturized, high tenacity, polyester filament yarns, and so on. The organization has its own Research and Development Department. The organization diversified into the manufacture of Portland Cement and, as a result, Division 2 (i.e., the Cement Works Division) was created.

The organization is headed by the Executive Director who is the owner of the organization. Next to him are two General Managers. Under the General Managers (GMs) are a number of managers and assistant managers. However, the managers of the Personnel and Management Information Departments report directly to the Executive Director. Next to the Assistant Managers is a large chain of engineers/officers and assistant officers. Below the assistant officers are supervisors and/or trainees.

This organization can be categorized as efficient on the basis of various statistics available. The total turnover in 1979 was about 15,000, which has now reached 26,000. The profit in 1979 was Rs 17.5 million; this figure was Rs 19.5 million at the time of the study.

Departmental heads or GMs are allotted offices from where they can observe everyone in the office through a glass window. Because of the heavy workload, officers work late in the evening. They are well paid for extra work. They get proper rewards (or fringe benefits) in terms of money, bonus and verbal appreciation. There is smooth communication between the management and subordinates. Subordinates can go to their bosses and talk freely to them about their problems, and the management also pays sufficient attention to their problems and welfare. Tea and refreshments are served free of charge to everyone at their desks. The organization is fully air-cooled. All types of facilities (such as accommodation, medical benefits, loans and travelling allowance) are available to the members of the organization. Since it is making a lot of profit, the organization shares its profit with the members in terms of a large bonus once in a year—generally on Diwali. There have been no strikes here. The organization has neither an officers' association nor any workers' union. Group membership in the organization is based on the workplace and the nature of work. People share their joys and sorrows with one another. In order to enrich and enlarge the life of their workforce, the organization has established hospitals/dispensaries, a supermarket, sports stadium and an open-air auditorium.

For the purpose of this study, three subdivisions of the cement works were selected: the Sales Department, White Cement Accounts, and Technical. In addition, the Personnel and Management Information Department participated in the study.

Summary

A summary of the data of the seven organizations under study is given in Table 2.1.

Table 2.1 *Data Summary Regarding the Organizations Under Study*

	Organization Number						
	1	2	3	4	5	6	7
Ownership	PB	PR	PR	PB	PB	PB	PR
Nature	SM	S	S	M	M	M	M
Established in	1940s	1910s	1950s	1970s	1950s	1970s	1930s
Profit/Loss	L	P	P	P	P	L	P
Efficiency	I	E	E	E	E	E	E
Approximate size of staff:	4,150	470	270	3,225	10,820	3,530	4,000
Executives	150	50	33	645	1,203	262	80
Non- executives	4,000	420	237	2,580	9,617	3,268	3,920

Note: PB = public; PR = private; S = service; SM = semi-manufacturing; M = manufacturing; P = profit; L= loss; E = efficient; I = inefficient.

As can be seen from Table 2.1 the organizations were heterogeneous, thus meeting my objectives. That is, some represented the public sectors while others were privately managed; some were manufacturing concerns, others service organizations; some turned out to be large ones, others small ones; and some were known to be efficient, while others were inefficient. Having such a heterogeneous sample of organizations was a deliberate attempt on my part to generalize the survey findings in significantly different settings.

The Sample

Altogether, 440 executives representing seven organizations participated in the study. These were predominantly males (90 per cent). Two main strategies were adopted in drawing the sample: main sections or divisions of an organization were covered, and only those executives were sampled who had at least two subordinates directly under them.

Based on the salary range, the number of levels of management, and subjective status allocation within an organization, the sampled executives were classified into low, middle and top levels. Details of this classification are provided in Table 2.2. As can be seen from Table 2.2, of the sampled 440 executives, the majority represented the low and middle levels of management (41 per cent) whereas only around 18 per cent constituted the top level.

Table 2.2 *Details of the Sample*

Organization	Levels			Total	Percentage
	Low	Middle	Top		
1	34	22	4	60	13.64
2	22	6	12	40	9.09
3	16	7	5	28	6.36
4	40	27	10	77	17.50
5	19	34	18	71	16.14
6	34	47	18	99	22.50
7	15	37	13	65	14.77
Total	180	180	80	440	
Percentage	40.91	40.91	18.18		100.00

The background facts about the respondents organization-wise and level-wise, respectively, are reported in Appendix I and Appendix II. The mean scores on the background facts are illustrated in Table 2.3. Each of the background characteristics was analyzed in a 2×2 ANOVA, with two levels of function (manufacturing/service) and two levels of ownership (public/private) of the organizations. For a further clarification of results, Dunn's multiple comparison procedure was used to test the significance of intercell comparisons of interest. All comparisons were tested at a $p < 0.01$ level of significance (Kirk, 1968).

Table 2.3   *Mean Scores on Background Characteristics: Ownership versus Function of Organizations*

Ownership: Functions	Organizations				
	PB M (n = 247)	PB S (n = 60)	PR M (n = 65)	PR S (n = 68)	Total Sample (N = 440)
Age (years)	38.00	42.40	37.09	34.29	37.89
Education*	3.01	3.13	3.43	3.16	3.11
Tenure in present position (years)	3.86	6.90	2.98	3.62	4.11
Tenure in present organization (years)	10.51	16.80	11.29	5.13	10.65
No. of promotions	1.96	1.23	2.44	1.54	1.87
No. of subordinates†	2.55	4.95	2.40	1.93	2.76
No. of other organizations worked for	1.31	0.72	1.05	1.50	1.22
Salary range**	4.80	5.10	4.77	1.91	4.39
Salary progress[a]	12.50	11.98	12.63	5.50	11.37

Note: PB = public; PR = private; M = manufacturing; S = service; * = 5-point scale; † = 9-point scale; ** = 11-point scale; [a] = (salary range/age) × 100.

Table 2.3 and Appendix I make it clear that the bulk of the respondents (69.4 per cent) were in the range of 26 to 45 years ($M = 37.9$). However, a clear interaction between functions and ownership, $F (1,436) = 12.57$, $p < 0.01$, was evident. Dunn's analyses clarified that whereas those executives who were employed in the public service organizations were significantly older than those employed in other organizations, the executives in the private service organizations appeared to be the youngest ones. The pattern in general suggested that the public sector executives were significantly older than the private sector executives, $F (1,436) = 19.75$, $p < 0.01$.

The role of ownership and function was not very critical to the formal education attained by the respondents. On the whole, the analysis suggested that over 50 per cent of the sampled executives were graduates (i.e., holding a bachelor's degree). A few (18 per cent) had master's degrees, and some were found to hold professional degrees (e.g., a Ph.D.).

The executives were seen to differ significantly in terms of their tenure in the present position and tenure in the present organization.

Table 2.3 shows that the executives in public sector organizations had longer tenure in both the present position, $F(1,436) = 27.06$, $p < 0.01$, and present organization, $F(1,436) = 61.77$, $p < 0.01$, than those in private organizations. The interactions between ownership and function were also apparent with regard to tenure in the present position, $F(1,436) = 8.94$, $p < 0.01$, and present organization, $F(1,436) = 80.71$, $p < 0.01$. Executives in public service organizations appeared to have both tenures significantly longer than executives in other organizations. On the whole, 67 per cent of the respondents were working in their present positions for about four years (or less) and 31 per cent were in the range of 5 to 14 years. Similarly, the majority of executives (67 per cent) were found to have served their present organizations for 5 to 19 years.

The results also revealed that about 66 per cent of the respondents were promoted during their professional career at least once or twice; some of them (about 28 per cent) had even been promoted three or four times. Table 2.3 also makes it evident that manufacturing organizations have provided promotional opportunities to their executives significantly more often, $F(1,436) = 22.33$, $p < 0.01$, than the service organizations.

Regarding the span of control, about 66 per cent of the executives were supervising 1 to 9 subordinates. An inspection of Table 2.3 also suggests that executives had a significantly smaller span of control in private service organizations, whereas they had a greater span of control in public service organizations—suggesting a clear interaction, $F(1,436) = 29.29$, $p < 0.01$.

Other findings on the demographic facts are as follows: About 43 per cent of the respondents did not serve any other organizations. While 42 per cent had worked for 1 or 2 organizations, about 13 per cent had worked for 3 or 4 organizations in their adult career. About 55 per cent of the executives were in a salary range of Rs 1,501 to 2,700 per month, whereas about 24 per cent were in the range of Rs 2,701 to 3,600. One important finding (see Table 2.3) was that executives in public manufacturing organizations were getting a higher salary than their counterparts in other organizations, whereas executives in private service organizations had the lowest salary system. This interaction was significant, $F(1,436) = 35.57$, $p < 0.01$. A similar interaction pattern, $F(1,436) = 31.17$, $p < 0.01$, can be observed for the salary progress of the respondents. The salary range also varied a lot across organizations, $F(6,433) =$

249.12, $p < 0.01$. Organizations 2 and 3 had the lowest salary system; this may be because both were charitable hospital organizations. Further, a number of executives work here on nominal payment and many head nurses and sisters receive only a small honorarium. Except for the doctors, the rest of the staff are low-paid. The salary level was the highest for Organizations 1 and 4, both of which were large public sector organizations.

The relationships between the background facts are presented in Table 2.4. It did not require any close scrutiny to discover that the background factors were as related as one would expect on theoretical grounds. For example, age, tenure in present organization, tenure in present position, span of control, salary, number of promotions and hierarchical level were all significantly tied up with one another. This means that the executives at the top level were older, had longer tenure in their present position and present organization, were promoted significantly more often, had a greater span of control, and were in a higher salary range. Education was also seen to be positively related to the salary scale, hierarchical level and number of promotions.

Table 2.4 *Intercorrelations Among Background Facts*

	1	2	3	4	5	6	7	8	9
Age	X								
Education	06	X							
Tenure in present organization	65[b]	−07	X						
Tenure in present position	31[b]	−04	41[b]	X					
No. of subordinates	23[b]	01	20[b]	15[b]	X				
Salary scale	48[b]	25[b]	45[b]	07	16[b]	X			
No. of promotions	50[b]	12[a]	49[b]	−01	10[a]	44[b]	X		
No. of other organizations worked for	30[b]	08	−04	02	07	06	17[b]	X	
Level	35[b]	33[b]	20[b]	−01	01	64[b]	43[b]	14[b]	X

Note: $N = 440$;
　　　decimal points have been omitted;
　　　[a]$p < 0.05$; [b]$p < 0.01$.

The Survey Questionnaire

On the basis of various studies available in current literature, a questionnaire booklet was prepared consisting of several tests and measures. The questionnaire consisted of four sections. Section I dealt with items concerning the ways of dealing with subordinates in day-to-day affairs (for instance, downward influence tactics). Section II assessed the ways of dealing with immediate superiors (that is, upward influence tactics). Section III assessed the perceptions and observations about the organization (or, the organizational climate). Finally, section IV had items concerning the personal and demographic characteristics of the respondents (for instance, leadership styles). A summary of the measures employed in the study is contained in Table 2.5.

Table 2.5   *Survey Questionnaires Employed in the Study*

Section	Measure(s)	No. of Items	Scales
I	1. Downward influence tactics	60	5-point
I	2. Bases of power	7	5-point
II	1. Leader behavior	50	5-point
II	2. Upward influence tactics	55	5-point
II	3. Bases of power	7	5-point
III	1. Organizational climate	30	5-point
IV	1. Leadership style	45	5-point
IV	2. Background data	11	SIM

Note: SIM = Single item measures having different scale-points.

This questionnaire was a revision of an earlier pilot questionnaire from which unreliable, unclear and irrelevant questions had been omitted. During this phase of analysis, some items were modified and some new ones were added. The final questionnaire was sixteen printed pages and contained as many as 265 questions or scales (see Appendix III). Details about the questionnaire concerning its psychometric properties (such as, factor structures and reliabilities) are outlined in the following chapters.

The Procedure

Two female Research Assistants, both with master's degrees in psychology and experienced in interviewing, conducted the interviews with executives. Prior to the actual data collection, they were trained by me for three weeks. Their training included the following major components. Some preliminary lectures were given on the projects dealing with the general aims and procedures of the proposed survey. Role-playing sessions were arranged. The Assistants acted out, in turn, the roles of interviewer and respondent using a draft questionnaire. A pilot study was conducted where each interviewer was asked to contact at least five managers from an organization. A discussion was initiated regarding the pilot study, including the problems related to item construction, length of time spent in interviewing and general problems of communication.

After training, the interviewers were allocated to organizations from the sampling frame. Data were collected during the fall of 1984 and spring of 1985. Executives were assured complete *anonymity* of their individual responses, and the importance of frank and sincere replies was emphasized. The average time for a complete interview was approximately 90 minutes.

The Statistical Analyses

In the best interest of the survey, the following statistical techniques were employed.

Some preliminary analyses were conducted to examine the psychometric properties of the measures employed in the study. Most of the measures were subjected to a varimax rotated factor analysis, that is, a partial test of the construct validity. Nie *et al.* (1975) have described five methods of factoring of which two commonly used methods are: principal factoring without iteration (PA1) and principal factoring with iteration (PA2). In this study, all the measures which were subjected to factor analysis were analyzed using the PA2 method, i.e., principal factoring with iteration for communality and varimax rotation. The PA2 method of factoring was used because, according to Nie *et al.* (1975), it has two advantages over the PA1 method. First, it automatically replaces the main diagonal elements of the correlation matrix with communality estimates. In this the user gets the so-called inferred factors. Second, it employs an iteration procedure for improving the estimates of communality. Varimax rotation was used as the emphasis in this method is on cleaning up the factors rather than the variables. For each factor, varimax rotation tends to yield high loadings for a few variables. The rest of the loadings in the factors are expected to be near zero. In this way, one is able to infer factors in a neat and clean way.

The selection of items to be retained in the scale (after factor analysis) was made on the basis of two criteria. In the first place, the solution was constrained using the criterion of eigenvalues greater than 1.00, and meeting the criteria of factor loadings not less than 0.35 on the defining component and no cross-loadings greater than 0.25. In cases where an item was loaded heavily (0.35 or greater) with two factors, it was retained at both places. In the second place, items were selected on the basis of an examination of each item's correlation with other items representing the factor and their correlations with items in the remaining factors. Only those items were included in the final analysis which had high inter-correlation within a factor and low intercorrelation with the remaining factors. During this preliminary analysis, Cronbach's coefficients alpha and descriptive statistics (such as, means and standard deviations of the scales) were also computed.

Second, researchers have used different analytical strategies to identify moderators in leadership studies. According to Howell, Dorfman and Kerr (1986), different strategies (such as, ANOVA, median split sample with correlation coefficients and hierarchical multiple regression) yield different information and the techniques may have been used inappropriately. For example, the median split sample approach using zero-order correlations gives information regarding the degree and direction of the relationship between the two variables, whereas the hierarchical regression approach provides information regarding the form or pattern of a relationship between the two variables. In any event, both Arnold (1982) and Stone and Hollenbeck (1984) have strongly recommended the use of a hierarchical regression approach as the appropriate strategy to identify moderator(s). Since the position taken in this study is slightly different from the one recommended in the foregoing, a note is in order.

In a hierarchical regression analysis, a moderator is identified through interaction. For each interaction pair, scores on the predictor and moderator are first converted to z scores and then a product term is formed. If the moderator hypothesis is to be confirmed, the beta weight of the product term (that is, interaction) should be significant. Significant interactions are then analyzed graphically (Hunt, Osborn and Larson, 1975). It should also be mentioned that the use of such a regression approach generally requires that the data in each pair are obtained on interval scales. In this analysis, the stepwise multiple regression strategy was adopted because the moderator was split into two groups based on company climate scores. Each of the seven organizations was located in a 'high' or 'low' category on each of the three climate dimensions based on an inspection of the organization's mean score on the dimension (see Chapter 3, section on Organizational Climate Measures). It should be mentioned that this was an 'organizational level' analysis; the objective was to study how differences in organizational environments moderate the predictor-criterion relationship, not how individual perceptions of the environment affect this relationship. In view of this assumption, five organizations were classified as having a favorable climate (that is, they had higher scores on all the climate factors) and two were classified as having an unfavorable climate (that is, they had lower scores on all the three climate dimensions). Thus, two sets of regression analysis were employed—one in a favorable and another in an unfavorable climate—to examine the patterns of relationships between predictors and the use of influence strategies.

All statistical analyses were performed using the *SPSS* manual (Nie *et al.*, 1975) on the DEC 1090 system available at the Indian Institute of Technology, Kanpur.

3 Managing Subordinates

Chapter 2 outlined the broad objectives and strategy of investigations. The proposed relationships between the study variables are examined and tested in this and following chapters. This chapter specifically presents data on how managers influence their subordinates.

Measures Used

A brief description of the measures used in this chapter follows. This description includes the properties of the scales and a discussion on psychometric results. The questionnaire items are provided in Appendix III. The interrelationships of all the variables included in the study are given in Appendix IV.

Downward Influence Strategy Measures

Sixty single-statement items were drawn from the current literature (Falbo, 1977; Falbo and Peplau, 1980; Kipnis *et al.*, 1980) to tap the respondents' downward influence strategies. Respondents were asked to indicate on a 5-point scale (1 = never; 5 = very often) the *frequency* with which during the past six months they engaged in the behaviors indicated by the scale items. They were instructed to respond in terms of what they generally did, and *not* what they would like to do. The distribution of items across strategies is given in Table 3.1.

Table 3.1   *Distribution of Items of Downward Strategy Measures*

Strategies	Code	Number of Items
Assertion	A	6
Coalition	C	4
Diplomacy	D	3
Exchange of benefits	E	5
Ingratiation	I	5
Manipulation	M	3
Personalized help	P̃	4
Persuasion	P	2
Rationality	R	5
Sanctions (positive)	S	4
Sanctions (negative)	Ś	5
Showing dependency	D̲	3
Showing expertise	Ĕ	4
Threats	T	3
Upward appeal	U	4
Total		60

A partial test of the construct validity of the scales employed a varimax rotated factor analysis. Table 3.2 shows the factor loadings obtained. It can be seen from Table 3.2 that the measures were constrained to seven interpretable factors (consisting of a total of 28 significant items), accounting for a total of 76.5 per cent of the variance. It is also evident that, for the most part, the items loaded rather cleanly (that is, loadings above .36 on the appropriate sub-scale, with loadings below .25 on the remaining sub-scales). The items having significant loadings on more than one factor were credited to the factor on which the loading was the highest, except for item 46 which was allowed to stay on two factors (that is, factors 4 and 6). Three influence strategies—positive sanction, negative sanction, and threats—did not emerge at all as distinct configurations. In fact, their items were not clustered on any particular factor either. Hence these factors were reconstituted by having 13 of their original items, which were not loaded on other factors.

Table 3.2   *Factor Analysis Results—Downward Strategy Measures (N= 440)*

Items	Factor						
	1	2	3	4	5	6	7
13. I promised to help them to get further advancement if they helped me now	*0.54*	0.20	0.12	0.03	0.07	0.14	0.08
15. I told them the reasons why my plan was the best	−0.08	*0.41*	0.20	0.05	0.11	0.15	0.06
16. I showed that I was concerned about their welfare	0.03	*0.38*	0.20	0.08	0.13	0.11	0.01
17. I offered an exchange of favor	*0.58*	0.01	0.16	−0.02	0.13	0.20	0.12
20. I obtained the informal support of higher-ups	0.11	0.05	−0.01	0.13	−0.01	*0.58*	−0.03
22. I obtained my boss's approval before making the request	0.17	−0.04	0.02	0.17	0.02	*0.40*	0.11
25. At times I showed my knowledge of the specific issue	0.11	*0.49*	0.17	0.00	−0.05	0.06	0.07
26. I got the support of someone higher to back my request	0.13	0.01	0.13	0.05	0.10	*0.63*	0.05
28. I made an impression that I cannot really work without their help	0.18	0.06	0.05	0.21	*0.56*	−0.06	−0.07
29. I got everyone else to agree with me before I made the request	0.05	0.07	0.01	*0.58*	0.09	0.15	−0.00
31. I repeatedly reminded them about what I wanted	0.04	0.23	0.04	0.13	0.15	0.13	*0.42*
33. I showed that I sought their help	0.06	0.13	0.16	−0.07	*0.70*	0.05	−0.02
34. I helped them even in personal matters	0.07	0.15	*0.62*	0.07	0.10	0.00	0.12
37. I called a staff meeting to back my request	0.15	0.15	0.14	*0.49*	0.14	0.19	0.07
39. I influenced them because of my competence	0.12	*0.65*	0.05	−0.03	0.09	−0.03	−0.14
40. I reminded them of some past favor I did for them	*0.66*	0.09	0.05	0.07	0.04	0.06	0.05
42. I argued my points logically	−0.16	*0.45*	0.05	0.18	0.04	−0.02	0.21
45. My knowledge of the technical issues won their favor for me	−0.03	*0.59*	0.08	0.13	0.11	−0.06	0.16
46. I obtained the support of co-workers to back my request	0.18	0.14	0.11	*0.41*	0.08	*0.40*	0.13
47. I made them realize that I needed their help	0.11	−0.01	0.22	0.32	*0.60*	0.08	0.06
48. I challenged their ability (e.g., 'I bet you can't do that')	*0.46*	0.04	−0.13	0.16	0.01	0.09	0.00

(Table 3.2 contd...)

Items	Factor						
	1	2	3	4	5	6	7
49. I asked them to cooperate to get the work done while promising extra benefits for it	*0.60*	−0.03	0.19	0.09	0.10	0.03	0.11
50. I simply ordered them to do what was asked	0.17	−0.06	0.11	−0.12	−0.17	−0.04	*0.37*
53. I went out of my way to help them at the time of their need	0.04	0.18	*0.46*	0.04	0.17	−0.00	0.05
55. I told them exactly why I needed their help	0.02	0.17	0.16	0.08	*0.41*	0.09	0.04
57. I encouraged them to discuss even their personal problems	−0.02	0.13	*0.69*	0.14	0.10	−0.02	−0.01
59. I pointed out that the rules required that they comply	0.18	0.17	0.12	0.05	0.06	0.05	*0.57*
60. I usually got my way by making them feel that it was their idea	0.01	0.13	0.11	*0.54*	0.10	−0.09	0.11
Eigenvalue	8.65	4.05	2.09	1.73	1.26	1.18	1.14
Percentage of variance	32.9	15.4	8.0	6.6	4.8	4.5	4.3

Note: Factor 1 = exchange and challenge; factor 2 = expertise and reasons; factor 3 = personalized help; factor 4 = coalition and manipulation; factor 5 = showing dependency; factor 6 = upward appeal; factor 7 = assertion.

Descriptive statistics, scale characteristics, reliability coefficients and inter-relationships among the scales are presented in Table 3.3. It is important to note that the scales exhibited well over the 0.50 reliability levels suggested by Nunnally (1978) as a minimum level for acceptable reliability. Six of the scales ranged in their reliability from 0.59 to 0.76. Only one factor—assertion—had its reliability just below the required level. This might be because it was composed of just three items.

Table 3.3 also suggests that the average correlation between the factors used as scales was 0.26, indicating a reasonable level of scale independence. However, some overlap in the factors was expected partly because of some spread-over effects from one strategy to another and partly because of the fact that measures were perceptual ones. Table 3.3 makes it clear that only 6 out of the 45 coefficients of correlation were not significant; one was significant at the 0.05 level; the rest were significant at the 0.01 level. However, only two correlations were in the 0.50s; five were in the 0.40s; and rest of others were below 0.40. This fact again indicates a considerable non-overlapping variance in the dimensions.

Table 3.3 also shows that the exchange and challenge scale exhibits an average inter-item correlation of 0.39, which is far greater than the correlation of index items versus all other items ($r = 0.12$). A similar pattern can be observed in the case of other scales. The fact that for each scale the average inter-item correlation is significantly greater than the index items versus all the other items may be interpreted as partial evidence for the discriminant validity of the scales.

Table 3.3 *Descriptive Statistics, Scale Characteristics, Reliabilities and Intercorrelations Among Downward Strategy Measures*

Strategies	1	2	3	4	5	6	7	8	9	10
1. Exchange and challenge	(76)									
2. Expertise and reasons	14[b]	(71)								
3. Personalized help	19[b]	39[b]	(70)							
4. Coalition and manipulation	29[h]	29[b]	26[b]	(65)						
5. Showing Dependency	26[b]	27[b]	35[b]	33[b]	(69)					
6. Upward appeal	40[b]	15[b]	14[b]	56[b]	22[b]	(65)				
7. Assertion	32[b]	22[b]	20[b]	19[b]	10[a]	25[b]	(48)			
8. Positive sanction	45[b]	33[b]	45[b]	31[b]	35[h]	34[b]	25[b]	(51)		
9. Negative sanction	51[b]	03	02	15[b]	06	29[b]	33[b]	21[b]	(59)	
10. Threats	43[b]	-02	00	23[b]	07	37[b]	30[b]	28[b]	49[b]	(62)
No. of items	5	6	3	4	4	4	3	4	5	3
M	9.21	20.47	9.60	9.84	11.35	9.40	8.80	11.39	7.78	4.58
SD	3.71	3.93	2.55	3.26	3.12	3.29	2.36	2.77	2.64	1.92
Among index items correlations	0.39	0.29	0.43	0.32	0.36	0.33	0.23	*	*	*
Index items vs. all others correlations	0.12	0.11	0.14	0.16	0.13	0.14	0.11	*	*	*
Split-half reliability	0.76	0.71	0.69	0.65	0.69	0.66	0.47	0.52	0.60	0.63

Note: Decimal points in matrix and alpha are omitted.

Figures in brackets indicate coefficients alpha reliability; $N = 440$; [a]$p < 0.05$; [b]$p < 0.01$.

* Information not available—generated factors.

Bases of Power Measures

The measures employed seven items, each referring to a particular base of power. The items were drawn from the work by Hersey *et al.* (1979). The subjects were asked to answer the question: 'What makes you influential?' They were required to describe on a 5-point scale (1 = almost no extent; 5 = to a very great extent) the *extent* to which each statement was true with respect to their immediate subordinates/immediate superior. Although they lack psychometric properties, such single-item measures to study bases of power have been shown to have concurrent or predicative validity in a number of previous studies (see, for instance, Adler, 1983; Cobb, 1980; Martin and Hunt, 1980; Student, 1968).

Table 3.4 provides the intercorrelations among the bases of power measures. It can be seen from Table 3.4 that the scales were moderately intercorrelated (average *r* in each matrix, above the diagonal or below the diagonal, was 0.21), indicating a reasonable level of scale independence. It is also evident that both sets of correlations had a similar pattern in their deliberations. It is interesting to note that respondents perceived their bases of power similarly with respect to both immediate subordinates and immediate superior. In other words, respondents reported that they had similar bases of power with regard to both the targets of influence. With regard to the referent, information and connection bases of power, this similarity is much more evident (see coefficients of correlation in brackets in Table 3.4). This fact may be attributed partly to the common method variance.

Table 3.4 *Intercorrelations Among the Bases of Power*

Bases	1	2	3	4	5	6	7	M	SD
1. Reward	(13[a])	29[b]	24[b]	16[a]	11[a]	35[b]	26[b]	3.98	0.89
2. Coercion	4	(26[b])	33[b]	8	7	26[b]	28[b]	1.73	0.94
3. Legitimate	26[b]	27[b]	(13[a])	17[b]	28[b]	12[b]	24[b]	3.21	1.03
4. Referent	25[b]	8	17[b]	(52[b])	38[b]	17[b]	16[b]	3.55	0.86
5. Expert	27[b]	4	16[b]	37[b]	(40[b])	7	12[b]	4.01	0.84
6. Information	14[b]	34[b]	22[b]	22[b]	16[b]	(51[b])	30[b]	2.67	1.16
7. Connection	11[a]	39[b]	22[b]	22[b]	8	47[b]	(61[b])	2.11	1.17
M	2.80	2.35	3.21	3.70	4.16	2.86	2.43		
SD	1.00	1.03	1.10	0.91	0.73	1.05	1.23		

Note: The matrix above the diagonal indicates downward bases of power; the matrix below the diagonal indicates upward bases of power. Decimal points in correlation coefficients are omitted. Figures in brackets indicate the relationship between the same bases of power (e.g., reward *vs* reward). *N* = 440; [a]$p < 0.05$; [b]$p < 0.01$.

The mean scores (see Table 3.4) quickly disclosed that executives possessed more expert and referent power when influencing subordinates, and expert and reward power when influencing an immediate superior. On the other hand, regardless of the target of influence, they possessed little connection and coercive power.

Leadership Style Measures

Based upon the recent work by Ansari (1986), Hassan (1986), and Sinha (1980), 45 single-statement items were employed to tap the respondents' self-reported leadership styles. The items represented five styles: authoritarian, participative, nurturant, task-oriented and bureaucratic, each composed of nine items. The respondents rated each statement on a 5-point scale (1 = quite false; 5 = quite true), according to whether it was true or false to them.

The set of items with their appropriate scores was then submitted to a varimax rotated factor analysis. The factor loadings obtained are reported in Table 3.5. It is evident from this table that the measures constrained to three meaningful and interpretable factors (with a total of 17 significant items), accounting for a total of 60.4 per cent of the variance. On the whole, the items loaded rather cleanly. The only exception was observed in the case of item 15 which was allowed to stay on two factors (i.e., factors 2 and 3). Surprisingly, authoritarian style did not emerge at all as a distinct configuration. Nor did its items cluster on any particular factor. Consequently, this factor was generated by having its original items which were not loaded on other factors.

Table 3.5   *Factor Analysis Results—Leadership Style (Self-Reported) Measures* (N= 440)

Items	Factor		
	1	*2*	*3*
1. I take special care that work gets top priority	0.04	*0.49*	0.11
4. I believe in strict division of labor, even in a work group	0.05	0.16	*0.45*
5. I expect my subordinates to increase their knowledge on the job	0.07	*0.62*	0.18
6. I drive myself really hard	0.10	*0.61*	−0.01
10. I think that these days power and prestige are necessary so that subordinates will listen to me	−0.03	0.09	*0.36*

(Table 3.5 contd...)

Items		Factor		
		1	2	3
13.	I always keep track of the progress of work	0.05	*0.47*	0.19
15.	If clear job descriptions are available, there will be less conflicts in an organization	−0.01	*0.36*	*0.42*
18.	I believe that one can really grow up by learning to do a job well	0.14	*0.51*	0.04
25.	I treat all group members as my equal	*0.42*	0.06	−0.02
28.	I grant full freedom and autonomy to the subordinates so that they can work best	*0.57*	0.22	−0.08
29.	As and when necessary, I give specific directions to my subordinates	0.15	*0.40*	0.12
31.	I try to confine myself to my own jurisdiction	−0.03	0.03	*0.43*
36.	I see that subordinates work to their capacity	0.25	*0.48*	0.07
37.	I go by the joint decisions of my group	*0.74*	0.16	0.05
38.	I believe that the area of responsibility should be clearly demarcated according to rank and position	0.10	0.18	*0.67*
39.	I provide all information to my subordinates and let them jointly find the solution to a problem	*0.61*	0.14	0.04
40.	I always follow standard rules and regulations	0.06	0.20	*0.46*
Eigenvalue		7.26	3.05	1.27
Percentage of variance		37.9	15.9	6.6

Note: Factor 1 =participative; factor 2= task-oriented; factor 3= bureaucratic.

Table 3.6 provides the descriptive statistics, psychometric properties and intercorrelations of the scales. It should be noted that the scales documented acceptable reliability coefficients which were in the range of 0.68 to 0.77. From Table 3.6 it can also be inferred that the scales were moderately intercorrelated (average r = 0.33), indicating a considerable non-overlapping variance in the scales. However, some spread-over effects were apparent from one factor to another. Since two of the factors—authoritarian and bureaucratic—were conceptually close, they were closely tied with each other. Task-oriented style was positively related with all the other style dimensions. Interestingly, the participative and the authoritarian styles were independent of each other. Table 3.6 quickly reveals that the average inter-item correlations were all above 0.25—a restriction placed by Nunnally (1978)— and they were significantly greater than the index items versus all others correlations, a fact that may be interpreted as partial evidence for the discriminant validity of the scales.

Table 3.6 *Descriptive Statistics, Scale Characteristics, Reliabilities and Inter-correlations Among Leadership Style (Self-Reported) Measures*

Style	1	2	3	4
1. Participative	(0.69)			
2. Task-oriented	0.35[b]	(0.76)		
3. Bureaucratic	0.10[a]	0.49[b]	(0.68)	
4. Authoritarian	−0.01	0.37[b]	0.68[b]	(0.71)
No. of items	4	8	6	9
M	14.96	33.40	22.30	31.91
SD	2.37	3.48	3.46	5.02
Among index items correlations	0.36	0.29	0.27	*
Index items *vs* all others correlations	0.11	0.18	0.14	*
Split-half reliability	0.69	0.77	0.69	0.72

Note: Figures in brackets indicate coefficients alpha reliability; $N = 440$; [a]$p < 0.05$; [b]$p < 0.01$.
    * Information not available—generated variable.

The mean scores revealed that task-oriented followed by participative styles were predominant in Indian organizations, while the authoritarian style was least endorsed by the executives.

Leadership Behavior Measures

Fifty single-statement items were drawn from recent work by Ansari (1986), Hassan (1986) and Sinha (1980) to measure the leadership styles of the immediate superior. Five style dimensions were incorporated—authoritarian, participative, nurturant, task-oriented and bureaucratic—each dimension consisting of 10 items. Respondents were asked to rate each statement on a 5-point scale (1 = quite false; 5 = quite true) according to whether it was true or false in relation to their immediate superior.

A partial test of the construct validity of the scales employed a varimax rotated factor analysis. Table 3.7 contains the factor loadings obtained. It is evident from Table 3.7 that the measures constrained to four meaningful and interpretable factors (with a total of 26

Table 3.7   *Factor Analysis Results—Leader Behavior Measures (N = 440)*

Items	Factor			
	1	*2*	*3*	*4*
4. He helps his subordinates to grow up and assume greater responsibility	*0.49*	*0.35*	0.10	−0.06
6. He makes his subordinates feel free even to disagree with him	0.23	*0.61*	0.06	−0.13
8. He provides all information to his subordinates and lets them jointly find the solution to a problem	0.19	*0.61*	0.14	−0.10
11. He interacts with his subordinates as if they are equal	0.18	*0.63*	0.03	−0.07
13. He goes by the joint decisions of his group	0.24	*0.57*	0.12	−0.17
14. He takes special care that work gets top priority	*0.67*	0.19	0.21	0.02
16. He believes that most of the interpersonal troubles start because people try to be over-friendly and informal on the job	0.06	−0.02	0.06	*0.42*
17. He maintains a high standard of performance	*0.71*	0.18	0.24	0.00
19. He thinks that clear job descriptions are necessary for the effective functioning of the employee	*0.42*	0.21	0.24	0.02
21. He does not think that his subordinates deserve to be officers	−0.22	−0.23	−0.01	*0.39*
22. He openly shows affection to those subordinates who work hard	*0.44*	*0.36*	0.13	− 0.02
25. He believes that one can really grow up by learning to do a job well	*0.67*	0.24	0.05	−0.16
28. He always follows standard rules and regulations	0.28	0.13	*0.75*	0.01
29. He grants full freedom and autonomy to his subordinates so that they can work best	*0.37*	*0.55*	0.15	−0.18
30. He rules with an iron hand in order to get work done	0.06	−0.18	0.17	*0.56*
31. He wants to have full power and control over his subordinates	−0.07	−0.25	0.14	*0.54*
33. He believes that all of us have more or less equal potentialities	0.16	*0.56*	0.10	−0.08
34. He drives himself really hard	*0.57*	0.14	0.10	0.14
37. As and when necessary, he gives specific directions to his subordinates	*0.54*	0.22	0.11	0.05
44. He is a friendly type	0.25	*0.56*	0.05	− 0.20
45. He always goes by the rules and procedures	0.18	0.09	*0.78*	0.03
46. He maintains a strict division of labor even in his own group	0.23	0.15	*0.49*	0.13

(Table 3.7 contd...)

Items	Factor			
	1	*2*	*3*	*4*
47. He finds time to listen to the personal problems of subordinates	*0.39*	*0.46*	0.04	− 0.12
48. He does not tolerate any interference from his subordinates	−0.05	−0.25	0.16	*0.37*
49. He has affection for his subordinates	*0.44*	*0.45*	0.11	−0.12
50 He believes that if he does not watch out, there are many people who will pull him down	−0.08	−0.04	0.00	*0.41*
Eigenvalue	14.08	3.60	1.39	1.21
Percentage of variance	58.7	14.6	5.8	5.1

Note: Factor 1 = nurturant-task; factor 2 = participative; factor 3 = bureaucratic; factor 4 = authoritarian.

significant items), accounting for a total of 84.2 per cent of the variance. It can also be seen from Table 3.7 that, for the most part, the items loaded rather cleanly. The overall strategy was that the items bearing significant loadings on more than one factor were credited to the factor on which the loading was the highest, except for five items (items 4, 22, 29, 47 and 49) which were allowed to stay on two factors (factors 1 and 2). Apparently, as indicated by the percentages of variance explained, the first two factors were the strongest ones whereas the last two factors were the weak ones.

Descriptive statistics, scale characteristics, reliability coefficients and interrelationships among the scales are contained in Table 3.8. It should be noted that the four scales documented fairly adequate reliability coefficients, ranging from 0.68 to 0.89.

Table 3.8 also indicates that the average correlation between the factors used as scales was 0.26, indicating a reasonable level of scale independence. However, some overlap in the factors was obvious partly because of some spread-over effects from one factor to another and partly because of the fact that measures were perceptual ones. The ovelap is clear as to the first two scales: nurturant-task and participative. A possible reason may be that the two scales had at least five common items in their configurations. Participative behavior, as one would expect on theoretical grounds, was inversely related to authoritarian behavior. Nurturant-task behavior was closely and positively related with the bureaucratic behavior but negatively with authoritarian behavior. While participative behavior showed a positive relationship with bureaucratic behavior, the latter and autocratic behavior were positively inter-related.

Table 3.8   *Descriptive Statistics, Scale Characteristics, Reliabilities and Intercorrelations Among Leader Behavior Measures*

Style	1	2	3	4
1. Nurturant-task	(0.89)			
2. Participative	0.85^b	(0.89)		
3. Bureaucratic	0.46^b	0.36^b	(0.77)	
4. Authoritarian	-0.23^b	-0.37^b	0.11^a	(0.69)
No. of items	11	11	3	6
M	40.50	38.23	10.10	18.20
SD	7.42	7.73	2.53	4.10
Among index items correlations	0.42	0.42	0.53	0.26
Index items *vs* all others correlations	0.26	0.26	0.21	0.01
Split-half reliability	0.89	0.89	0.77	0.68

Note: Figures in brackets indicate coefficients alpha reliability; $N = 440$; $^a p < 0.05$; $^b p < 0.01$.

A quick look at Table 3.8 indicates that the average inter-item correlations were all above 0.25 and were significantly greater than the index items versus all others correlations. This fact may be interpreted as partial evidence for the discriminant validity of the scales.

The mean scores disclosed that nurturant-task and participative styles were highly endorsed by the executives, whereas bureaucratic and authoritarian behavior were the least endorsed ones.

Organizational Climate Measures

A modified version of Litwin and Stringer's (1968) organizational climate questionnaire was used to tap the respondents' perceptions of the organizational climate. The climate questionnaire was modified by Schnake (1983) with the idea that removing the affective component from responses to an organizational climate questionnaire would improve the discriminant validity of the instrument, and would lead to a more objective measure of organizational climate.

Subjects were given a set of 30 statements concerning their perceptions and observations about the organization in which they were working. They rated each item on a 5-point scale (1 = almost no extent; 5 = to a very great extent) the *extent* to which it was true for their organization. The set of items with their appropriate scores was then submitted to a varimax rotated factor analysis. The factor analysis results are provided in Table 3.9. It is clear from Table 3.9 that climate measures constrained to three neat and meaningful factors (with a total of 13 significant items), accounting for a total of 86.7 per cent of the variance. It is also quite clear that the items loaded rather cleanly (i.e. loadings above 0.42 on the appropriate sub-scale, with no cross-loadings greater than 0.26).

Table 3.9   *Factor Analysis Results—Climate Measures*

Items	Factor		
	1	*2*	*3*
1. The assignments to this organization are clearly defined	0.26	*0.54*	0.09
2. In this organization, we set very high standards for performance	0.18	*0.57*	0.08
6. The policies and goals of this organization are clearly understood	0.24	*0.79*	0.17
7. The goals I am supposed to achieve in my area are realistic	0.17	*0.65*	0.04
11. People in this organization don't really trust each other very much(R)	0.16	0.15	*0.69*
13. In this organization, I am given a chance to participate in setting the performance standards for my job	*0.46*	0.26	−0.13
14. In this organization, people don't seem to take much pride in the excellence of their performance (R)	0.08	0.19	*0.51*
16. We have a promotion system that helps the best person rise to the top	*0.73*	0.24	0.07
17. People in this organization tend to be cool and aloof towards each other (R)	−0.10	0.08	*0.57*
21. In this organization, people are rewarded in proportion to the excellence of their job performance	*0.79*	0.26	0.07
26. There is a lot of warmth in the relationship between management and other personnel in this organization	*0.53*	0.16	0.10

(Table 3.9 contd...)

Items	Factor		
	1	*2*	*3*
28. In this organization, people are encouraged to initiate projects that they think are important	*0.68*	0.07	−0.06
30. I have a clear idea of what I am supposed to do in my job	0.13	*0.43*	0.10
Eigenvalue	6.68	2.93	1.39
Percentage of variance	52.6	23.1	11.0

Note: $N = 440$; (R) = scoring reversed.
Factor 1 = reward and participation; factor 2 = structure; factor 3 = warmth and support.

The descriptive statistics and psychometric properties of the scales and their inter-relationships can be seen in Table 3.10. It is important to note that the scales exhibited well over the 0.50 reliability levels suggested by Nunnally (1978) as a minimum level for acceptable reliability. Table 3.10 also suggests that the average correlation between the factors used as scales was 0.29, indicating a reasonable level of scale independence.

Table 3.10 *Descriptive Statistics, Scale Characteristics, Reliabilities and Intercorrelations Among Climate Measures*

Climate	*1*	*2*	*3*
1. Reward and participation	(0.80)		
2. Structure	0.47[b]	(0.78)	
3. Warmth and support	0.11[a]	0.28[b]	(0.64)
No. of items	5	5	3
M	12.91	17.07	9.72
SD	4.34	3.90	2.54
Among index items correlations	0.40	0.41	0.40
Index items *vs* all other correlations	0.19	0.22	0.11
Split-half reliability	0.77	0.78	0.64

Note: Figures in brackets indicate coefficients alpha reliability; $N = 440$; [a]$p < 0.05$; [b]$p < 0.01$.

Some evidence of discriminant validity can also be seen at the bottom of Table 3.10. It is interesting to note that all the average inter-item correlations were greater than or equal to 0.40, which were significantly greater than the correlations of index items versus all the other items. In sum, the climate measures documented fairly adequate internal consistency reliability and internal validity.

It was of interest to see if the seven organizations had significantly different climates. The mean scores and F-ratios are given in Table 3.11. The differences were highly significant on all the climate factors.

Table 3.11   *Mean Scores on Climate Factors and Significance of their Differences*

Organizations	Climate		
	Reward and Participation	*Structure*	*Warmth and Support*
1	12.18	16.45	9.18
	(6)	(6)	(6)
2	12.43	18.48	9.83
	(5)	(2)	(4)
3	14.11	19.18	11.71
	(2)	(1)	(1)
4	13.56	18.35	9.36
	(3)	(3)	(5)
5	13.01	17.77	10.38
	(4)	(4)	(2)
6	11.61	14.71	9.13
	(7)	(7)	(7)
7	14.46	17.17	9.86
	(1)	(5)	(3)
$F(6,433)$	4.04	11.82	5.65

Note: All F-ratios are significant at the 0.01 level; Figures in brackets indicate ranks—the higher the rank the less favorable the climate.

A cursory look at Table 3.11 reveals that organizations 1 and 6 had the most unfavorable climate while the remaining organizations had a favorable climate. On the whole, these mean scores were consistent with the information drawn from other sources (see Chapter 2). One notable finding is that almost all the organizations were relatively structured with warmth and support (i.e., above the median), but all of them fell less than the median score on the reward and participation dimensions of climate. In sum, organizations 1 and 6 were in the public sector and were indeed considered to be inefficient on various objective statistics of efficiency.

On the favorable side were organizations 2, 3, 4, 5 and 7. They were considered to be efficient and found to have better working conditions. Thus, in the final analysis, organizations 1 and 6 were classified as having an unfavorable climate and the rest were classified as having a favorable climate. Finally, a one-way *ANOVA* was computed for the climate scores to check if a significant difference between the two types of organizations existed. Once again, scores on all the climate dimensions reflected a highly significant difference ($p < 0.001$) between the classified organizations.

In summary, the organizational environment scores were based on the collective judgments of the climates in the particular organization, of which the individual was a part. Such an analytical strategy has been adopted in much previous research (see, for instance, Ansari *et al.*, 1982 and Baumgartel *et al.*, 1978). Accordingly, the organizational (objective) climate was conceptualized as 'the sum total of the particular attributes of the organization as a system as well as those values and norms which symbolize the on-going pattern of the organization and its sub-units' (Ansari, 1980, p. 94), whereas the psychological climate was conceptualized as the attributes of the organization as perceived by individual members.

This study employed both psychological (perceived) and organizational (objective) climates. While examining direct effects the psychological climate was used, while in the case of moderating effects the organizational climate was employed.

Direct Effects

In this section, our results are displayed in the form of various factors as directly associated with the downward influence processes in organizations. Four sets of factors were examined—bases of power, leadership styles, leadership behavior and perceived organizational climate. The zero-order correlations between the predictors and criterion variables are contained in Table 3.12. The intercorrelations among the predictors are shown in Appendix IV. The information contained in Appendix IV suggests that, in general, there is a great deal of independence among the scales. That is, they do not appear to limit the subsequent analyses owing to the problem of multicollinearity.

Table 3.12 *Interrelationships Between Downward Influence Strategies (Criterion Variables) and Bases of Power, Leadership Style, Leader Behavior and Organizational Climate (Predictors)*

Variables/Strategies	DS_1	DS_2	DS_3	DS_4	DS_5	DS_6	DS_7	DS_8	DS_9	DS_{10}
Bases of Power										
Reward	29[b]	4	17[a]	9	12[a]	13[a]	22[b]	28[b]	13[a]	16[a]
Coercion	19[b]	−3	2	7	−8	11[a]	30[b]	13[a]	27[b]	27[b]
Legitimate	9	13[a]	8	11[a]	10[a]	5	18[b]	11[a]	9	6
Referent	11[a]	26[b]	25[b]	8	6	2	5	17[a]	−13[a]	−10[a]
Expert	−2	31[b]	15[a]	−2	10[a]	−10[a]	5	8	−9	−17[a]
Information	19[b]	11[a]	12[a]	20[b]	5	18[b]	19[b]	21[b]	10[a]	16[a]
Connection	25[b]	−1	14[a]	20[b]	5	22[b]	20[b]	20[b]	16[a]	14[a]
Leadership Style										
Participative	8	11[a]	27[b]	17[a]	17[a]	9	−1	22[b]	−4	0
Task-oriented	2	24[b]	19[b]	7	4	0	14[a]	15[a]	−8	−8
Bureaucrat	13[a]	9	7	13[a]	−5	14[a]	27[b]	10[a]	2	4
Authoritarian	18[b]	9	11[a]	5	−10[a]	10[a]	29[b]	14[a]	10[a]	10[a]
Leader Behavior										
Nurturant-task	11[a]	−2	6	2	4	12[a]	16[a]	12[a]	−3	8
Participative	7	−3	6	2	5	13[a]	8	7	4	10
Bureaucrat	14[a]	−3	5	15[a]	7	18[b]	15[a]	10[a]	9	6
Authoritarian	21[b]	7	9	9	−4	3	23[b]	15[a]	17[a]	8
Organizational Climate										
Reward & participation	13[a]	−5	5	32[b]	15[a]	20[b]	11[a]	11[a]	5	12[a]
Structure	6	11[a]	7	10[a]	4	5	7	8	−5	−3
Warmth & support	−12[a]	−8	−4	−16[a]	1	−12[a]	−8	−10[a]	−17[a]	−10[a]

Note: Decimal points have been omitted.
$N = 140$; [a] $p < 0.05$; [b] $p < 0.01$; DS_1 = exchange and challenge; DS_2 = expertise and reasons; DS_3 = personalized help; DS_4 = coalition and manipulation; DS_5 = showing dependency; DS_6 = upward appeal; DS_7 = assertion; DS_8 = positive sanctions; DS_9 = negative sanctions; DS_{10} = threats.

Bases of Power, Leadership and Influence Strategies

Where does power come from? What is it that gives a manager influence over others? Probably the earliest answer to these questions was a five-category classification scheme proposed by French and Raven (1959). The term 'bases of power' refers to what the manager has that provides him or her power (such as, reward or coercion). In other words, a power base is a source of influence in a social relationship. It should be noted that the contingency model of leadership (Fiedler, 1967) seems to be limited to positional power which is similar to legitimate power. Recently, the use of power is seen to be incorporated in the situational leadership theory. Hersey *et al.* (1979) postulate that

> power bases are potentially available to any leader as a means of inducing compliance or influencing the behavior of others. Some leaders have a great deal of power while others have very little. Part of the variance in actual power is due to the organization, and part is due to individual differences among the leaders themselves (p. 5).

According to them, effective leaders should not only vary their styles depending on the maturity level of their subordinates, but they should also vary the use of power in order to be effective. They further suggest that some bases of power (reward, coercion and connection) are used for inducing *compliance,* others (referent, expert and information) for *influencing* others, and it is only legitimate power which is used for *both*—inducing compliance and influencing others. Finally, they contend (1979, p. 4): 'with people of below-average maturity the emphasis is on compliance; with people of average maturity it is on compliance and influence; and with people of above-average maturity the emphasis is on influence'.

Unfortunately, not much is known about the relationship between bases of power and leadership styles. However, one systematic study is of special interest that empirically examined the influence of bases of power on leader behavior. In this study by Martin and Hunt (1980), it was found that both initiating structure and consideration leader behaviors were significantly affected by expert power. Whereas legitimate power negatively influenced consideration, referent power positively affected initiating structure. However, reward power and coercive power had no significant impact on either leader behavior.

A quick look at the foregoing discussion suggests that it is too early to draw any definite conclusion with respect to the link between power bases and leadership. It is important to mention that, in the Martin and Hunt study, it was only the impact of expert power which was replicated for the two samples employed in the study. Other effects held true for one sample only—that is, the effects were not cross-validated. Following Martin and Hunt's empirical study and that of Hersey *et al.*'s proposition, one general hypothesis may be advanced:

The higher the leader is on participative behavior, the more he or she will perceive to have influence (expert and referent bases of power); whereas the higher the leader is on autocratic behavior, the more he or she will perceive those bases of power (e.g., reward, coercion, and connection) which induce compliance.

Now, the question arises: How do managers vary their influence strategies depending on their own leadership inclinations? Unfortunately, there is not much that can be found in organizational behavior literature as to how influence strategies are affected by leadership styles. However, there are some empirical studies available which I shall now consider. Since these studies have already been reviewed in Chapter 1, only the highlights will be presented here.

Kipnis (1958) was probably one of the earliest researchers who investigated the exercise of power by a leader. His main conclusion was that participative leadership was more effective than directive leadership in both the reward and control groups, but less effective in a punishment group. Mulder *et al.* (1977) reported that the relationship between the exercise of influence and leadership styles was significantly moderated by situation. Leaders were found to exert more formal power, referent power, expert power and upward influence, and less open consultations in crisis than in non-crisis situations. Furthermore, Mulder *et al.* (1983) suggested that a good consultant (like any good leader) must be able to exert forceful power as well as be able to maintain personal open relationships with others when confronted with difficult requirements, some of which may involve a crisis. Finally, the experimental study of Kipnis *et al.* (1981) is of particular interest. Their principal finding was that leaders who were expected to act autocratically or democratically used controlling or non-controlling influence tactics, respectively.

Based on the studies just highlighted, one general hypothesis may be forwarded:

The higher the leader is on participative behavior, the more will be the use of non-controlling influence tactics (e.g., ingratiation, personalized help, etc.); whereas the higher the leader is on autocratic behavior, the more will be the use of controlling tactics (e.g., assertiveness, sanctions, etc.).

Controlling tactics refer to those tactics in which a leader retains decision-making power, whereas non-controlling tactics are those in which subordinates are allowed to participate in decision-making (Kipnis *et al.*, 1981). The hypothesized relationships between bases of power, leadership and influence strategies are depicted in Figure 3.1.

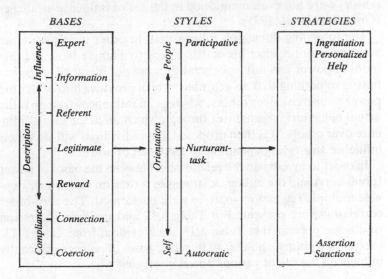

Figure 3.1 *Posited Relationships Between Bases of Power, Leadership and Influence Strategies*

Bases of Power and Influence Strategies

Before we test the above hypotheses, let us first examine the relationship between bases of power and influence strategies. According to Kipnis and Schmidt (1983), with few exceptions (e.g., Cartwright, 1965; Dahl, 1957), the distinction between resources (or bases) and behavioral strategies has not been made explicit. Instead, an implicit assumption has developed that bases of power and power strategies go hand in hand (Tedeschi, Schlenker and Bonoma, 1973). This implies that negative sanctions (such as, threats or demotions) are used when the base of power is coercive and that positive sanctions (such as, promotions or pay raises) are used when the base of power is reward. This assumption may be incorrect (Kipnis & Schmidt, 1983). As a matter of fact, several studies (e.g., Goodchilds *et al.*, 1975; Kapoor, 1986; Kipnis *et al.*, 1980; Singh, 1985) revealed that people do not use all of the behavioral strategies described by the bases of power schemes (French & Raven, 1959;

Kelman, 1958). For example, it was found that people used influence strategies which were not even mentioned in these schemes (Kipnis *et al.*, 1980), whereas several bases (such as, the use of expert power) were not even mentioned in the list of influence strategies (Goodchilds *et al.*, 1975).

The foregoing discussion follows that, in order to influence, an actor need not restrict his or her choice to a single base and that bases of power and influence strategies are not identical. A power base is something that an actor has, which provides him or her the power to exercise over others, whereas an influence strategy is the actual behavioral mechanism through which an actor exerts influence over others. It is then proposed that individuals will vary their influence strategies depending on the bases of power.

In order to investigate the relationship between the bases of power (predictors) and the influence strategies (criterion variables), stepwise multiple regression analyses were performed. The zero-order correlations are presented in Table 3.12 and multiple regression results are presented in Table 3.13. As is evident from Table 3.13, except for legitimate power, all the other bases of power significantly influenced the use of various power strategies.

Table 3.13   *Stepwise Multiple Regression Analysis Results— Bases of Power (Predictors) and Downward Strategies (Criterion Variables)*

Strategies	Bases						
	Reward	Coercion	Legitimate	Referent	Expert	Information	Connection
Exchange and Challenge							
R^2	0.08	0.12	0.13	0.13	0.13	0.13	0.12
Beta	0.21[b]	0.07	−0.01	0.07	−0.09	0.05	0.17[b]
Order	1	3	7	5	4	6	2
Expertise and Reasons							
R^2	0.14	0.14	0.14	0.12	0.10	0.13	0.13
Beta	−0.03	−0.07	0.07	0.17[b]	0.24[b]	0.11[a]	−0.09
Order	7	5	6	2	1	4	3
Personalized Help							
R^2	0.08	0.09	*	0.06	0.09	0.09	0.09
Beta	0.12[a]	−0.06	*	0.20[b]	0.05	0.03	0.08
Order	2	4	*	1	5	6	3
Coalition and Manipulation							
R^2	0.07	0.07	0.06	0.07	0.07	0.06	0.04
Beta	−0.01	−0.04	0.09	0.05	−0.09	0.15[b]	0.15[b]
Order	7	6	3	5	4	2	1

(Table 3.13 contd...)

Strategies	Bases						
	Reward	Coercion	Legitimate	Referent	Expert	Information	Connection
Showing Dependency							
R^2	0.01	0.03	0.04	0.04	0.04	0.04	0.04
Beta	0.12[a]	−0.16[b]	0.09	0.01	0.06	0.03	0.03
Order	1	2	3	7	4	6	5
Upward Appeal							
R^2	0.08	0.08	0.08	0.08	0.06	0.08	0.05
Beta	0.05	0.03	0.01	0.02	−0.15[b]	0.11[a]	0.18[b]
Order	4	5	7	6	2	3	1
Assertion							
R^2	0.11	0.09	0.12	0.12	0.12	0.12	0.12
Beta	0.11[a]	0.21[b]	0.06	−0.02	0.01	0.07	0.08
Order	2	1	5	6	7	4	3
Positive Sanction							
R^2	0.08	0.11	*	0.11	*	0.11	0.10
Beta	0.20[b]	0.01	*	0.10[a]	*	0.08	0.11[a]
Order	1	5	*	3	*	4	2
Negative Sanction							
R^2	0.11	0.07	0.11	0.10	0.11	0.11	0.11
Beta	0.05	0.23[b]	0.02	−0.15[b]	−0.07	0.02	0.10[a]
Order	5	1	7	2	4	6	3
Threat							
R^2	0.12	0.07	*	0.13	0.11	0.13	0.14
Beta	0.09[a]	0.22[b]	*	−0.09	−0.17[b]	0.08	0.07
Order	3	1	*	4	2	5	6

Note: $N = 440$; [a]$p < 0.05$; [b]$p < 0.01$.
* Tolerance level insufficient for further computation.

The exchange and challenge strategy was significantly influenced by the reward and connection bases of power; together they accounted for a total of 12 per cent of the variance. The expertise and reasons strategy was significantly affected by such bases of power as expert, information and referent. The reward and referent bases of power affected significantly (8 per cent of the variance) the use of personalized help, whereas the strategy of coalition and manipulation was the product of the information and connection bases of power (6 per cent). Whereas reward power positively affected the use of showing dependency, coercive power had its negative impact on this strategy. The strategy of upward appeal was significantly and positively affected by such bases of power as information and connection, but it was negatively influenced by expert power. The technique of assertiveness was best predicted by the reward and coercive bases of power, explaining 11 per cent of the variance. While positive sanction was significantly explained (11 per cent) by the reward, referent and connection bases of power, negative sanction was positively influenced by the coercive and connection bases of power but negatively by referent power. Finally, the threat strategy was significantly predicted by the reward, coercion and expert bases of power; the last having a negative beta weight.

Bases of Power and Leadership Style

Now we return to the question posed earlier: What is it that gives a manager (with a particular style) influence over his or her subordinates? This question leads us to examine the relationship between the bases of power and leadership styles. The zero-order correlations between bases of power (predictors) and leadership styles (criterion variables) can be seen in Table 3.12. The stepwise multiple regression analysis results are displayed in Table 3.14. It is evident from Table 3.14 that except for legitimate information and reward, all the other bases of power significantly affected leadership styles.

The results disclosed that whereas participative style was significantly affected by referent power, authoritarian style was significantly influenced by coercive power. Expert power significantly affected the use of task-oriented style, whereas both coercive and connection bases of power significantly affected the bureaucratic style.

Leadership Styles and Influence Strategies

We shall now consider how influence strategies vary with respect to leadership styles. It was hypothesized that participative and authoritarian leaders would employ non-controlling (such as, personalized help) and controlling (such as, assertiveness) influence strategies, respectively. The zero-order correlations between leadership styles (predictors) and influence strategies (criterion variables) are presented in Table 3.12 and the stepwise multiple regression results are reported in Table 3.15.

Table 3.14   *Stepwise Multiple Regression Analysis Results—Downward Bases of Power (Predictors) and Self-Reported Styles (Criterion Variables)*

Styles	Bases						
	Reward	Coercion	Legitimate	Referent	Expert	Information	Connection
Participative							
R^2	0.04	0.04	0.04	0.03	0.04	0.03	0.04
Beta	0.05	−0.06	−0.02	0.12[a]	0.08	0.07	0.02
Order	5	4	7	1	3	2	6
Task-Oriented							
R^2	*	0.08	0.08	0.07	0.06	0.09	0.09
Beta	*	0.06	0.04	0.09	0.19[b]	0.03	0.03
Order	*	3	4	2	1	5	6
Bureaucratic							
R^2	0.06	0.05	*	0.06	0.06	0.06	0.04
Beta	−0.01	0.12[a]	*	−0.02	0.08	0.06	0.14[b]
Order	6	2	*	5	3	4	1
Authoritarian							
R^2	0.07	0.04	0.07	*	0.07	0.06	0.07
Beta	0.06	0.13[a]	0.04	*	0.03	0.10	0.08
Order	4	1	5	*	6	2	3

Note: $N = 440$; [a]$p < 0.05$; [b]$p < 0.01$.
    * Tolerance level insufficient for further computation.

It can be seen from Table 3.15 that the exchange and challenge strategy was best explained by three leadership styles—authoritarian, participative, and task-oriented—the last having a negative beta weight. As expected, task-oriented style affected significantly the use of such influence tactics as expertise and reasons. The strategy of personalized help was strongly predicted by participative style of leadership (7 per cent); authoritarian style added to it by contributing 1 per cent of the variance. It is interesting to note that both participative and bureaucratic styles affected significantly the use of such non-rational influence tactics as coalition and manipulation.

As anticipated, participative style positively influenced the use of showing dependency, and authoritarian style negatively affected the use of this strategy. The strategy of upward appeal was significantly and positively influenced by bureaucratic and participative leadership styles, but negatively influenced by task-oriented leadership style. As expected, assertiveness was strongly influenced by bureaucratic and authoritarian styles. Interestingly, positive sanction

Table 3.15 *Stepwise Multiple Regression Analysis Results—Self-Reported Styles (Predictors) and Downward Strategies (Criterion Variables)*

Strategies	Styles			
	Participative	Task-oriented	Bureaucratic	Authoritarian
Exchange and Challenge				
R^2	0.04	0.05	0.05	−0.03
Beta	0.12[a]	−0.12[a]	0.05	0.19[b]
Order	2	3	4	1
Expertise and Reasons				
R^2	0.06	0.06	0.06	0.06
Beta	0.04	0.24[b]	−0.05	0.03
Order	2	1	3	4
Personalized Help				
R^2	0.07	0.09	0.09	0.08
Beta	0.24[b]	0.10	−0.09	0.13[a]
Order	1	3	4	2
Coalition and Manipulation				
R^2	0.03	0.05	0.04	0.05
Beta	0.17[b]	−0.06	0.17[a]	−0.04
Order	1	3	2	4
Showing Dependency				
R^2	0.03	0.04	*	0.04
Beta	0.16[b]	0.02	*	−0.11[a]
Order	1	3	*	2
Upward Appeal				
R^2	0.03	0.04	0.02	0.04
Beta	0.12[a]	−0.14[a]	0.17[a]	0.04
Order	2	3	1	4
Assertion				
R^2	0.10	*	0.10	0.09
Beta	−0.02	*	0.14[a]	0.20[b]
Order	3	*	2	1
Positive Sanction				
R^2	0.05	0.07	0.07	0.07
Beta	0.22[b]	0.04	−0.06	0.17[b]
Order	1	4	3	2
Negative Sanction				
R^2	0.03	0.03	0.03	0.01
Beta	0.01	−0.13[a]	−0.04	0.18[b]
Order	4	2	3	1
Threat				
R^2	0.03	0.03	0.03	0.01
Beta	−0.01	−0.16[b]	−0.01	0.18[b]
Order	3	2	4	1

Note: $N = 440$; [a]$p < 0.05$; [b]$p < 0.01$.

* Tolerance level insufficient for further computation.

was positively influenced by participative leadership style, whereas negative sanction and threats were significantly influenced by authoritarian leadership. It is interesting to note that task-oriented leadership negatively influenced the use of both negative sanctions and threats.

Discussion and Conclusions

We shall now examine what our survey data suggest regarding the relationships between downward influence processes in organizations. We shall also present a discussion and some conclusions regarding the findings obtained thus far.

The results suggest three general themes in the data. The first, concerning bases of power and influence strategies, indicates that although there is a meaningful correspondence between the two (for instance, reward *vs* positive sanction, coercion *vs* negative sanction and threat, expert *vs* expertise and reasons, and referent *vs* personalized help) as one would expect on the basis of French and Raven's classification, this correspondence is not mutually exclusive. In fact, the findings make it evident that a manager with a particular base of power can use a set of strategies, and that a particular strategy may be the product of several bases of power. For example, having reward power does not mean only the use of positive sanction (such as, promotions), but it may also prompt a manager to use several other strategies like personalized help, exchange and showing dependency. Conversely, the strategy of positive sanction may not be guided only by reward power but by other bases of power as well, such as, referent and connection.

In sum, the findings are consistent with our hypotheses as well as with previous findings (Kapoor, 1986; Schlenker and Tedeschi, 1973; Singh, 1985). It can, then, be concluded that bases of power are a crucial determinant of influence strategies.

The second theme, concerning the relationship between bases of power and leadership styles, makes it evident that there is a meaningful relationship between the two. For example, those bases of power which induce compliance (such as, connection and coercion) were related to bureaucratic and authoritarian styles, and referent power (which is used to influence) was associated with participative style. Our findings in this study can be compared with those of Martin and Hunt (1980). Reward power, in our study, was not found to be related with any of the styles. This was true of Martin and Hunt's study as well. However, in their study, coercive power was also not related to either leader behavior—consideration or initiating structure. While in their study, legitimate power did negatively affect consideration behavior, our study discovered no significant relationship between legitimate power and any leadership style. In sum, the relationship between bases and style found in our study is as consistent as one would expect on theoretical grounds.

The third theme, relating to the relationship between leadership styles and influence strategies, indicates that the relationships, for the most part, between the two are meaningful and in tune with the hypothesis. For example, task-oriented managers were found to employ such influence strategies significantly more often as expertise and reasons, but they reported a less frequent use of such non-rational influence tactics as exchange and challenge, upward appeal, negative sanction and threats. Participative managers were found to use a mix of rational (such as, personalized help) and non-rational (such as, upward appeal) influence tactics in order to get their way. In general, bureaucratic and authoritarian managers were seen to influence their immediate subordinates significantly more often by employing non-rational strategies. Thus, our findings here generally support the earlier contention.

Our findings so far are summarized in Figure 3.2. One general conclusion is that there is a meaningful correspondence between bases of power, leadership styles and influence strategies. For example if a participative manager has referent power, then he makes frequent use of such tactics as personalized help, showing dependency and positive sanction. Likewise, a task-oriented manager with expert power very often employs influence strategies such as expertise and reasons. The bureaucratic manager often relies on such tactics as exchange and challenge, upward appeal, and coalition and manipulation. Similarly, an authoritarian manager with coercive power relies more often on negative sanction and threat. These findings are clear and unambiguous, as one would expect.

However, let us have a look at the other side of the coin. The data suggest that participative managers use non-rational tactics (such as, exchange and challenge, and upward appeal) in the same way as authoritarians and bureaucrats employ rational influence tactics (such as, positive sanction and personalized help).

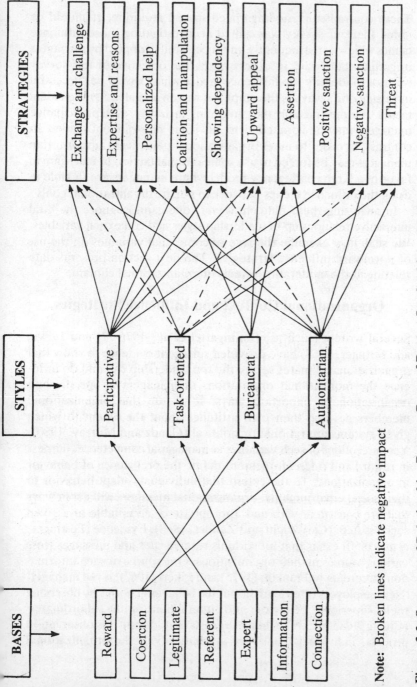

Note: Broken lines indicate negative impact

Figure 3.2 Summary of Relationships Between Bases of Power, Leadership and Influence Strategies

These contradictory findings need special attention. It should be noted that our survey was aimed at investigating those influence tactics which were frequently and successfully adopted by managers in getting their way. In other words, the objective of this survey was not to identify the influence tactics which would be successful in getting one's way, as the emphasis was on actual *rather than* ideal tactics. It is then possible that, in getting their way, even participative managers may be compelled to use some non-rational tactics. In contrast, in order to meet organizational objectives, authoritarian managers may be forced to use some rational tactics. In fact, I am in favor of a large contingency model where managers are flexible in using the influence tactics in order to pursue organizational goals.

In analyzing these data, however, one cannot ignore the vital interactive relationship of leadership styles and contextual variables. We shall now examine the role of contextual variables on the use of downward influence strategies. The next section presents data relating to the moderating effects of organizational climate.

Organizational Context and Influence Strategies

Several writers (such as, Baumgartel *et al.*, 1976-77; and Litwin and Stringer, 1968) have provided sufficient evidence to show that organizational climates set by the top leadership can and do influence the motivational orientations of managers in specific and organizationally important ways. It is true that organizational members develop their own attitudes about the extent to which given systems are rational or political (Gandz and Murray, 1980). Yet perceptions of such variables as managerial competence, fairness in reward and rule-enforcement define the prevalence of behavior in organizations. To the extent that individuals adapt behavior to their social environments, organizational members will act in ways that are consistent with and appropriate or acceptable in a given social system (Cartwright and Zander, 1968). Evidence (Festinger, *et al.*, 1950) exists that individuals receive cues and messages from various sources in their organizations. One source of such information, according to Franklin (1975) and Likert (1967), is the manager. 'New employees often learn about the behavioral norms by observing their superiors' behavior and interactions with subordinates' (Cheng, 1983, p. 339). Cheng suggests that, during this observation process, individuals construct a reality about the organizational environment and *adapt* their behavior accordingly (Festinger, 1950; Salancik and Pfeffer, 1978).

There is some evidence that certain organizational situations tend to be intrinsically 'political'. Madison *et al.* (1980) found that some situations are high in political activity (such as, organizational changes, personnel changes and budget allocation). According to them, rule and procedure changes, establishment of individual performance standards and purchase of major items are low in political activity. Some studies (such as, Ansari and Rehana, 1986; Ansari and Kapoor, 1987; Cheng, 1983; and Kapoor et al., 1986) have clearly indicated that the use of upward influence tactics is a function of the organizational context.

In this study, two contextual factors—leader behavior and perceived organizational climate—were employed. In line with the earlier discussions, both the contextual factors are expected to play a part in the use of downward influence strategies. Accordingly, two general hypotheses follow:

Having an autocratic boss, managers would employ more often such non-rational tactics as negative sanctions and threats in influencing their immediate subordinates. Conversely, the participative boss would encourage the managers to adopt such rational tactics as positive sanctions and personalized help.

The managers would more often use such rational influence tactics as expertise and reasons when they perceive their organizational climate as favorable. Those perceiving their climate as unfavorable would use more often such non-rational tactics as upward appeal, coalition and manipulation.

Leader Behavior and Influence Strategies

The zero-order correlations between leader behavior (predictors) and downward influence strategies are contained in Table 3.12. The stepwise multiple regression results are shown in Table 3.16. It can be seen from Table 3.16 that, with two exceptions (expertise and reasons, and showing dependency), the influence strategies were significantly predicted by the immediate superiors' leadership styles.

Those managers who perceived their immediate boss as authoritarian relied significantly more often on a combination of rational

Table 3.16   *Stepwise Multiple Regression Analysis Results—Leader Behavior (Predictors) and Downward Strategies (Criterion Variables)*

Strategies	Styles			
	Nurturant-Task	Partici-pative	Bureau-cratic	Authori-tarian
Exchange and Challenge				
R^2	0.07	0.07	0.07	0.04
Beta	0.07	0.08	0.05	0.25[b]
Order	2	4	3	1
Expertise and Reasons				
R^2	*	0.01	0.01	0.00
Beta	*	0.02	−0.05	0.08
Order	*	3	2	1
Personalized Help				
R^2	0.01	0.02	*	0.01
Beta	0.02	0.09	*	0.13
Order	3	2	*	1
Coalition and Manipulation				
R^2	0.03	0.03	0.02	0.03
Beta	0.10	0.07	0.16[b]	0.07
Order	3	4	1	2
Showing Dependency				
R^2	0.01	0.01	0.00	0.01
Beta	−0.04	0.04	0.08	0.04
Order	4	3	1	2
Upward Appeal				
R^2	0.04	0.04	0.03	0.04
Beta	−0.04	0.14	0.14[a]	0.06
Order	4	2	1	3
Assertion				
R^2	0.10	0.10	0.10	0.05
Beta	0.23[a]	−0.02	0.02	0.28[b]
Order	2	4	3	1
Positive Sanction				
R^2	0.04	0.04	0.04	0.02
Beta	0.13	0.03	0.01	0.18[b]
Order	2	3	4	1
Negative Sanction				
R^2	0.06	0.04	0.07	0.03
Beta	−0.32[b]	0.36[b]	0.08	0.22[b]
Order	3	2	4	1

(Table 3.16 Contd...)

Strategies	Styles			
	Nurturant-Task	Partici-pative	Bureau-cratic	Authori-tarian
Threat				
R^2	0.03	0.01	*	0.03
Beta	−0.07	0.21[b]	*	0.14[a]
Order	3	1	*	2

Note: $N = 440$; [a]$p < 0.05$; [b]$p < 0.01$.
* Tolerance level insufficient for further computation.

and non-rational tactics (such as, personalized help, positive sanction, exchange and challenge, negative sanction, and threats). Surprisingly, under the participative boss, managers used significantly more often such strategies as negative sanctions and threats. As expected, under the bureaucratic boss, managers relied significantly more often on such strategies as coalition and manipulation and upward appeal. Another expected finding was that, under the nurturant-task boss, managers were seen to use significantly more often assertiveness to influence their subordinates. However, they reported a less frequent use of negative sanctions (i.e., a significant negative beta weight). In sum, leader behavior was seen to affect significantly the downward influence strategies of managers.

Organizational Climate and Influence Strategies

In order to examine the impact of perceived organizational climate (predictors) on the use of influence strategies (criterion variables), stepwise multiple regression analyses were computed (see Table 3.17). The zero-order correlations between predictors and criteria can be had from Table 3.12.

The results make it clear that perceived organizational climate does account for a significant amount of variance in the use of influence strategies. As can be seen in Table 3.17, the reward and participation climate significantly and positively affected a number of such influence strategies as exchange and challenge, coalition and manipulation, showing dependency, upward appeal, and threats. However, it was seen to affect negatively such influence tactics as expertise and reasons. The climate of structure was seen to affect significantly only one influence strategy—expertise and reasons. It

Table 3.17 *Stepwise Multiple Regression Analysis Results—Climate (Predictors) and Downward Strategies (Criterion Variables)*

Strategies	Climate		
	Reward and Participation	Structure	Warmth and Support
Exchange and Challenge			
R^2	0.02	0.04	0.04
Beta	0.12[a]	0.05	−0.15[b]
Order	1	3	2
Expertise and Reasons			
R^2	0.04	0.01	0.03
Beta	−0.13[a]	0.21[b]	−0.13[a]
Order	3	1	2
Personalized Help			
R^2	0.01	0.00	0.01
Beta	0.02	0.08	−0.06
Order	3	1	2
Coalition and Manipulation			
R^2	0.11	*	0.14
Beta	0.35[b]	*	−0.20[b]
Order	1	*	2
Showing Dependency			
R^2	0.02	0.02	*
Beta	0.16[b]	−0.03	*
Order	1	2	*
Upward Appeal			
R^2	0.04	0.06	0.06
Beta	0.22[b]	−0.01	−0.14[b]
Order	1	3	2
Assertion			
R^2	0.01	0.02	0.02
Beta	0.09	0.06	−0.11[a]
Order	1	3	2
Positive Sanction			
R^2	0.01	0.03	0.02
Beta	0.09	0.08	−0.13[b]
Order	1	3	2
Negative Sanction			
R^2	0.03	0.04	0.03
Beta	0.09	−0.04	−0.17[b]
Order	2	3	1

(*Table 3.17 contd...*)

Strategies	Climate		
	Reward and Participation	Structure	Warmth and Support
Threat			
R^2	0.01	0.03	0.03
Beta	0.16^b	−0.07	$−0.10^a$
Order	1	3	2

Note: $N = 440$; [a]$p < 0.05$; [b]$p < 0.01$.
  * Tolerance level insufficient for further computation.

is interesting to note that the climate of warmth and support significantly but negatively affected almost all the influence strategies except personalized help and showing dependency. It is also important to note that personalized help was an influence strategy which was not significantly related to either organizational climate.

Discussion and Conclusions

Our findings in general supported the contextual perspective (Rousseau, 1978; Salancik and Pfeffer, 1978) that the organizational context makes a significant contribution to the variance in downward influence strategies. This effect has been noted in previous studies (for instance, Ansari and Kapoor, 1987; Ansari and Rehana, 1986; Cheng, 1983; Kapoor et al., 1986) also, as far as the use of upward influence strategies is concerned. However, the findings in this study are not as consistent with the hypothesis as expected. In fact, some of the findings are difficult to interpret.

Leader behavior did affect the use of influence strategies, but the findings were not in keeping with the hypothesis. For example, under an authoritarian boss, managers were seen to get their way by using a number of rational (for instance, positive sanctions) and non-rational (like negative sanctions and threats) influence strategies. The finding regarding the use of softer tactics like personalized help is consistent with that of Kipnis et al. (1981), who also found that an autocratic superior encourages the use of ingratiation. The finding that under a participative boss managers use negative sanction and threat, is rather difficult to explain. However, two findings are in line with the hypotheses and make sense. First, under the nurturant-task manager, managers rely more often on assertion and less on negative sanctions. Second, bureaucratic managers cultivate the use of such devious means as coalition and manipulation and upward appeal in their subordinates.

The findings regarding the role of perceived organizational climate on the use of downward influence strategies are meaningful but unexpected. Although the three climate measures (see Appendix IV) were found to be positively related to one another, their relationships with the influence strategies are not similar. One finding is clear and unambiguous: the higher the structured climate, the greater the use of such strategies as expertise and reasons. However, the other findings are not in expected directions. For example, the climate of reward and participation encourages the use of non-rational tactics, whereas the climate of warmth and support affects negatively the use of almost all the strategies.

Two general themes can be derived from our data. The first, concerning these unexpected results, suggests that contextual factors might be more useful and salient in predicting the use of upward influence strategies than predicting the use of downward strategies. The second theme is that contextual variables may interact significantly with the managers' own style in affecting the use of downward influence strategies. While the first theme has been dealt with in the next chapter, the second theme is examined in the next section.

Moderating Effects of Organizational Climate

Most leadership theories today include one or more moderators. For example, the contingency model (Fiedler, 1967) includes such moderators as leader-member relations, position power, and task structure. The path-goal theory (House, 1971; House and Dessler, 1974) includes such moderators as the personal characteristics of the subordinates and environmental processes and task demands while the life cycle model (Hersey and Blanchard, 1977) includes the subordinates' maturity level as a moderator. These are but few examples. One could find the role of moderator(s) in other leadership paradigms as well (e.g., Vroom and Yetton, 1973; Yukl, 1981).

The prime objective of this section is to investigate the moderating effect of organizational climate on the relationship between leadership styles (or leader behavior or bases of power) and downward influence strategies. The rationale for choosing organizational climate as a moderator is based on the assumption that it has been found to be related to several variables, such as, job satisfaction, leader behaviors, and the quality of work group interactions (for details, see Schnake, 1983). Of particular significance about the Indian sector is that climate affects most significantly whether or not a manager attempts to apply what he or she has learned upon returning to the job following a management development experience (Baumgartel, 1981).

As has been mentioned earlier, most of the current leadership paradigms include at least one moderator. However, much of the research on moderators has been unsystematic (Miner, 1980) because 'they fail to focus on the *mechanisms* by which moderators operate' (Howell *et al.*, 1986, p. 88, emphasis in original). In view of this complexity, managers report greater difficulties in attempting to apply the contingency model of leadership. Recently, Howell *et al.*, (1986) have proposed leadership neutralizers/enhancers as moderators. According to them, both enhancers and neutralizers are two varieties of the same basic type of moderator. The only difference between the two is that 'enhancers represent a positive moderating influence ... while neutralizers represent a negative moderating influence' (p. 90). In this study, the predictor-criterion relationship is expected to vary as a function of organizational climate. In one climate, this relationship might be stronger (enhancer), whereas in another the same relationship might be substantially weaker (neutralizer). The moderating effects of organizational climate are presented in the next section.

Leadership Style and Influence Strategies

In order to test for the effects that objective organizational climate might have on the leadership style-influence strategies relationship, two separate sets of stepwise multiple regression analyses were performed. The zero-order correlations are reported in Table 3.18. Table 3.19 shows the findings in term of the particular combination of influence tactics that best predicted each leadership style. In addition, Table 3.19 reports the multiple regression coefficients of these influence tactics with each leadership style.

Even a cursory look at the tables would make it clear that climate does moderate the relationship between leadership and influence tactics. A summary of the significant relationships follows. Participative managers, in an unfavorable climate, reported a frequent use of coalition and manipulation tactics to influence their subordinates. In contrast, they relied more often on personalized help

Table 3.18 *Zero-Order Correlations Between Leadership Style and Downward Influence Strategies—Sub-Group Analysis*

Strategies/ Styles	Unfavorable Climate[d]				Favorable Climate[c]			
	P	T	B	F	P	T	B	F
Exchange and challenge	0	−14	6	10	13[a]	11[a]	18[b]	23[b]
Expertise and reasons	11	19[a]	12	−3	11[a]	27[b]	8	16[b]
Personalized help	26[b]	16[a]	15	11	28[b]	20[b]	3	11[a]
Coalition and manipulation	32[b]	9	15	−6	7	6	12[a]	10
Showing dependency	18[a]	0	−1	−8	15[b]	7	−7	−11[a]
Upward Appeal	6	−4	19[a]	−1	11[a]	3	12[a]	16[b]
Assertion	5	15	39[b]	39[b]	−4	13[a]	20[b]	24[b]
Positive Sanctions	24[b]	8	15	7	22[b]	19[b]	8	19[b]
Negative Sanctions	−3	−8	4	8	−4	−8	1	10
Threat	−4	−9	9	12	3	−8	0	9

Note: Decimal points are omitted.
[a]$p < 0.05$; [b]$p < 0.01$; [c]$N = 281$; [d]$N = 159$.
P = participative; T = task-oriented; B = bureaucratic; F = autocratic.

Table 3.19 *Regression Coefficients Between Leadership Styles and Downward Influence Strategies—Sub-Group Analysis*

Leadership Style	Unfavorable Climate		Favorable Climate	
	Strategies	Beta	Strategies	Beta
Participative	Coalition and manipulation	0.35	Personalized help	0.21
			Positive sanctions	0.09*
			Assertion	−0.13
		$R = 0.33$		$R = 0.31$
Task-oriented			Expertise and reasons	0.19
			Positive sanctions	0.10*
			Negative sanctions	−0.15
				$R = 0.31$
Bureaucratic	Assertion	0.37	Assertion	0.19
			Exchange and challenge	0.21
			Negative sanctions	−0.12*
			Showing dependency	−0.15
		$R = 0.39$		$R = 0.29$

(Table 3.19 contd...)

Leadership Style	Unfavorable Climate		Favorable Climate	
	Strategies	Beta	Strategies	Beta
Autocratic	Assertion	0.44	Assertion	0.15
			Exchange and challenge	0.17
			Showing dependency	−0.23
	R = 0.39		R = 0.33	

Note: *$p > 0.05$; all other coefficients are significant beyond the 0.05 level.
Strategies are listed in the order of their entry into the stepwise multiple regression equations.

to influence their subordinates in a favorable climate. However, they reported a less frequent use of assertion strategy. Whereas none of the influence tactics was associated with task-oriented style in an unfavorable climate, expertise and reasons and negative sanctions were, respectively, associated positively and negatively with this style in a favorable climate. Further, bureaucratic managers made frequent use of the assertion technique in an unfavorable climate, whereas in addition to assertion they made frequent use of such tactics as exchange and challenge in a favorable climate. Additionally, showing dependency was negatively associated with this style in a favorable climate. A similar trend as for bureaucratic managers was found for autocratic managers. Although autocratic and bureaucratic managers made frequent use of assertion in both the climates, they were significantly more assertive in an unfavorable climate than in a favorable one.

Bases of Power and Influence Strategies

Data are presented here on how organizational climate affects the relationship between bases of power and downward influence strategies. Table 3.20 reports the zero-order correlations. Table 3.21 reports the multiple regression coefficients of influence tactics with each base of power.

Table 3.21 clearly demonstrates the role of organizational climate as a significant moderator of the bases of power–influence strategies relationship. Having reward power, managers reported a frequent use of such influence strategies as positive sanctions and showing

Table 3.20   Zero-Order Correlations Between Bases of Power and Downward Influence Strategies—Sub-Group Analysis

Strategies/ Bases	Unfavorable Climate[d]							Favorable Climate[c]						
	B1	B2	B3	B4	B5	B6	B7	B1	B2	B3	B4	B5	B6	B7
Exchange and challenge	22[b]	11	-9	-7	-21[b]	-2	22[b]	32[b]	24[b]	19[b]	21[b]	7	31[b]	27[b]
Expertise and reasons	4	-13	12	25[b]	34[b]	15	-15	3	4	13[a]	26[b]	29[b]	9	7
Personalized help	19[a]	8	17[a]	23[b]	24[b]	15	23[b]	16[b]	0	3	27[b]	10	10	10
Coalition and manipulation	4	-4	17[a]	16[a]	10	16[a]	20[a]	13[a]	13[a]	8	3	-8	21[b]	20[b]
Showing dependency	27[b]	-15	6	19[a]	14	17[a]	11	0	-2	12[a]	-4	7	-2	1
Upward appeal	11	4	6	4	-11	12	17[a]	14[a]	16[b]	4	1	-10	22[b]	25[b]
Assertion	15	26[b]	18[a]	3	3	4	23[b]	28[b]	32[b]	19[b]	6	7	26[b]	18[b]
Positive sanctions	38[b]	16[a]	13	9	16[a]	15	17[a]	22[b]	12[a]	9	20[b]	4	25[b]	22[b]
Negative sanctions	19[a]	29[b]	6	-18[a]	-10	0	16[a]	10	25[b]	11[a]	-9	-7	15[b]	*16[b]*
Threat	24[b]	33[b]	7	-16[a]	19[a]	2	03	13[a]	23[b]	6	-6	-15[b]	22[b]	20[b]

Note: Decimal points are omitted.

[a] $p < 0.05$; [b] $p < 0.01$; [c] $N = 281$; [d] $N = 159$;

B1 = reward; B2 = coercion; B3 = legitimate; B4 = referent; B5 = expert; B6 = information; B7 = connection.

Table 3.21 *Regression Coefficients Between Power Bases and Downward Influence Strategies—Sub-Group Analysis*

Power Bases	Unfavorable Climate		Favorable Climate	
	Strategies	*Beta*	*Strategies*	*Beta*
Reward	Positive sanctions	0.30	Exchange and	
	Threat	0.15*	challenge	0.28
	Showing dependency	0.21	Assertion	0.21
	R = 0.43		R = 0.36	
Coercion	Threat	0.25	Assertion	0.23
	Assertion	0.18		
	Showing dependency	−0.21		
	Positive sanctions	0.21		
	Expertise and			
	reasons	−0.19		
	R = 0.48		R =0.32	
Legitimate	Assertion	0.10*	Exchange and	
	Exhange and		challenge	0.15
	challenge	−0.30	Assertion	0.14
	R = 0.22		R = 0.23	
Referent	Expertise and		Personalized help	0.16
	reasons	0.18	Expertise and	
			reasons	0.20
			Showing dependency	−0.18
			Exchange and	
			challenge	0.30
			Negative sanctions	−0.20
	R = 0.25		R = 0.43	
Expert	Expertise and		Expertise and	
	reasons	0.29	reasons	0.31
	Exchange and		Coalition and	
	challenge	−0.23	manipulation	−0.15
			Threat	−0.14*
			Exchange and	
			challenge	0.16
	R = 0.41		R = 0.37	
Information			Exchange and	
			challenge	0.20
			Assertion	0.14
			Coalition and	
			manipulation	0.11*
			Showing dependency	−0.15
			R = 0.39	

(Table 3.21 contd...)

Power Bases	Unfavorable Climate		Favorable Climate	
	Strategies	*Beta*	*Strategies*	*Beta*
Connection	Assertion	0.22	Exchange and challenge	0.16
	Expertise and reasons	−0.37		
	Personalized help	0.21.		
	R = 0.41		*R* = 0.27	

Note: * $p > 0.05$, all other coefficients are significant beyond the 0.05 level. Strategies are listed in order of their entry into the stepwise multiple regression equations.

dependency in an unfavorable climate. On the other hand, with the same base of power, in a favorable climate, they made frequent use of the exchange and challenge and assertion strategies. The higher the coercive base of power, the more frequent the use of threats, assertion, and positive sanctions and the less frequent the use of showing dependency and expertise and reasons in an unfavorable climate. In contrast, only the assertion technique was associated with the coercive base of power in a favorable climate. Legitimate power was negatively associated with the tactics of exchange and challenge in an unfavorable climate, whereas it was positively associated with both exchange and challenge and assertion methods of downward influence in a favorable climate. An interesting finding was that referent power was correlated only with expertise and reasons in an unfavorable climate, whereas it was associated with a number of influence tactics in a favorable climate—positively with personalized help, expertise and reasons, and exchange and challenge, and negatively with showing dependency and negative sanctions.

Expert power was positively associated with expertise and reasons in both the climates. But it was positively related to exchange and challenge in a favorable climate and negatively in an unfavorable climate. In addition, the use of coalition and manipulation was negatively associated with expert power in a favorable climate. None of the influence tactics was associated with information power in an unfavorable climate, whereas at least three influence strategies—exchange and challenge, coalition and manipulation, and showing dependency—were associated with this base of power in a favorable climate, the last one having a negative impact.

The connection base of power was positively associated with such influence tactics as exchange and challenge in a favorable climate, whereas it was associated with tactics like assertion, expertise and reasons, and personalized help in an unfavorable climate—the second having a negative beta coefficient.

Leader Behavior and Influence Strategies

We shall now examine how superiors' leadership styles are related to downward influence tactics as a function of organizational climate.

Table 3.22 shows the zero-order correlations between leader behavior and influence tactics and Table 3.23 presents a summary of the stepwise multiple regression analysis. As expected, some interesting findings did emerge from the data.

Table 3.22 *Zero-Order Correlations Between Leader Behavior and Downward Influence Strategies—Sub-Group Analysis*

Strategies/ Behavior	Unfavorable Climate[d]				Favorable Climate[c]			
	NT	P	B	F	NT	P	B	F
Exchange and challenge	5	−2	4	12	14[a]	12[a]	19[b]	25[b]
Expertise and reasons	−2	−5	−6	5	−4	−2	−3	8
Personalized help	2	3	0	15	9	7	8	6
Coalition and manipulation	2	0	20	18[a]	17[b]	3	12[a]	4
Showing dependency	−3	0	−2	−7	8	8	12[a]	−1
Upward appeal	18[a]	15	13	1	8	12[a]	20[b]	5
Assertion	23[b]	14	14	25[b]	13[a]	6	17[b]	22[b]
Positive sanctions	5	−1	2	9	13[a]	10	13[a]	18[b]
Negative sanctions	−3	−4	10	10	−1	10	10	20[b]
Threat	15	19[a]	9	0	4	6	6	11[a]

Note: Decimal points are omitted.
[a]$P < 0.05$; [b]$P < 0.01$; [c]$N = 281$; [d]$N = 159$.
NT = nurturant-task; P = participative; B = bureaucratic; F = autocratic.

None of the influence tactics were associated with nurturant-task behavior in a favorable climate, whereas two strategies—assertion and upward appeal—were associated with this behavior in an unfavorable climate. Participative behavior was significantly associated with such influence tactics as threats and upward appeal

Table 3.23   *Regression Coefficients Between Leader Behavior and Downward Influence Strategies—Sub-Group Analysis*

Leader Behavior	Unfavorable Climate		Favorable Climate ·	
	Strategies	Beta	Strategies	Beta
Nurturant-task	Assertion	0.25		
	Upward appeal	0.23		
	$R = 0.26$			
Participative	Threat	0.21		
	Negative sanctions	−0.13*		
	Assertion	0.14*		
	Upward appeal	0.24		
	$R = 0.28$			
Bureaucratic	Coalition and manipulation	0.26	Upward appeal	0.17
	$R = 0.20$		$R = 0.20$	
Autocratic	Assertion	0.21	Exchange and challenge	0.17
	Coalition and manipulation	0.25	Assertion	0.13
	Showing dependency	−0.24		
	$R = 0.32$		$R = 0.29$	

Note: * $p > 0.05$; all other coefficients are significant beyond the 0.05 level.
Strategies are listed in order of their entry into the stepwise multiple regression equations.

in an unfavorable climate, whereas it was associated with none of the tactics in a favorable climate. Bureaucratic behavior gave rise to coalition and manipulation in an unfavorable climate, whereas it gave rise to upward appeal in a favorable climate. Autocratic behavior was positively associated with assertion and coalition and manipulation, and negatively with showing dependency in an unfavorable climate. However, it was positively associated with such tactics as exchange and challenge, and assertion in a favorable climate.

Discussion and Conclusions

The findings in the study generally support the hypothesis that organizational climate moderates the relationship between leadership style (behavior) and influence strategies, and between bases of power and influence strategies. These findings are summarized as follows:

Organizational climate does appear to represent an important moderator of the leadership style–influence strategies relationship. For example, participative managers are found to make frequent use of such devious means as coalition and manipulation in order to get their way with subordinates in an unfavorable climate. On the other hand, they report a more frequent use of personalized help and a less frequent use of assertion in a favorable climate. Expertise and reasons are used more often and negative sanctions less often by task-oriented managers in a favorable climate, whereas none of the influence tactics relate significantly to this style in an unfavorable climate. The use of strong tactics (such as, assertion) relates significantly to both styles—autocratic and bureaucratic—in both the climates. However, the data do suggest that both bureaucratic and autocratic managers are more assertive in an unfavorable climate than in a favorable one. In addition, both types of managers report a more frequent use of exchange and challenge and a less frequent use of showing dependency in a favorable climate.

It was expected that organizational climate would affect the relationship between bases of power and influence strategies. Such an expectation seems to be substantiated with the data, that is, climate does appear to modify the relationship. Managers with reward power report a frequent use of showing dependency, with a blend of positive sanctions to influence their subordinates in an unfavorable climate. However, they rely quite often on exchange and challenge and assertion tactics in a favorable climate. The coercive base of power gives rise to one single strategy—i.e., assertion in a favorable climate—whereas it gives rise to many tactics in an unfavorable climate.

Exchange and challenge tactics relate negatively to legitimate power in an unfavorable climate and positively in a favorable climate. Referent power gives rise to such tactics as expertise and reasons in an unfavorable climate but it relates to many other techniques in a favorable climate. Rational tactics (such as, expertise and reasons) are positively associated with expert power in both the climates. Yet, some interesting variations are apparent. Managers with expert power report a less frequent use of exchange and challenge in an unfavorable climate and a more frequent use of this strategy in a favorable climate. In addition, they report, as expected, a less frequent use of coalition and manipulation in a favorable climate. The information power has no influence in an unfavorable climate but does affect several tactics in a favorable climate. The connection base of power relates positively with exchange and challenge tactics in a favorable climate, whereas it is associated positively with assertion and personalized help and negatively with expertise and reasons tactics in an unfavorable climate.

The moderating effect of climate is probably much more salient in the data with respect to the leader behavior – influence strategies relationship. Interestingly, organizational climate appears to neutralize the relationship in a favorable climate for two types of leader behavior—nurturant-task and participative—whereas it appears to enhance this relationship in an unfavorable climate. Tactics such as coalition and manipulation are frequently employed under a bureaucratic boss to influence subordinates in an unfavorable climate. On the other hand, the use of upward appeal is more frequent under such boss in a favorable climate. Autocratic behavior relates to three strategies in an unfavorable climate and two strategies in a favorable climate, the assertion technique being common to both climates.

One theme is clear and unambiguous in the data: organizational climate does modify the forementioned sets of relationships—leadership style *vs* influence tactics, bases of power *vs* influence tactics, and leader behavior *vs* influence tactics. The conclusion is that it is not the style, base of power, or leader behavior alone which makes a significant variance in influence attempts. Rather, the *interaction* between style, base or leader behavior and organizational climate is much more important as it predicts the effective use of leaders' influence tactics.

Downward Influence as Function of Ownership and Hierarchical Levels

We shall examine now the role of ownership and hierarchical levels on the use of downward influence tactics. Although no empirical evidence is available which shows the impact of ownership on the use of influence strategies, one study (Kipnis *et al.*, 1980) illustrates the relationship between job levels and influence strategies. Kipnis *et al.* concluded that the higher the respondents' own job status, the more likely is the use of more direct tactics of influence. In view of this finding, it is hypothesized that job levels would explain a significant amount of variance in the use of downward influence tactics.

Similarly, the main effect of ownership is predicted in view of some obvious differences in the patterns of management between public and private sector organizations (Sinha, 1973). However, no prediction about the interaction effect is being made.

The hypotheses mentioned earlier were tested by employing a 2 × 3 (ownership by level) ANOVA of unequal *n*s. The summary of statistics is given in Tables 3.24 and 3.25.

Table 3.24   *Effects of Hierarchical Level and Ownership on the Use of Downward Strategies—Mean Scores*

Strategies	Public			Private		
	Low (*n* = 127)	*Middle* (*n* = 130)	*Top* (*n* = 50)	*Low* (*n* = 53)	*Middle* (*n* = 50)	*Top* (*n* = 30)
Exchange and challenge	9.41	8.75	7.90	11.64	8.90	8.73
Expertise and reasons	19.76	21.12	21.18	20.40	19.58	21.07
Personalized help	9.58	9.74	9.84	10.21	8.92	8.80
Coalition and manipulation	10.30	9.73	10.56	9.25	9.06	9.50
Showing dependency	11.30	11.29	11.50	12.30	10.14	11.90
Upward appeal	9.66	9.18	8.60	10.04	9.92	8.50
Assertion	8.83	8.93	7.76	9.77	8.10	9.27
Positive sanctions	11.26	11.00	10.94	12.32	11.80	12.03
Negative sanctions	7.61	7.58	8.00	9.04	7.52	7.27
Threats	4.60	4.46	3.98	5.51	4.64	4.20

Main Effects of Ownership

As is evident from Tables 3.24 and 3.25, ownership made a significant difference in the use of 5 out of 10 influence strategies. Managers

Table 3.25 *Effects of Hierarchical Level and Ownership on the Use of Downward Strategies—ANOVA Analysis*

Strategies		Level (A) $(df = 2)$	Owner-ship (B) $(df = 1)$	$A \times B$ $(df = 2)$	Residual $(df = 434)$
Exchange and	MS	2.68	1.72	0.56	0.232
challenge	F	11.55[b]	7.41[b]	2.41	
Expertise and	MS	0.59	0.17	0.62	0.273
reasons	F	2.16	0.62	2.27	
Personalized	MS	0.22	0.25	0.42	0.116
help	F	1.90	2.16	3.62[a]	
Coalition and	MS	0.21	1.28	0.03	0.189
manipulation	F	1.11	6.77[b]	0.16	
Showing	MS	0.72	0.01	0.62	0.172
dependency	F	4.19[a]	0.06	3.60[a]	
Upward appeal	MS	0.93	0.18	0.09	0.193
	F	4.82[b]	0.93	0.47	
Assertion	MS	0.41	0.44	0.75	0.096
	F	4.27[a]	4.58[a]	7.81[b]	
Positive	MS	0.09	1.45	0.01	0.136
sanctions	F	0.66	10.66[b]	0.07	
Negative	MS	0.36	0.07	0.61	0.123
sanctions	F	2.93	0.57	4.96[b]	
Threats	MS	0.47	0.28	0.09	0.064
	F	7.34[b]	4.38[a]	1.41	

Note: [a] $p < 0.05$; [b] $p < 0.01$.

in the private sector, compared to those in the public sector, reported a more frequent use of such influence tactics as exchange and challenge, assertiveness, positive sanctions and threat. However, they reported a less frequent use of coalition and manipulation than their counterparts in public sector organizations.

Main Effects of Job Levels

Tables 3.24 and 3.25 also suggest that influence strategies are a function of the respondents' job status. Compared to those with a higher job status, respondents with a lower job status reported a frequent use of exchange and challenge, upward appeal, assertiveness and threat in influencing their subordinates. However, showing dependency was associated more with either lower level or top level managers than with middle ones. There was a slight trend in the data, although non-significant, that the higher the job status of the respondents the more frequent the use of expertise and reasons when influencing the subordinates.

Interaction Effects

Of interest were the effects of interaction between ownership and level on the use of influence strategies. Significant interactions are illustrated in Figure 3.3.

The first interaction shown in the figure suggests that, compared to those with higher job status, respondents with low job status reported a more frequent use of personalized help in private sector organizations. However, the difference in the reported use of this strategy between middle and top managers was not significant. In addition, top and middle managers in the public sector reported a more frequent use of this strategy than their counterparts in private sector organizations. The remaining comparisons were not significant beyond chance.

The second interaction gives clear evidence that, compared to those at the middle level, managers at the lower and top levels made frequent use of showing dependency in private organizations. Additionally, lower level managers in private sector organizations reported a more frequent use of this strategy than their counterparts in public sector organizations. There was no significant difference in the use of this strategy because of job status in public sector organizations. This was also the case with other mean comparisons.

The third interaction makes it clear that managers at the lower or top level of management in private organizations made more frequent use of assertiveness, whereas top managers in public sector organizations reported a less frequent use of this strategy. However, top managers in private organizations used this strategy more frequently than their counterparts in public sector organizations. Other differences were non-significant.

Finally, the fourth interaction suggests that the higher the hierarchical level, the less frequent the use of negative sanctions in private organizations. However, the difference between middle and top managers was not significant. Hierarchical levels made no difference in the use of this strategy in private organizations. However, top managers in public organizations, compared to their counterparts in private organizations, made more frequent use of this strategy. There were no other significant mean differences.

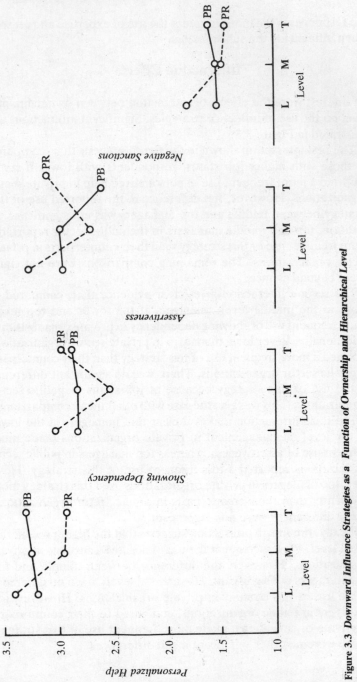

Figure 3.3 *Downward Influence Strategies as a Function of Ownership and Hierarchical Level*

Note: L = Low;   M = Middle;   T = Top;   PB = Public;   PR = Private..

Discussion and Conclusions

The findings regarding the main effects generally supported the hypothesis. The first finding that ownership makes a significant contribution to the variance in the use of influence strategies can be explained in terms of the inbuilt differences between public and private sector organizations. Some empirical evidence (Sinha, 1973) suggests that the private sector is predominantly task-oriented, drives its executives hard to maximize output, and in the process strains them to an extent not conducive to organizational health in the long run. In contrast, although the public sector has attempted to introduce participative management, it has been crippled by the bureaucracy and political interference. Some authors (for instance, Datt and Sundharam, 1985) have sarcastically referred the public enterprises as 'colonies for bureaucrats' (p. 168).

In view of these differences between the enterprises, it is natural to have such a trend in the results. For example, because of the presence of 'bureaucratic blood' in the public sector, managers make more frequent use of coalition and manipulation when influencing their subordinates. And, since productivity is top priority for managers in the private sector, the frequent use of such influence strategies as exchange and challenge, assertiveness, positive sanctions and threat is likely. Thus, direct influence strategies are more frequently used in the private sector, whereas indirect strategies are employed more frequently in the public sector.

The second finding concerning the role of job status (i.e., hierarchical levels) is interesting but somewhat inconsistent with the previous research (e.g., Kipnis *et al.*, 1980). The finding suggests that the lower the job status of the respondents, the more frequent the use of such influence methods as exchange and challenge, upward appeal, assertiveness and threat when influencing the subordinates. There is a slight trend in the data showing that such direct strategies as expertise and reasons are more often used by respondents with higher job status than those with low status. This trend is consistent with previous research (Kipnis *et al.*, 1980). However, the finding of the frequent use of assertiveness and threat by respondents with lower job status is not supported by the Kipnis *et al.* study. One more finding is difficult to explain—that is, managers in middle positions report a less frequent use of showing dependency than those in a low or top position. The difference in the findings here and those of Kipnis *et al.* may be attributed to the fact that the two studies differed greatly in terms of sample and also in terms of the list of influence strategies. Yet, some of these complexities in the results may also be explained in terms of the interaction between level and ownership.

Although not predicted, some significant interactions of ownership with job status on the use of influence strategies are interesting. This fact suggests that it is not ownership or job status alone *but* their interaction that makes a significant contribution to the variance in influence strategies. Such significant interactions were found for four strategies. One pattern is clear and unambiguous in the data and is similar across strategies—compared to those with higher job status, respondents with low job status in the private sector reported a more frequent use of personalized help, showing dependency, assertiveness and negative sanctions. It might be reasoned that (*i*) the private sector attaches top priority to task accomplishment, and (*ii*) it is the lower level managers who are generally hard-pressed to deliver the goods from their subordinates. Under such conditions, it is but natural to use a combination of rational (e.g., assertiveness) and non-rational tactics (e.g., negative sanctions) when influencing subordinates. However, the finding that the top managers in the public sector make less frequent use of assertiveness is difficult to explain. This finding also contradicts that of Kipnis *et al.* (1980). It can be reasoned that since public enterprises carry the 'blood of bureaucracy', the top managers rely on other tactics more often than on assertiveness.

4 Managing Superiors

There is an abundance of research on the strategies used by managers (that is, downward influence) to influence subordinates. Unfortunately, research on the strategies used by subordinates (or, upward influence) to influence managers is relatively much less (Schilit and Locke, 1982). The topic 'upward influence has seldom received concerted attention from those in the OB field and, indeed, has always been in the shadow of its "big brothers," namely, downward influence... and lateral influence' (Porter *et al.*, 1981, p.110). Recently, many researchers (Gabarrow, 1979; Kanter, 1977; Weinstein, 1979) have proposed that the understanding of how a subordinate influences his or her supervisor may be an essential ingredient of organizational effectiveness. Indeed, if this is so important, it alone makes the topic especially interesting.

This chapter deals with the upward influence process in organizations. The first section describes the upward influence measures used in the study. The second and the third sections, respectively, deal with direct and moderating effects on the use of upward influence strategies. Finally, the fourth section examines the process of upward influence as a function of organizational characteristics.

Upward Influence Strategy Measures

A total of 55 items were contained in the upward influence strategy measures. The items, were drawn from recent works by Falbo (1977), Falbo and Peplau (1980), and Kipnis *et al.* (1980). Respondents were asked to indicate on a 5-point scale (1= never; 5 = very often) the *frequency* with which during the past six months they engaged in the behaviors described by the scale items to influence their immediate superior at work. They were instructed to answer in terms of what they generally did, *not* what they would like to do. The distribution of items across strategies is presented in Table 4.1.

Table 4.1 *Distribution of Items of Upward Strategy Measures*

Strategies	Code	Number of Items
Blocking	B	4
Coalition	C	5
Defiance	D̄	5
Diplomacy	D	4
Exchange of benefits	E	5
Ingratiation	I	4
Manipulation	M	4
Personalized help	P̄	3
Persuasion	P	3
Reasoning	R	5
Showing dependency	D̿	3
Showing expertise	Ē	4
Upward appeal	U	3
Unclassified	Ū	3
Total		55

The factor structure (i.e., a partial test of construct validity) of the scales was examined by employing a varimax rotated factor analysis. Table 4.2 contains the factor loadings obtained. It is evident from Table 4.2 that the measures constrained to five interpretable factors (consisting of a total of 29 significant items), accounting for a total of 80.5 per cent of the variance. It is also evident that, for the most part, the items loaded rather cleanly (i.e., loadings above 0.40 on the appropriate sub-scale). Personalized help, as a method of influence, did not emerge at all as a distinct configuration. In fact, its items were not clustered on any particular factor either. Since the importance of this strategy has been emphasized in previous research (such as, Ansari *et al.*, 1984;

Table 4.2 *Factor Analysis Results—Upward Strategy Measures (N = 440)*

Items	Factor				
	1	*2*	*3*	*4*	*5*
1. At times I explained the reasons for my request	0.02	*0.48*	0.03	0.01	0.13
6. I praised him with superlatives	0.14	–0.01	*0.49*	0.10	0.16
8. I used logic to convince him	–0.09	*0.68*	0.04	0.00	0.09
9. I got my way by convincing him that my way was the best way	–0.02	*0.57*	–0.04	0.11	0.11
11. I obtained the support of my subordinates to back my request	0.19	0.03	0.07	*0.63*	0.09
12. I showed a feeling of dislike towards him	*0.61*	–0.14	0.01	–0.05	0.02
13. I provided sufficient information in support of my view	–0.15	*0.65*	–0.06	0.16	0.02
15. I engaged in a work slowdown until he did what I wanted	*0.55*	–0.10	0.16	0.13	0.12
17. I told him the reasons why my plan was the best	–0.05	*0.65*	0.12	0.15	–0.05
18. I voiced my wishes loudly	*0.49*	0.16	0.03	0.09	0.03
19. I influenced him because of my competence	0.03	*0.53*	0.17	–0.17	–0.05
21. I convinced him by explaining the importance of the issue	–0.10	*0.62*	0:23	–0.02	0.01
23. At times I tried to persuade him that my way was the best way	0.06	*0.63*	–0.05	0.02	0.02
25. I made him feel important	–0.01	0.13	*0.63*	0.08	0.22
26. I repeatedly persuaded him to comply with my arguments as they were the need of the time	0.22	*0.50*	0.11	0.15	0.12
27. I offered to help if he would do what I wanted	*0.44*	–0.03	0.19	0.18	0.03
30. At times I showed my knowledge of the specific issue	0.05	*0.51*	0.26	–0.19	0.13

(Table 4.2 contd...)

Items		Factor				
		1	2	3	4	5
31.	I acted very humbly to him while requesting my point	–0.12	0.13	*0.48*	0.03	–0.00
34.	I obtained the support of co-workers to back my request	0.28	–0.07	0.12	*0.60*	0.18
35.	I made a show that I had respect for him	0.11	0.10	0.19	0.16	*0.61*
36.	I acted unfriendly or did not cooperate with him	*0.63*	–0.00	–0.10	0.13	0.07
37.	I pretended that I cared for him	0.21	0.06	0.20	0.10	*0.64*
42.	I stopped the work in between if my demands were not met	*0.76*	–0.08	0.02	0.15	–0.02
44.	I distorted or lied about the reasons why he should do what I wanted	*0.61*	–0.11	0.01	0.17	0.14
46.	I got everyone else (my colleagues) to agree with me before I made the request	0.18	0.08	0.16	*0.60*	0.03
48.	I offered to work harder in the future	–0.00	0.06	*0.53*	0.18	0.08
50.	My expertise in technical issues won his favor for me	–0.01	*0.44*	0.16	–0.01	0.00
52.	I challenged his ability	*0.59*	0.07	–0.18	0.17	0.07
53.	I kept track of his omissions and commissions	*0.54*	–0.06	0.00	0.13	0.13
Eigenvalue		10.05	4.79	2.98	1.42	1.27
Percentage of variance		39.4	18.8	11.7	5.6	5.0

Note: Factor 1 = blocking and defiance; factor 2 = expertise and reasons; factor 3 =ingratiation and exchange; factor 4 = coalition; factor 5 = diplomacy.

Singh, 1985), it was reconstituted by having 3 of its original items which were not loaded on other factors.

The descriptive statistics, scale characteristics, reliabilities, and inter-relationships of the scales are provided in Table 4.3. It is important to note that the scales exhibited fairly high reliability coefficients, ranging from 0.69 to 0.84.

It can also be seen from Table 4.3 that the scales were only moderately intercorrelated (average $r = 0.27$), indicating a reasonable level of scale independence. However, some overlap was natural partly because of some spread-over effects from one strategy to another and partly because of the fact that the measures were perceptual ones. An inspection of Table 4.3 suggests that out of the 15 coefficients of correlation, 13 were significant at or beyond the 0.01 level of confidence. However, none of the significant correlations exceeded 0.50. This fact, once again, indicates that the factors may be taken as orthogonal.

Table 4.3 *Descriptive Statistics, Scale Characteristics, Reliabilities and Inter-correlations Among Upward Strategy Measures*

Strategies	1	2	3	4	5	6
1. Blocking and defiance	(0.83)					
2. Expertise and reasons	0.00	(0.84)				
3. Ingratiation and exchange	0.15[b]	0.24[b]	(0.67)			
4. Coalition	0.44[b]	0.09[a]	0.31[b]	(0.73)		
5. Diplomacy	0.31[b]	0.19[b]	0.38[b]	0.33[b]	(0.70)	
6. Personalized help	0.32[b]	0.20[b]	0.47[b]	0.32[b]	0.37[b]	(0.69)
No. of items	9	11	4	3	2	3
M	13.86	37.11	11.50	6.40	5.12	7.73
SD	5.35	6.74	3.30	2.70	2.18	2.73
Among index items correlations	0.37	0.33	0.34	0.48	0.54	*
Index items *vs* all others correlations	0.07	0.04	0.11	0.15	0.17	*
Split-half reliability	0.84	0.84	0.67	0.73	0.70	0.69

Note: Figures in brackets indicate coefficients alpha reliability;
$N = 440$; [a]$p < 0.05$; [b]$p < 0.01$.
* Information not available—generated variable.

Some evidence of discriminant validity can also be seen at the bottom of Table 4.3. For example, the blocking and defiance scale exhibits an average inter-item correlation of 0.37, which is far greater than the correlation of index items versus all other items ($r = 0.07$). A similar pattern can be observed in the case of other scales.

Direct Effects

This section specifically deals with how various personal and contextual variables directly relate to the upward influence process in organizations. Four sets of factors were examined—bases of power, leadership styles, leadership behavior and perceived organizational climate. The zero-order correlations between predictors and criterion measures are illustrated in Table 4.4. The intercorrelations among the predictors are contained in Appendix IV.

Table 4.4 *Interrelationships Between Upward Influence Strategies (Criterion Variables) and Bases of Power, Leadership Style, Leader Behavior and Organizational Climate (Predictors)*

Variables/Strategies	US_1	US_2	US_3	US_4	US_5	US_6
Bases of Power						
Reward	-11^a	22^b	24^b	-1	-7	22^b
Coercion	32^b	14^a	13^a	26^b	21^b	21^b
Legitimate	15^a	15^a	15^a	13^a	14^a	16^a
Referent	-2	26^b	25^b	3	7	22^b
Expert	-12^a	35^b	16^a	-5	-1	14^a
Information	19^b	18^b	20^b	19^b	22^b	25^b
Connection	34^b	11^a	22^b	32^b	31^b	34^b
Leadership Style						
Participative	-8	7	16^a	10^a	7	11^a
Task-oriented	-32^b	21^b	13^a	-9	-3	10^a
Bureaucratic	-5	9	32^b	5	16^a	18^b
Authoritarian	-3	7	33^b	7	16^a	17^a
Leader Behavior						
Nurturant-task	-21^b	-8	16^a	-4	7	8
Participative	-20^b	-7	13^a	-8	5	5
Bureaucratic	-12^a	-7	24^b	10^a	6	9
Authoritarian	20^b	11^a	20^b	14^a	6	12^a
Organizational Climate						
Reward and participation	19^b	0	8	25^b	11^a	17^a
Structure	-11^a	4	7	2	-8	11^a
Warmth and support	-26^b	-12^a	-9	-17^a	-19^b	-10^a

Note: Decimal points are omitted.

$N = 440$; $^a p < 0.05$; $^b p < 0.01$; US_1 = blocking and defiance; US_2 = expertise and reason; US_3 = ingratiation and exchange; US_4 = coalition; US_5 = diplomacy; US_6 = personalized help.

Bases of Power, Leadership and Influence Strategies

Bases of Power and Influence Strategies

The point has already been made clear in Chapter 3 that bases of power and influence strategies do not always go hand-in-hand. Although a meaningful correspondence between the two was found, this correspondence was not mutually exclusive. Thus, it was concluded that a manager with a particular downward base of power could employ a set of influence strategies to influence his or her subordinates, and that a particular influence strategy could be a product of more than one base of power.

Table 4.5 *Stepwise Multiple Regression Analysis Results—Bases of Power (Predictors) and Upward Strategies (Criterion Variables)*

Strategies	Bases						
	Reward	Coercion	Legitimate	Referent	Expert	Information	Connection
Blocking and Defiance							
R^2	0.18	0.16	0.20	0.20	0.19	0.20	0.11
Beta	-0.14[b]	0.20[b]	0.09	-0.03	-0.12[a]	0.03	0.26[b]
Order	3	2	5	6	4	7	1
Expertise and Reasons							
R^2	0.15	0.17	0.17	0.14	0.12	0.16	0.17
Beta	0.09	-0.07	0.06	0.11[a]	0.26[b]	0.11	0.01
Order	3	5	6	2	1	4	7
Ingratiation and Exchange							
R^2	0.09	0.13	0.13	0.06	0.13	0.12	0.12
Beta	0.16[b]	0.03	0.03	0.14[b]	0.04	0.06	0.12[a]
Order	2	6	7	1	5	4	3
Coalition							
R^2	0.14	0.13	0.13	0.14	0.13	0.14	0.10
Beta	-0.04	0.15[b]	0.05	-0.02	-0.07	0.03	0.25[b]
Order	5	2	4	7	3	6	1
Diplomacy							
R^2	0.12	0.11	0.12	*	0.11	0.11	0.10
Beta	0.03	0.08	0.05	*	-0.07	0.08	0.24[b]
Order	6	2	5	*	4	3	1
Personalized Help							
R^2	0.15	0.17	0.17	0.16	0.17	0.17	0.12
Beta	0.15[b]	0.08	0.02	0.09	0.03	0.05	0.24[b]
Order	2	4	7	3	6	5	1

Note: $N = 440$;
[a] $p < 0.05$; [b] $p < 0.01$.
* Tolerance level insufficient for further computation.

Going by this rationale, it is hypothesized that a similar relationship between bases of power and influence strategies should be observed in an upward influence attempt. Thus, the relationship between the two was examined by employing stepwise multiple regression analyses. The zero-order correlations can be seen in Table 4.4 and multiple regression results can be seen in Table 4.5.

As is evident from Table 4.5, there exists a meaningful relationship betweeen the upward bases of power and upward influence tactics. The strategy of blocking and defiance was positively influenced by the coercive and connection bases of power, and negatively by reward and expert power. The four bases of power contributed a total of 18 per cent of the variance in the use of blocking and defiance. The expert and referent bases of power significantly (14 per cent of the variance) affected the use of expertise and reasons. The tactics of ingratiation and exchange were the product of three bases of power—reward, referent and connection (12 per cent). The coalition strategy was positively influenced by the coercive and connection bases of power (12 per cent). Diplomacy, as an influence strategy, was influenced positively only by the connection base of power (10 per cent). Finally, personalized help was a product of both the reward and connection bases of power (15 per cent). As expected, legitimate power did not contribute significantly to any upward influence strategies.

Leadership Styles and Influence Strategies

We shall now examine how influence strategies with regard to upward influence vary with respect to own leadership styles. Table 4.4 presents the zero-order correlations between leadership styles (predictors) and influence strategies (criterion variables). The stepwise multiple regression results are summarized in Table 4.6.

As can be seen in Table 4.6, task-oriented style was negatively associated with the blocking and defiance strategy (10 per cent) and positively with expertise and reasons. Ingratiation and exchange was such a strategy that it was associated with all the leadership styles. Except for task-oriented style, it had positive regression coefficients with all the styles. Taken together, a total of 16 per cent of the variance was explained by leadership styles in this strategy. Coalition strategy was positively predicted by the participative style and negatively by task-oriented style (3 per cent of the variance).

Table 4.6 *Stepwise Multiple Regression Analysis Results—Self-Reported Styles (Predictors) and Upward Strategies (Criterion Variables)*

Strategies	Styles			
	Partici-pative	Task-Oriented	Bureau-cratic	Authori-tarian
Blocking and Defiance				
R^2	0.12	0.10	0.11	0.12
Beta	0.05	-0.40^b	0.10	0.06
Order	3	1	2	4
Expertise and Reasons				
R^2	0.04	0.04	0.04	*
Beta	-0.01	0.22^b	-0.02	*
Order	3	1	2	*
Ingratiation and Exchange				
R^2	0.14	0.15	0.15	0.11
Beta	0.18^b	-0.12^a	0.19^b	0.25^b
Order	2	4	3	1
Coalition				
R^2	0.01	0.03	0.05	0.05
Beta	0.18^b	-0.23^b	0.08	0.10
Order	1	2	4	3
Diplomacy				
R^2	0.05	0.04	0.03	0.06
Beta	0.12^a	-0.19^b	0.17^a	0.11
Order	3	2	1	4
Personalized Help				
R^2	0.04	0.05	0.03	0.05
Beta	0.11^a	-0.03	0.11^a	0.11
Order	2	4	1	3

Note : $N = 440$; $^a p < 0.05$; $^b p < 0.01$.
    * Tolerance level insufficient for further computation.

The participative and bureaucratic styles significantly and positively affected the strategy of diplomacy, whereas the task-oriented style negatively influenced it. Personalized help was significantly associated with the bureaucratic and participative styles of leadership.

Discussion and Conclusions

The findings suggest two general themes in the data. The first, concerning upward bases of power and upward influence strategies, suggests that a meaningful correspondence between the two does exist (e.g., reward *vs* personalized help, coercive *vs* blocking and defiance, expert *vs* expertise and reasons, connection *vs* coalition, etc.). However, this correspondence is not always mutually exclusive. In fact, the results suggest that a manager with a particular base of power can use a number of upward influence strategies. For example, the connection base of power was found to be associated with almost all the strategies, except expertise and reasons. Thus the findings are in expected directions. It is interesting to note that the two bases of power—legitimate and information— were not associated with any of the upward influence strategies. It is understandable that a person may not have legitimate power over his or her immediate boss. But the non-significant finding with regard to informational power is difficult to explain.

The second theme, concerning the relationship between leadership styles and bases of power, indicates that the relationship, for the most part, between the two is meaningful and is in the expected direction. For example, authoritarian managers were found to employ significantly more often such upward strategies as ingratiation and exchange. Bureaucrats relied more often on such strategies as ingratiation and exchange, diplomacy and personalized help. Task-oriented managers relied more often on a single strategy, i.e., expertise and reasons. But, at the same time, they did not encourage such strategies as blocking and defiance, ingratiation and exchange, coalition and diplomacy. Participative managers were found to frequently employ a combination of tactics such as ingratiation and exchange, coalition, diplomacy and personalized help.

One general conclusion is obvious from the findings that managers are highly flexible in using the methods of influence. It is not that participative managers use one set of strategies and autocratic managers use another set of strategies. In fact, a combination of strategies may be used by a manager with a particular style. For example, participative managers are found to use not only the personalized help strategy but they are also found to use such devious means as coalition. In contrast, autocratic managers are seen to strongly prefer such strategies as ingratiation and exchange. The ingratiation and exchange strategy has been found to be positively associated with almost all the styles (except task-oriented). Task-oriented managers prefer only the expertise and reasons strategy. But bureaucrats frequently use a combination of strategies like ingratiation and exchange, diplomacy, and personalized help. Such a trend in the results might be possible because the emphasis in this study was on actual *rather than* ideal tactics.

Organizational Context and Upward Influence Strategies

The manner in which the climate of an organization can and does influence the motivational orientations of managers has been emphasized by several writers (such as, Baumgartel, Dunn and Sullivan, 1976-77; and Litwin and Stringer, 1968). Evidence exists that individuals develop their own attitudes about the extent to which given systems are rational or non-rational (Gandz and Murray, 1980). Nevertheless, perceptions of the climate define the prevalence of their behavior in organizations. Thus, the role of contextual factors cannot be denied. Some studies (such as, Ansari and Rehana, 1986; Ansari and Kapoor, 1987; and Cheng, 1983) clearly indicate that the use of upward influence tactics is a function of the organizational context, of which the individual is a part.

This study employed two contextual variables: leader behavior and perceived organizational climate. Ansari and Kapoor (1987) examined the role of leader behavior on the use of upward influence tactics. In their experimental study, it was clearly demonstrated that subordinates responding to the authoritarian manager showed a greater tendency to employ such non-rational tactics as blocking, upward appeal and ingratiation. In contrast, those responding to the nurturant-task or participative manager showed a greater tendency to choose such rational strategies as rational persuasion. In line with the study, it is hypothesized that 'having an autocratic boss, managers would employ more often such non-rational tactics as blocking and defiance, ingratiation and exchange, and coalition. In contrast, those having a participative boss would employ such rational tactics as expertise and reasons.'

The second factor influencing the use of upward influence tactics relates to the perceived organizational climate. In an experimental study, Cheng (1983) hypothesized that individuals working in a rational climate would more frequently employ such tactics as rationality, and those working in a political climate would more frequently employ such non-rational tactics as ingratiation or threat. He labeled rationality (or reasons) as rational tactics, and ingratiation, upward appeal, threat, blocking, and exchange as political tactics. His experimental data showed reasonable evidence to conclude that the use of a particular strategy is a function of the context (climate) of the organization of which the individual is a part. The findings of Cheng (1983) were replicated in a more recent study by Ansari and Rehana (1986). In line with these findings, it is hypothesized that 'perceived climate would make a significant difference in the use of upward influence tactics. Managers would more often use rational tactics when they perceive their organizational climate as favorable. Those perceiving their climate as unfavorable would more often use non-rational tactics.'

Leader Behavior and Influence Strategies

The zero-order correlations between leader behavior and influence strategies are found in Table 4.4. A summary of the stepwise multiple regression results appears in Table 4.7. The table suggests that the strategy of blocking and defiance was positively influenced by autocratic behavior and negatively by nurturant-task behavior. The expertise and reasons strategy was significantly affected only by autocratic behavior. This was the case with the personalized help strategy as well. Bureaucratic, participative, and autocratic behavior determined the use of the ingratiation and exchange strategy. The coalition strategy was influenced only by bureaucratic behavior. Diplomacy was not associated with any leader behaviors.

Organizational Climate and Influence Strategies

The zero-order correlations between organizational climate and influence strategies are illustrated in Table 4.4. A summary of the stepwise multiple regression results is provided in Table 4.8.

The results suggest that climate did account for a significant amount of variance in the use of upward influence tactics. As is evident from Table 4.8, the three climates accounted for 15 per cent

Table 4.7 *Stepwise Multiple Regression Analysis Results—Leader Behavior (Predictors) and Upward Strategies (Criterion Variables)*

Strategies	Styles			
	Nurturant-task	Participative	Bureaucratic	Authoritarian
Blocking and Defiance				
R^2	0.04	0.07	0.07	0.07
Beta	−0.16[a]	0.02	−0.08	0.18[b]
Order	1	4	3	2
Expertise and Reasons				
R^2	0.02	0.02	0.02	0.01
Beta	−0.04	−0.04	−0.08	0.12[a]
Order	3	4	2	1
Ingratiation and Exchange				
R^2	0.10	0.11	0.06	0.09
Beta	0.04	0.12[a]	0.15[b]	0.23[b]
Order	4	3	1	2
Coalition				
R^2	*	0.03	0.03	0.02
Beta	*	−0.09	0.12[a]	0.10
Order	*	3	2	1
Diplomacy				
R^2	0.00	0.01	0.01	0.01
Beta	0.04	0.04	0.01	0.08
Order	1	3	4	2
Personalized Help				
R^2	0.03	*	0.03	0.01
Beta	0.11	*	0.02	0.14[b]
Order	2	*	3	1

Note: $N = 440$;
[a] $p < 0.05$; [b] $p < 0.01$.
* Tolerance level insufficient for further computation.

of the variance in the use of the blocking and defiance strategy. The two strategies—expertise and reasons and ingratiation and exchange —were both negatively affected by the climate of warmth and support. The two climates—reward and participation and warmth and support—significantly affected the use of coalition and personalized help strategies; but the regression coefficients were positive and negative, respectively. Diplomacy was significantly affected by all the climates (8 per cent of the variance).

Table 4.8   *Stepwise Multiple Regression Analysis Results—Climate (Predictors) and Upward Strategies (Criterion Variables)*

Strategies	Climate		
	Reward and Participation	Structure	Warmth and Support
Blocking and Defiance			
R^2	0.12	0.14	0.07
Beta	0.31[b]	–0.19[b]	–0.24[b]
Order	2	3	1
Expertise and Reasons			
R^2	0.02	0.02	0.02
Beta	–0.03	0.10	–0.15[b]
Order	3	2	1
Ingratiation and Exchange			
R^2	0.02	0.02	0.01
Beta	0.06	0.07	–0.11[a]
Order	3	2	1
Coalition			
R^2	0.06	0.11	0.10
Beta	0.30[b]	–0.07	–0.18[b]
Order	1	3	2
Diplomacy			
R^2	0.05	0.06	0.04
Beta	0.18[b]	–0.11[a]	–0.18[b]
Order	2	3	1
Personalized Help			
R^2	0.03	0.05	0.04
Beta	0.15[b]	0.07	–0.13[b]
Order	1	3	2

Note: $N = 440$;
[a]$p < 0.05$; [b]$p < 0.01$.

Discussion and Conclusions

The findings generally support the contextual perspective (Rousseau, 1978; and Salancik and Pfeffer, 1978) that the context of an organization accounts for a significant amount of variance in the use of influence strategies. Although such contextual effects have been reported in previous studies, the findings in this study are not very consistent with the hypothesis. In some cases, the findings with regard to the role of climate are even difficult to interpret.

The findings regarding the role of leader behavior are, by and large, consistent with those of previous studies. For example, managers influenced their autocratic boss by frequently employing almost all the influence strategies, i.e., a combination of rational and non-rational tactics. The frequent use of the ingratiation and exchange strategy to influence the autocratic boss is completely in line with that of previous studies (Ansari and Kapoor, 1987; Kipnis *et al.*, 1981). Kipnis *et al.* pointed out that an autocratic superior encourages the use of ingratiation, which was similar to the view of Ralston (1985). The findings in this study are supported by that of Kumar (1986). In a field study, Kumar also found that subordinates used ingratiation tactics more often to influence their authoritarian supervisor than to influence a non-authoritarian one. The use of the blocking and defiance strategy is also congruent with the findings of Ansari and Kapoor. However, the findings with regard to the use of expertise and reasons and personalized help are not in keeping with those of Ansari and Kapoor. Although the frequency of these strategies was not high, it seems reasonable to conclude that autocratic managers do demand some rational tactics in addition to non-rational ones.

As expected, managers used only non-rational tactics (such as, ingratiation and exchange and coalition) in influencing their bureaucratic boss. In an experimental study, Ansari and Kapoor (1987) found that the participative boss was often influenced by the use of rational persuasion tactics. The difference in the results might be attributed to the fact that the two studies were different in terms of sample and research design. Finally, managers did not relish using such non-rational tactics as blocking and defiance to influence the nurturant-task-oriented superior. This finding was expected and is consistent with that of Ansari and Kapoor (1987).

The findings with regard to the role of perceived climate on the use of upward influence tactics are meaningful but somewhat unexpected. Although it can be recalled (see Appendix IV) that the three climate measures were positively intercorrelated, their impact on the use of influence tactics are not similar—a fact which will now be dealt with.

Some conclusions are clear and expected in the data: the higher the structured climate, the less frequent the use of such non-rational upward influence tactics as blocking and defiance and diplomacy; the more the organization is perceived as reward and participation oriented, the more frequent the use of such influence tactics as personalized help; and the more the organization encourages warmth and support, the less frequent the use of such influence tactics as blocking and defiance, ingratiation and exchange, coalition, and diplomacy. These findings are consistent with those of Ansari and Rehana (1986) and Cheng (1983). Up to this point, it can be concluded that the more favorable the climate, the less frequent use of non-rational tactics and the more frequent the use of rational tactics; whereas the reverse holds true for the unfavorable or less favorable climate.

However, some other findings are not in expected directions. For example, the more the organization is perceived as reward and participation oriented, the more frequent the use of such non-rational tactics as blocking and defiance, coalition, and diplomacy. This finding is rather difficult to interpret. However, it can be reasoned that since reward is tied with participation, some devious means may be the likely consequences. There is some information available to suggest that, in order to meet organizational objectives, subordinates influence their immediate superior by employing both rational and non-rational tactics (Ansari and Kapoor, 1987).

Another finding is also somewhat puzzling, that is, the more the warmth and support in the organization, the less frequent the use of expertise and reasons and personalized help. It might be reasoned, however, that in a highly supportive climate, subordinates do not want to influence their superiors by showing expertise, giving reasons, or helping at a personal level. In fact, the climate of warmth and support is found to relate to all the influence tactics but in negative directions.

No matter how difficult interpretation of the present findings may be, one message is clear—the perceived climate contributes a significant amount of variance to the use of upward influence strategies.

Moderating Effects of Organizational Climate

We shall now examine the moderating effects of objective climate on the relationship between leadership styles (or leader behavior or bases of power) and upward influence strategies. The rationale for treating the role of climate as a potential moderator has already been dealt with, in Chapter 3. The moderating effects of climate are presented under three separate heads.

Leadership Styles and Influence Strategies

Two separate sets of stepwise multiple regression analyses were performed in order to test for the effects that climate might have on the relationship between leadership style and influence tactics. Table 4.9 shows the zero-order correlations and Table 4.10 presents the findings in terms of the particular combination of upward influence tactics that best predicted each leadership style.

Table 4.9   *Zero-Order Correlations Between Leadership Style and Upward Influence. Strategies—Sub-Group Analysis*

Strategies/Styles	Unfavorable Climate[a]				Favorable Climate[c]			
	P	T	B	F	P	T	B	F
Blocking and defiance	−10	−41[b]	−18[a]	−14	−7	−27[b]	2	3
Expertise and reasons	11	10	2	−1	4	27[b]	13[a]	11[a]
Ingratiation and exchange	27[b]	18[a]	29[b]	18[a]	10	11[a]	34[b]	41[b]
Coalition	15	−9	0	−3	7	−10	9	12[a]
Diplomacy	4	−7	24[b]	16[a]	9	0	12[a]	16[b]
Personalized help	14	7	23[b]	20[a]	9	12[a]	15[b]	17[b]

Note : Decimal points are omitted.
   [a]$p < 0.05$; [b]$p < 0.01$; [c]$N = 281$; [d]$N = 159$.
   P = participative; T = task-oriented; B = bureaucratic; F = autocratic.

As can be seen in Table 4.10, there is a meaningful relationship between leadership style and influence tactics as a function of objective organizational climate. Some of the significant findings are summarized above.

In the first place, highly participative managers were less likely to use such tactics as blocking and defiance irrespective of whether the climate was favorable or unfavorable. But they reported a frequent use of ingratiation and exchange tactics when influencing their boss in an unfavorable climate. Secondly, task-oriented managers reported a less frequent use of blocking and defiance tactics in order to influence their boss in both the climates. But they did make more frequent use of such tactics as expertise and reasons and personalized help in a favorable climate. Further, highly bureaucratic managers made frequent use of ingratiation and exchange tactics in both the climates. But they also made more frequent use of such tactics as diplomacy and personalized help and less frequent use of such tactics as blocking and defiance in an unfavorable climate. Finally, the autocratic style was significantly associated with such tactics as personalized help and blocking and defiance in an unfavorable climate, the latter having a negative impact. This style was, however, only strongly associated with ingratiation and exchange tactics in a favorable climate.

Table 4.10 *Regression Coefficients Between Leadership Styles and Upward Influence Strategies—Sub-Group Analysis*

Leadership Style	Unfavorable Climate		Favorable Climate	
	Strategies	*Beta*	*Strategies*	*Beta*
Participative	Ingratiation and exchange	0.22	Ingratiation and exchange	0.04*
	Blocking and defiance	−0.20	Blocking and defiance	−0.16
	$R = 0.30$		$R = 0.13$	
Task-oriented	Blocking and defiance	−0.48	Expertise and reasons	0.22
			Blocking and defiance	−0.30
			Personalized help	0.16
	$R = 0.41$		$R = 0.41$	
Bureaucratic	Ingratiation and exchange	0.23	Ingratiation and exchange	0.33
	Blocking and defiance	−0.29		
	Diplomacy	0.21		
	Personalized help	0.18		
	$R = 0.44$		$R = 0.34$	
Autocratic	Personalized help	0.20	Ingratiation and exchange	0.40
	Blocking and defiance	−0.22		
	$R = 0.29$		$R = 0.41$	

Note: * $p > 0.05$; all other coefficients are significant beyond the 0.05 level; strategies are listed in order of their entry into the stepwise multiple regression equations.

Bases of Power and Influence Strategies

We shall now examine the relationship between bases of power and upward influence tactics as a function of organizational climate. Table 4.11 shows the zero-order correlations and Table 4.12 presents the regression coefficient of influence tactics with each base of power.

Table 4.11 *Zero-Order Correlations Between Bases of Power and Upward Influence Strategies—Sub-Group Analysis*

Strategies/ Bases	Unfavorable Climate[d]							Favorable Climate[c]						
	B1	B2	B3	B4	B5	B6	B7	B1	B2	B3	B4	B5	B6	B7
Blocking and defiance	-20[a]	31[b]	8	-5	-14	16[a]	34[b]	-7	33[b]	17[b]	-1	-11[a]	22[b]	34[b]
Expertise and reasons	23[b]	5	16[a]	25[b]	32[b]	23[b]	8	21[b]	-1	14[a]	27[b]	37[b]	16[b]	13[a]
Ingratiation and exchange	21[b]	10	16[a]	29[b]	28[b]	30[b]	18[a]	25[b]	15[b]	13[a]	21[b]	11[a]	15[b]	25[b]
Coalition	-1	22[b]	20[a]	4	2	28[b]	34[b]	-2	29[b]	8	0	-9	15[b]	32[b]
Diplomacy	-3	28[b]	9	9	9	24[b]	32[b]	14[a]	16[b]	17[b]	5	-8	21[b]	31[b]
Personalized help	19[a]	32[b]	17[a]	22[b]	23[b]	34[b]	42[b]	24[b]	14[a]	15[b]	20[b]	9	20[b]	30[b]

Note: Decimal points are omitted.
[a]$p < 0.05$; [b]$p < 0.01$; [c]$N = 281$; [d]$N = 159$;
B1 = reward; B2 = coercion; B3 = legitimate; B4 = referent; B5 = expert; B6 = information; B7 = connection.

As is evident from Table 4.12, the objective climate did make a significant difference to the relationship between power bases and upward influence tactics. Details of some of the significant results are summarized below.

Expertise and reasons and personalized help were such influence tactics which were positively associated with the reward base of power in both the climates. In addition, managers with reward power reported a less frequent use of blocking and defiance tactics in an unfavorable climate but a more frequent use of ingratiation and exchange tactics in a favorable climate. Managers with coercive power reported the greater use of personalized help, blocking and defiance, and diplomacy tactics in an unfavorable climate, whereas they showed a frequent use of blocking and defiance and coalition tactics in a favorable climate. None of the upward influence tactics were associated with legitimate power in an unfavorable climate,

Table 4.12   *Regression Coefficients Between Power Bases and Upward Influence Strategies—Sub-Group Analysis*

Power Bases	Unfavorable Climate		Favorable Climate	
	Strategies	Beta	Strategies	Beta
Reward	Expertise and reasons	0.20	Ingratiation and exchange	0.18
	Blocking and defiance	−0.26	Expertise and reasons	0.14
	Personalized help	0.25	Personalized help	0.18
	$R = 0.39$		$R = 0.33$	
Coercion	Personalized help	0.25	Blocking and defiance	0.25
	Blocking and defiance	0.17	Coalition	0.17
	Diplomacy	0.18		
	$R = 0.40$		$R = 0.37$	
Legitimate			Blocking and defiance	0.15
			Expertise and reasons	0.13
			$R = 0.23$	
Referent	Ingratiation and exchange	0.20*	Expertise and reasons	0.23
	Expertise and reasons	−0.18	Ingratiation and exchange	0.15
			Personalized help	0.14
	$R = 0.32$		$R = 0.33$	
Expert	Expertise and reasons	0.26	Expertise and reasons	0.35
	Blocking and defiance	−0.22	Diplomacy	−0.15
	Personalized help	0.20		
	$R = 0.42$		$R = 0.39$	
Information	Personalized help	0.20	Blocking and defiance	0.16
			Expertise and reasons	0.14
	$R = 0.34$		$R = 0.28$	
Connection	Personalized help	0.32	Blocking and defiance	0.20
	Blocking and defiance	0.12*	Diplomacy	0.12
	Diplomacy	0.17	Personalized help	0.10*
	Coalition	0.18	Coalition	0.14
	$R = 0.50$		$R = 0.45$	

Note: * $p > 0.05$; all other coefficients are significant beyond the 0.05 level. Strategies are listed in order of their entry into the stepwise multiple regression equations.

whereas two strategies—blocking and defiance and expertise and reasons—were positively associated with this base of power in a favorable climate.

In addition, referent power was only associated with expertise and reasons in an unfavorable climate, whereas it was related positively to two additional strategies—ingratiation and exchange and per- sonalized help—in a favorable climate. Expert power, as expected, was positively associated with expertise and reasons tactics in both the climates. In addition, it was related to personalized help in an unfavorable climate. However, it was negatively associated with blocking and defiance and diplomacy in unfavorable and favorable climates, respectively. Information power was related to person-- alized help in an unfavorable climate and to blocking and defiance, and expertise and reasons in a favorable climate. The connection base of power was found to be associated with four strategies— personalized help, blocking and defiance, diplomacy, and coali- tion—in both the unfavorable and favorable climates.

Table 4.13 *Zero-Order Correlations Between Leader Behavior and Upward Influence Strategies—Sub-Group Analysis*

Strategies/ Behavior	Unfavorable Climate[d]				Favorable Climate[c]			
	NT	P	B	F	NT	P	B	F
Blocking and defiance	-18^a	-19^a	-16^a	8	-25^b	-22^b	-11^a	26^b
Expertise and reasons	-14	-15	-12	18^a	-4	-3	-4	9
Ingratiation and exchange	27^b	19^a	10	13	8	8	31^b	23^b
Coalition	-13	-16^a	5	24^b	0	-4	12^a	11^a
Diplomacy	11	3	3	7	4	7	7	6
Personalized help	18^a	12	8	12	0	-1	8	13^a

Note: Decimal points are omitted.

[a]$p < 0.05$; [b]$p < 0.01$; [c]$N = 281$; [d]$N = 159$; NT = nurturant-task; P = parti- cipative; B = bureaucratic; F = autocratic.

Leader Behavior and Influence Strategies

The relationship between a superior's leadership style and upward influence tactics in a favorable and an unfavorable climate is exam- ined here. Thus, two sets of stepwise multiple regression analyses were performed. The zero-order correlations between leader behavior and influence tactics are displayed in Table 4.13. Table 4.14 presents the summary of multiple regression analysis.

Table 4.14   *Regression Coefficients Between Leader Behavior and Upward Influence Strategies—Sub-Group Analysis*

Leader Behavior	Unfavorable Climate		Favorable Climate	
	Strategies	Beta	Strategies	Beta
Nurturant-task	Ingratiation and exchange	0.39	Blocking and defiance	−0.34
	Expertise and reasons	−0.30		
	Coalition	−0.21		
	Blocking and defiance	−0.18		
	R = 0.47		*R* = 0.25	
Participative	Blocking and defiance	−0.16*	Blocking and defiance	−0.29
	Ingratiation and exchange	0.32	Diplomacy	0.13
	Expertise and reasons	−0.26		
	Coalition	−0.21		
	R = 0.41		*R* = 0.27	
Bureaucratic	Blocking and defiance	−0.27	Ingratiation and exchange	0.33
	Coalition	0.15*	Blocking and defiance	−0.22
	Expertise and reasons	−0.21	Coalition	0.13
	R = 0.26		*R* = 0.37	
Autocratic	Coalition	0.22	Blocking and defiance	0.28
			Ingratiation and exchange	0.23
	R = 0.24		*R* = 0.32	

Note: * $p > 0.05$; all other coefficients are significant beyond the 0.05 level. Strategies are listed in order of their entry into the stepwise multiple regression equations.

Table 4.14 clearly suggests that the objective organizational climate has a powerful impact on the relationship between leader behavior and upward influence tactics. The significant results can be summarized. Managers reported a more frequent use of ingratiation and exchange and a less frequent use of expertise and reasons, coalition, and blocking and defiance tactics in order to influence their nurturant-task-oriented boss in an unfavorable climate. Blocking and defiance was the only strategy which was seen to be associated (negatively) with nurturant-task behavior in a favorable climate. Managers reported a more frequent use of ingratiation and exchange and a less frequent use of expertise and reasons and coalition tactics to influence their participative boss in an unfavorable climate, whereas they made less frequent use of blocking and defiance and more frequent use of diplomacy in a favorable climate. In order to influence the bureaucratic boss, respondents reported a less frequent use of blocking and defiance and expertise and reasons tactics in an unfavorable climate. On the other hand, in a favorable climate, they made greater use of ingratiation and exchange and coalition and less use of blocking and defiance tactics to influence the bureaucratic boss. Autocratic behavior was influenced by means of the coalition technique in an unfavorable climate, whereas this behavior was influenced by the frequent use of such tactics as blocking and defiance and ingratiation and exchange tactics in a favorable climate.

Discussion and Conclusions

A discussion on the findings regarding the role of organizational climate as a moderator follows. It was hypothesized that organizational climate would affect the relationship between leadership style (behavior) and upward influence strategies and between bases of power and upward influence strategies. The data mentioned in the foregoing clearly support this general hypothesis. The main findings are discussed below.

Participative managers report a more frequent use of ingratiation and exchange tactics in an unfavorable climate to influence their immediate superior, whereas in both the climates they report a less frequent use of blocking and defiance. Although task-oriented managers report a less frequent use of blocking and defiance in both the climates, they report a more frequent use of such tactics as expertise and reasons and personalized help in a favorable climate. Tactics of ingratiation and exchange are used in equal frequency by bureaucratic managers in both the climates. But diplomacy and personalized help (positively) and blocking and defiance (negatively) are also associated with bureaucrats in an unfavorable climate. Autocratic managers rely more often on ingratiation and exchange tactics to influence their boss in a favorable climate, whereas they rely more often on personalized help and less often on blocking and defiance in an unfavorable climate. Thus, climate significantly affects the use of influence tactics with respect to a leader's style.

A similar moderating effect is apparent as regards the relationship between bases of power and upward influence tactics. Having reward power, managers influence their immediate superior by employing the frequent use of such tactics as expertise and reasons and personalized help in both the climates. However, having this power, managers report a more frequent use of ingratiation and exchange tactics in a favorable climate and a less frequent use of blocking and defiance in an unfavorable climate. Coercive power leads to personalized help, blocking and defiance, and diplomacy tactics in an unfavorable climate, whereas it leads to blocking and defiance and coalition tactics in a favorable climate. Legitimate power is unrelated to any tactics in an unfavorable climate, but it is related positively to two strategies—blocking and defiance and expertise and reasons—in a favorable climate. Referent power relates positively to expertise and reasons in both the climates, but it also gives rise to such tactics as ingratiation and exchange and personalized help in a favorable climate. Managers with expert base of power report the use of expertise and reasons but more frequently in a favorable climate. In addition, they make more frequent use of personalized help and less frequent use of blocking and defiance in an unfavorable climate, and they make more frequent use of diplomacy in a favorable climate. Having information power, managers rely more often on the personalized help strategy in an unfavorable climate, but they frequently use such tactics as blocking and defiance and expertise and reasons in a favorable climate. The connection base of power gives rise to similar tactics in both the climates.

The moderating effect of organizational climate is evident in that it interacts meaningfully and significantly with leader behavior (i.e., the immediate superior's leadership style) in explaining the use of upward influence tactics. Managers less often use such tactics as blocking and defiance to influence their nurturant-task-oriented boss in both the climates, but they also report a less frequent use of expertise and reasons and coalition and a more frequent use of ingratiation and exchange tactics in an unfavorable climate. Participative behavior is seen to be related positively with diplomacy and negatively with blocking and defiance in a favorable climate. In contrast, this behavior is tied positively with ingratiation and exchange and negatively with expertise and reasons and coalition tactics in an unfavorable climate. In order to influence a bureaucratic boss, managers report a less frequent use of blocking and defiance tactics in both the climates. But they report a less frequent use of expertise and reasons in an unfavorable climate, and a more frequent use of ingratiation and exchange and coalition tactics in a favorable climate. While influencing the autocratic boss, managers report a frequent use of coalition in an unfavorable climate, and blocking and defiance and ingratiation and exchange tactics in a favorable climate.

One point is clear from these findings: organizational climate does interact significantly with self-reported style, leader behavior, and bases of power in determining the use of upward influence tactics.

Upward Influence as a Function of Ownership and Hierarchical Levels

This section specifically examines the role of ownership of the organization and job status of the respondents (hierarchical levels) on the use of upward influence strategies. The rationale behind such effects can be seen in Chapter 3. It was hypothesized in the light of Kipnis *et al.'s* (1980) study that the job status of the respondents would make a significant difference in the use of upward influence tactics. More specifically, the higher the job status of the respondents, the more frequent the use of such direct strategies as expertise and reasons. Similarly, in the light of the difference in the patterns of management between the enterprises (see Chapter 3), it was hypothesized that ownership would also make a significant contribution to the variance in the use of upward influence tactics. However, no prediction about the interaction between ownership and level was ventured.

In order to investigate the above hypotheses, a 2 × 3 (ownership by hierarchical level) ANOVA of unequal *n*s was performed. The mean scores on strategies are displayed in Table 4.15 and the summary of ANOVA results is provided in Table 4.16.

Table 4.15   *Effects of Hierarchical Level and Ownership on the Use of Upward Strategies—Mean Scores*

Strategies	Public			Private		
	Low (n = 127)	Middle (n = 130)	Top (n = 50)	Low (n = 53)	Middle (n = 50)	Top (n = 30)
Blocking and defiance	14.07	13.42	12.38	16.30	13.78	13.23
Expertise and reasons	36.80	37.73	38.68	35.21	35.78	38.67
Ingratiation and exchange	11.68	11.25	10.40	12.83	11.36	11.50
Coalition	6.67	5.90	6.38	7.28	6.32	6.07
Diplomacy	5.53	4.82	4.34	5.75	5.14	4.87
Personalized help	8.02	7.18	7.26	9.02	7.96	6.97

Table 4.16   *Effects of Hierarchical Level and Ownership on the Use of Upward Strategies—ANOVA Analysis*

Strategies		Level (A) (df = 2)	Ownership (B) (df = 1)	A × B (df = 2)	Residual (df = 434)
Blocking and defiance	MS	2.94	1.97	0.48	0.502
	F	5.86^b	3.92^a	0.96	
Expertise and reasons	MS	3.79	2.10	0.54	0.804
	F	4.71^b	2.61	0.67	
Ingratiation and exchange	MS	0.91	0.93	0.17	0.191
	F	4.76^b	4.87^a	0.89	
Coalition	MS	0.45	0.09	0.12	0.129
	F	3.49^a	0.70	0.93	
Diplomacy	MS	0.55	0.19	0.02	0.083
	F	6.63^b	2.29	0.24	
Personalized help	MS	1.03	0.37	0.24	0.129
	F	7.98^b	2.87	1.86	

Note: [a]$p > 0.05$; [b]$p > 0.01$.

Main Effects

As can be seen in Tables 4.15 and 4.16, compared to those in the public sector, managers in the private sector reported a frequent use of such upward influence tactics as blocking and defiance and ingratiation and exchange. However, on the remaining tactics, managers from the two enterprises did not differ significantly.

Interestingly, the main effect of job status was significant for all the influence strategies (Tables 4.15 and 4.16). Compared to those with higher status, respondents with low status reported a frequent use of all tactics, except expertise and reasons, which was more frequently used by top managers than by middle and low level managers. In most cases (except blocking and defiance and expertise and reasons), the difference between the middle and top level managers was not significant in the use of influence tactics.

No significant interaction for any influence strategies was found.

Discussion and Conclusions

The results suggest that between the main effects of ownership and hierarchical level, it is the latter which has the stronger effect on the use of influence tactics. In addition, the interaction between the two makes no significant contribution to the variance in upward influence attempts. The finding that influence strategies (like blocking and defiance and ingratiation and exchange) are used more frequently by private sector managers points to the fact that, because managers in the private sector attach greater priority to productivity, they engage in such tactics when influencing their immediate superiors.

The finding that such direct tactics (as expertise and reasons) are used more often by top managers than by middle and low level managers is consistent with the study of Kipnis *et al.* (1980). The findings that indirect tactics (such as blocking and defiance, ingratiation, coalition, diplomacy, and personalized help) are used more often by respondents with low status than by those with higher status is also in keeping with those of Kipnis *et al.* (1981).

5   Knitting the Threads

This chapter integrates the findings reported in the last three chapters. It aims at understanding the popularity or endorsement of leadership styles (of the respondents and those of their immediate superiors) and influence strategies (downward and upward) in organizations in India. Further, it gauges the extent to which the dynamics of influence strategies are similar or dissimilar to the status of the target person: the immediate superior or the immediate subordinates.

Prominence of Leadership Styles and Influence Strategies

Leadership Styles

The prominence of leadership styles will now be dealt with. The summary statistics based on mean analysis are presented in Table 5.1.

As is evident from Table 5.1, among the four self-reported styles, the task-oriented style is the most frequently endorsed by managers. This is followed by the participative style. The bureaucratic and autocratic styles are the least preferred ones. The mean analysis of leader behavior (i.e., subordinates' ratings of superior's style)

Table 5.1. *Leadership Styles Ordered in Terms of Endorsement*

Endorsement	Leadership Styles	
	Self-Reported	*Subordinates' Ratings of Superior's Behavior*
Most prominent to least prominent	Task-oriented Participative Bureaucratic Autocratic	Nurturant-task Participative Bureaucratic Autocratic

indicates that nurturant-task behavior, followed by participative behavior, is most frequently endorsed, whereas bureaucratic and autocratic behavior are once again the least frequently mentioned ones.

A similar ordering has been reported in previous research. For instance, Hassan (1986) reported a greater endorsement of self-reported leadership styles like participative, task and supportive. On the other hand, power-oriented, authoritarian and bureaucratic styles were the least preferred. As regards leader behavior, Hassan found that task and nurturance orientations were endorsed most frequently, whereas authoritarian and impersonal orientations were mentioned least frequently. A similar trend was observed by Ansari (1986). The fact that there is a great deal of similarity between the ordering of leadership styles of this study and that of Ansari (1986) and Hassan (1986) may be considered partial evidence for the external validity of the present findings.

Influence Strategies

We shall now examine the popularity of influence tactics in Indian organizations. The summary analysis of influence strategies (downward and upward) with respect to their popularity is contained in Table 5.2.

Table 5.2 *List of Influence Strategies Ordered in Terms of Popularity*

Popularity	Influence Strategies	
	Downward	*Upward*
Most popular to least popular	Expertise and reasons Personalized help Assertion Positive sanction Showing dependency Coalition and manipulation Upward appeal Exchange and challenge Negative sanction Threat	Expertise and reasons Ingratiation and exchange Personalized help Diplomacy Coalition Blocking and defiance

Table 5.2 suggests that at least three influence strategies (expertise and reasons, exchange, and coalition) are common to both the influence strategies. It should be noted that the strategy of personalized help did emerge as a separate configuration in the list of downward influence strategies, but it did not appear at all in the list of upward influence strategies. Keeping in view, however, the relevance of this strategy in the Indian context, it was reconstituted. Similarly, three strategies — positive sanctions, negative sanctions, and threat — in the downward influence attempt did not emerge as separate configurations but were reconstituted (see Chapters 3 and 4). Apart from the three common ones, the remaining strategies are seen to be uniquely associated either with influencing subordinates or with influencing the immediate superior. Such a unique association of influence tactics with the status of the target person has also been reported in previous studies. Mowday (1978) found the differential use of manipulation (a power tactic) in effective and non-effective principals. Kipnis *et al.* (1980) reported eight methods of influence which varied with the relative power of the respondents and that of the target. The results of two recently conducted studies of Indian organizations are also in keeping with the present findings. For example, Singh (1985) identified two sets of eight downward and upward influence strategies. Two sets of strategies clearly varied with respect to the target of influence: the immediate senior or the immediate subordinates. Similarly, Kapoor (1986) factor-analytically derived eight dimensions of downward influence and five dimensions of upward influence strategies. In her analysis, only two dimensions were common to the two lists of influence tactics.

Table 5.2 also suggests that expertise and reasons are tactics which appear to be the most popular for influencing both immediate subordinates and the immediate superior. In contrast, such non-rational tactics as exchange and challenge, negative sanctions, threat (downward influence), coalition and blocking and defiance (upward influence) are the least frequently mentioned influence methods. The finding regarding the ordering of influence strategies can be directly compared with those obtained in previous studies. Kipnis *et al.* (1980) saw the use of rationality as the most popular strategy for influencing both superiors and subordinates. On the other hand, blocking and sanctions were found to be less frequently used by managers to influence superiors and subordinates, respectively. Kapoor (1986) also found reasons (or rationality) as the most popular influence tactic for influencing subordinates as well as the immediate superior. Less frequently used strategies in her study were threats and negative sanctions (downward influence) and conditional cooperation and confrontation (upward influence). Some experimental studies (e.g., Ansari and Kapoor, 1987; Ansari and Rehana, 1986) also support the findings of the present survey to the extent that the strategy of rationality or rational persuasion is used most frequently and the blocking strategy is used least frequently for influencing the immediate boss.

One theme is obvious in the present data: rational tactics are used more often and non-rational tactics are used less often in organizations. Evidence (e.g., Kipnis and Schmidt, 1984) also exists that managers in Australia, England and the United States use rational tactics more frequently than non-rational influence tactics in getting their way. Thus, the similarity between the present findings and those obtained in previous studies is obvious. It should be mentioned that although the various studies reported above differed greatly in terms of design, sample and even culture from the present one, the similarity in the findings is quite encouraging. This fact may be considered partial evidence for the external validity of the present measures as well as the findings.

Integration of Findings

This section integrates the earlier findings (Chapters 3 and 4) with respect to the correlates of influence strategies (downward and upward). The integration of findings appears under four heads, based on multiple regression analysis and the ANOVA results.

Bases of Power and Influence Strategies

The bases of power emerged as an important predictor of influence strategies. It was anticipated that the use of influence strategies would vary as a function of bases of power. Figure 5.1 presents a summary of the relationship between bases of power and influence tactics. As is evident from Figure 5.1, there is a meaningful relationship between the two. A close inspection of the findings suggests that bases of power significantly affect the use of down-

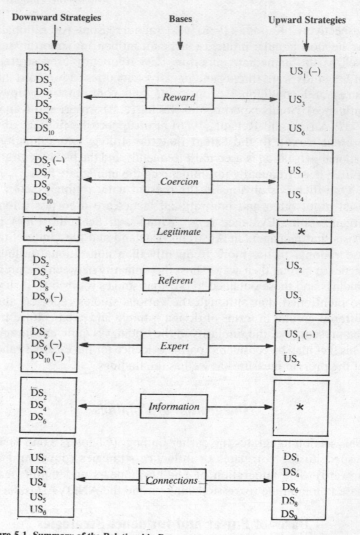

Figure 5.1 *Summary of the Relationship Between Bases of Power and Influence Strategies*

Note: Asterisks indicate the absence of any significant variables;
negative sings in brackets indicate negative impact

Abbreviations: DS$_1$ = exchange and challenge; DS$_2$ = expertise and reasons; DS$_3$ = personalized help; DS$_4$ = coalition and manipulation; DS$_5$ = showing dependency; DS$_6$ = upward appeal; DS$_7$ = assertion; DS$_8$ = positive sanction; DS$_9$ = negative sanction; DS$_{10}$ = threats; US$_1$ = blocking and defiance; US$_2$ = expertise and reasons; US$_3$ = ingratiation and exchange; US$_4$ = coalition; US$_5$ = diplomacy; US$_6$ = personalized help.

ward influence tactics in the same way as they affect the use of upward influence tactics. For example, both categories of influence tactics appear to be unaffected by the legitimate base of power. Whereas reward power is mostly associated with rational and positive tactics, coercive power is largely associated with non-rational and negative tactics. Similarly, both referent and expert bases of power are seen to affect the use of rational tactics in both the lists of strategies. One interesting finding is that the connection base of power affects most of the influence tactics in both the categories. Probably, in the Indian context, this base of power is more salient, since one of the dominant modes of power expression in Indians is power through proximity with powerful others (McClelland, 1975). The only inconsistency in the present findings is that information power does affect the use of at least three downward influence tactics but it does not affect any upward influence tactics.

Leadership Styles and Influence Strategies

A summary of the relationship between leadership styles and influence strategies is shown in Figure 5.2. This figure makes it clear that leadership styles affect downward influence tactics more or less in the same way as they affect the use of upward influence tactics. For example, participative managers are seen to use indirect techniques while influencing their immediate superior and immediate subordinates. Task-oriented managers use such direct techniques as expertise and reasons, no matter who the target of influence is: the subordinates or the superior. Other strategies are negatively associated with task-oriented style for both the targets. Such a similarity is evident for bureaucratic managers too. However, authoritarian managers are found to use a number of tactics when influencing their subordinates. But they rely quite often only on ingratiation and exchange when influencing their immediate superiors. Such a discrepancy may be due to the 'authoritarian submission' tendency in authoritarian managers (Adorno *et al.*, 1950).

Contextual Factors and Influence Strategies

The findings regarding the relationships of two contextual variables—leader behavior and perceived organizational climate—with the two lists of influence tactics—downward and upward—will now be dealt with.

Leader Behavior and Influence Strategies

Let us now examine to what extent the immediate superior's style

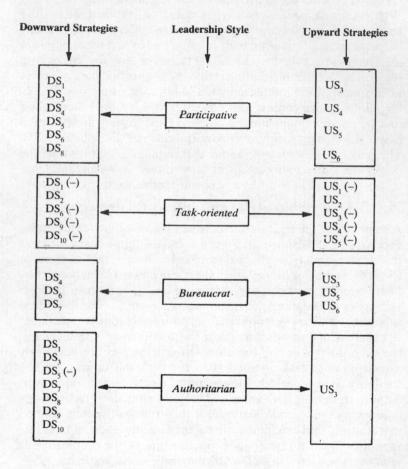

Figure 5.2 *Summary of the Relationship Between Leadership Styles and Influence Strategies*

Note: Negative signs in brackets indicate negative impact.

Abbreviations: DS_1 = exchange and challenge; DS_2 = expertise and reasons; DS_3 = personalized help; DS_4 = Coalition and manipulation; DS_5 = showing dependency; DS_6 = upward appeal; DS_7 = assertion; DS_8 = positive sanction; DS_9 = negative sanction; DS_{10} = threats; US_1 = blocking and defiance; US_2 = expertise and reasons; US_3 = ingratiation and exchange; US_4 = coalition; US_5 = diplomacy; US_6 = personalized help.

effect is similar to the managers' use of influence tactics with their immediate boss and immediate subordinates.

The summary of relationships between leader behavior and influence tactics (downward and upward) is shown in Figure 5.3. As can be seen from Figure 5.3, there is a substantial overlap in the managers' use of upward and downward influence tactics under a boss with a particular style. Under a nurturant-task-oriented boss, managers decline to use negative sanctions in influencing their subordinates in the same way as they decline to use blocking and defiance in influencing their immediate superior. However, they also report the frequent use of assertiveness while influencing their subordinates. Under a participative manager, managers report a more frequent use of such downward influence tactics as negative sanctions and threat and such upward influence tactics as ingratiation and exchange. Under a bureaucratic boss, managers report the use of similar influence tactics in influencing both their immediate superior and subordinates. Finally, under an authoritarian boss, a variety of influence tactics are used to influence both the targets.

Perceived Climate and Influence Strategies

Does perceived climate affect both upward and downward influence tactics in the same or similar ways? The summary of relationships is illustrated in Figure 5.4. It is readily seen that the managers' use of upward and downward influence tactics is affected by three climate factors in a similar fashion. For example, this similarity is more obvious with regard to the climate of warmth and support: it negatively affects almost all the tactics in both categories.

Organizational Characteristics and Influence Strategies

Of interest was the effect of job level and ownership of the organization on the use of influence tactics. Let us now see whether these organizational characteristics affect the two lists of influence strategies (downward and upward) in a similar way.

As can be seen in Chapter 3 (Tables 3.24 and 3.25) and Chapter 4 (Tables 4.15 and 4.16), there is a great deal of similarity in the use of upward and downward influence tactics as a function of job status and ownership. For example, compared to those with low

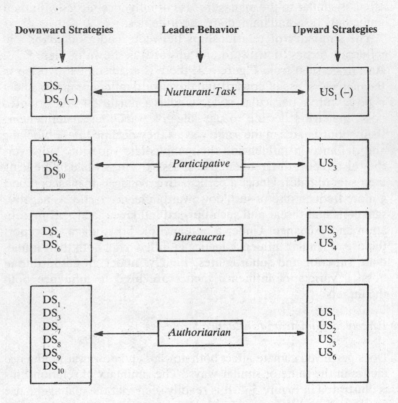

Figure 5.3 *Summary of the Relationship Between Leader Behavior and Influence Strategies*

Note: Negative signs in brackets indicate negative impact

Abbreviations: DS_1 = exchange and challenge; DS_2 = expertise and reasons; DS_3 = personalized help; DS_4 = coalition and manipulation; DS_5 = showing dependency; DS_6 = upward appeal; DS_7 = assertion; DS_8 = positive sanction; DS_9 = negative sanction; DS_{10} = threats; US_1 = blocking and defiance; US_2 = expertise and reasons; US_3 = ingratiation and exchange; US_4 = coalition; US_5 = diplomacy; US_6 = personalized help.

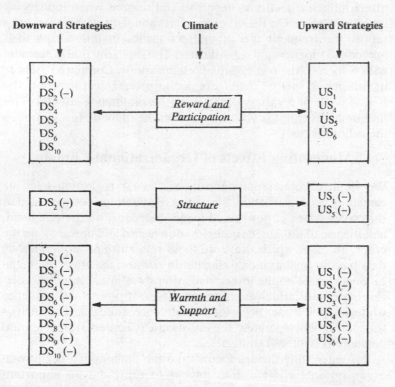

Figure 5.4 *Summary of the Relationship Between Climate and Influence Strategies*

Note: Negative signs in brackets indicate negative impact.

Abbreviations: DS_1 = exchange and challenge; DS_2 = expertise and reasons; DS_3 = personalized help; DS_4 = Coalition and manipulation; DS_5 = showing dependency; DS_6 = upward appeal; DS_7 = assertion; DS_8 = positive sanction; DS_9 = negative sanction; DS_{10} = threats; US_1 = blocking and defiance; US = expertise and reasons; US_3 = upgradation and exchange; US_4 = coalition; US_5 = diplomacy; US_6 = personalized help.

status, managers with higher status report the frequent use of such direct influence tactics as expertise and reasons when influencing both the targets. On the other hand, respondents with lower status report the frequent use of indirect tactics in influencing their immediate superior and subordinates. The similarity is also apparent with respect to the ownership of organizations. Compared to those in the public sector, managers in the private sector report the frequent use of a variety of tactics in their influence attempt. This finding holds true for both the targets: the immediate superior or the subordinates.

Moderating Effects of Organizational Climate

We shall now integrate our findings so far regarding how the climate of an organization affects the relationships between leadership style, bases of power and leader behavior, on the one hand, and the use of influence strategies (downward and upward), on the other. In other words, how are these relationships moderated by the objective organizational climate. In essence, the effect of organizational climate on the three relationships was investigated—leadership style and influence strategies, bases of power and influence strategies, and leader behavior and influence strategies. The analysis was performed separately for downward (Chapter 3) and upward influence (Chapter 4) strategies.

Two interesting themes follow from the findings. To begin with, organizational climate does appear to represent an important moderator of each of the three sets of relationships for this sample of Indian managers. Secondly, the moderating effect of climate is evident for both upward and downward influence attempts in a similar way. This implies, for example, that a manager with a particular style cannot influence (successfully) his or her immediate boss or subordinates without considering the role of the existing climate of the organization. That is, the emphasis in this study is on the effective use of a particular influence tactic rather than on the ideal one. In summary, then, this study adopts an interactionist stand in explaining the managers' use of influence tactics with regard to the superior and subordinates.

General Discussion and Conclusions

Taken as a whole, the findings suggest that the use of influence strategies is meaningfully related to the key variables identified in the study: leadership style, superiors' leadership style, bases of power, perceived climate of the organization, and organizational characteristics. What is more important is that the objective organizational climate (measured in terms of reward and participation, structure, and warmth and support) significantly affects the relationships between the key variables and the use of influence strategies. Taking organizational climate as a moderator has important implications for organizations. The implications are suggested in the next chapter. However, at this point, it is sufficient to note that a manager must know which types of moderators are present in the environment while developing an effective strategy to influence the subordinates or the superiors. The data of this study suggest that essentially the same key variable which enhances the effectiveness of an influence tactic in one climate also neutralizes it in another. Hence, there is a clear *interaction* between organizational climate and the key variables in determining the use of actual influence strategies.

This fact implies that human behavior (i.e., a choice of influence tactic) is so complex that it cannot be understood in terms of either the work environment (i.e., organizational climate) or the person (i.e., leadership style) alone *but* in terms of the interaction (or inter-relationship) between the two. Although this interactionist position in this problem area is sorely lacking, it is believed to most accurately represent the emergent nature of the real world of work organizations (Schneider, 1983). Literature is witness that 'both the trait and the situationist propositions are inaccurate and misleading and that a position stressing the interaction of the person and environment is both conceptually satisfying and empirically warranted' (Bowers, 1973, p. 307). Bowers is of the view that *'situations are as much a function of the person as the person's behavior is a function of the situation'* (p. 327, emphasis in original). Thus, situation and person are inseparable. No matter how sensible the interactionist position may be, only occasionally has statistical (algebraic) interaction been found in organizational behavior. The reality is that most studies fail to find support for the significance of the interaction term (Terborg, 1977). The failure to obtain the significant interaction terms, in most cases, is attributed to the fact that extremes of persons and contexts (or situations) rarely exist together. Thus, the real problem lies in the data analysis strategy.

Schneider (1983), like many others, feels that 'usual conceptualization of the word interaction as representing an algebraic term in ANOVA is quite narrow' (p. 12). The present study employed, instead of ANOVA, the stepwise multiple regression analysis to test the interaction or moderator hypothesis. However, a note of caution may be in order: 'Inclusion of an interaction term in data analysis does not make a piece of research interactional, nor does *lack* of such a term make the effort non-interactional' (Schneider, 1983, p. 9, emphasis in orginal).

Another interesting theme in the data is that the key variables (such as, bases of power and style) determine the use of both sets of influence tactics — upward and downward — in a similar fashion.

6 Summing Up

Background

What is it that managers actually do? They do nothing but exercise leadership. The exercise of leadership essentially involves the use of power—the use of power over subordinates as well as superiors. In view of this, this monograph has presented the concept of leadership as a particular type of power relationship. Leadership has been conceptualized as a 'reciprocal influence process' and power has been conceptualized as a 'potential influence'. The running thread between the two is 'influence,' whereas the distinguishing point between them is 'action connotation'. Whereas influence refers to a change in one person which has its origin in another person, action connotation refers to the actual behavioral mechanisms of influence.

The survey has presented data as to how leaders exercise power over their immediate subordinates and superiors. In the course of this presentation, five key elements are considered: bases of power, leadership style, leader behavior, perceived organizational climate, and organizational characteristics. These elements have been examined in relation to the actual use of a leader's power tactics. While examining the relationship between the first three key elements and influence tactics, the role of objective organizational climate has been treated as a moderator.

The survey in this study was conducted in seven heterogeneous organizations located in northern India. That is, some represented the public sector while others were privately managed; some were manufacturing concerns, others service organizations; some turned out to be large ones, others small ones; some were running in profit, others in loss; and some were known to be efficient, others inefficient. Having such a heterogeneous universe was a deliberate attempt to generalize the findings in significantly different settings. Altogether 440 executives representing seven organizations voluntarily participated in the study. The bulk of them were in the age range of 26 to 45 years, with a mean of 37.89 years. The average company tenure and the average tenure in present positions, respectively, were 10.65 and 4.11 years. Two female Research Assistants conducted the interviews with the executives. Data were collected during the fall of 1984 and the spring of 1985. The executives were interviewed individually and in private. They were assured complete *anonymity* of their individual responses.

The survey employed a number of measures to assess the key predictors and the criterion measures of downward and upward influence strategies. Before the measures were subjected to final analyses, their psychometric properties were thoroughly checked. In brief, each of the measures had substantial reliability and construct validity. Psychometric evidence was gathered with the help of descriptive statistics, correlations, varimax rotated factor analysis, and Cronbach's coefficient alpha. The final analyses testing the major hypotheses were subjected to multiple regression analysis and analysis of variance.

Summary

Some major findings emerged from the survey. First, the mean scores on the influence measures suggest the following. Among the four self-reported leadership styles in Indian organizations, task-oriented and participative are predominant, whereas the bureaucratic and authoritarian styles are the least endorsed by executives. As regards the subordinates' ratings on the immediate superior's leadership style (leader behavior), nurturant-task and participative are endorsed more by the executives, whereas bureaucratic and authoritarian behavior are the least endorsed ones. The executives perceive possessing more expert and referent power to influence subordinates, and expert and reward power to influence the immediate superior. On the other hand, regardless of the target of influence, they report possessing little of connection and coercive power. Irrespective of the target of influence (immediate subordinates or superior), executives report a more frequent use of rational influence tactics like expertise and reasons. In contrast, they report a less frequent use of such downward influence tactics as threats and negative sanctions, and such upward influence tactics as blocking and defiance.

Secondly, bases of power appear to be a crucial determinant of the managers' use of influence tactics. There is a meaningful correspondence between the bases of power and influence strategies (e.g., reward power *vs* positive sanctions and personalized help; coercive power *vs* negative sanctions, threats, and blocking and defiance; referent power *vs* positive sanctions and personalized help; expert power *vs* expertise and reasons; information power *vs* expertise and reasons; connection power *vs* upward appeal, coalition and manipulation). Legitimate power is found to be unrelated to any of the upward or downward influence tactics. Information power does relate to downward influence tactics, but it does not relate to any of the upward influence strategies. Also, there is an indication in the data that a manager with a particular base of power may adopt a variety of tactics in order to be effective, and that a particultar strategy may be a product of several bases of power. For example, having reward power does not mean the use of positive sanctions (e.g., promotion) only; it may cause a manager to use several other tactics like exchange and threats. Stated differently, the strategy of positive sanctions may not be guided by reward power only but also by some other bases of power (such as referent and connection.)

Further, leadership style appears to be a critical determinant of the use of influence strategies. Participative managers report the frequent use of a number of influence tactics (rational and non-rational) to influence their immediate subordinates and boss. Task-oriented managers report the more frequent use of such influence tactics as expertise and reasons to influence both the targets. Bureaucrats report the more frequent use of devious means to influence both the targets. Authoritarian managers report the frequent use of almost all the strategies (except expertise, reasons, and upward appeal) to influence subordinates, whereas they rely heavily on a single strategy—ingratiation and exchange—to influence the boss.

In addition, the use of influence strategies is found to be meaningfully affected by leader behavior (i.e., the superior's leadership style). Under a nurturant-task boss, managers appear to use assertiveness to influence the subordinates, and they report the less frequent use of devious means to influence both the targets. Under a participative boss, managers use negative sanction and threat with the subordinates and ingratiation and exchange with the immedite boss. Bureaucratic behavior gives rise to non-rational influence tactics (e.g., coalition and upward appeal) with both the targets. The autocratic boss gives rise to many rational and non-rational influence tactics to influence both the targets.

The perceived climate is also found to affect the use of influence tactics. The climate of reward and participation affects positively the use of non-rational tactics and negatively the use of expertise and reasons to influence both the targets. The climate of structure relates positively to such downward tactics as expertise and reasons and negatively to such upward tactics as blocking, defiance and diplomacy. The climate of warmth and support affects negatively almost all the upward and downward influence tactics.

Organizational characteristics also affect the use of influence tactics. Compared to those in the public sector, managers in the private sector report a frequent use of such upward influence tactics as blocking, defiance, ingratiation and exchange, and such downward influence tactics as exchange and challenge, assertiveness, positive sanction, and threat. However, managers in the public sector report a frequent use of coalition and manipulation tactics to influence subordinates. Compared to those with higher job status, managers with low job status report the more frequent use of a variety of influence tactics with both the targets. In contrast, those with higher status report the more frequent use of such rational tactics as expertise and reasons. Certain interactions between job level and ownership also make a significant amount of variance in the use of downward influence tactics.

Organizational climate appears to represent an important moderator in the relationship between leadership style and influence strategies. Participative managers report the more frequent use of influence tactics like coalition and manipulation for their subordinates and ingratiation and exchange for their boss in an unfavorable climate, whereas they report a more frequent use of personalized help for their subordinates and a less frequent use of blocking and defiance for their boss in a favorable climate. Task-oriented managers make more frequent use of expertise and reasons with both the targets in a favorable climate, but they report a less frequent use of blocking and defiance with their boss in an unfavorable climate. While influencing the subordinates, bureaucrats report the greater use of assertiveness in an unfavorable climate, and exchange and challenge tactics in a favorable climate. For the boss, they report a more frequent use of tactics like ingratiation, exchange, and diplomacy in an unfavorable climate, and ingratiation and exchange in a favorable climate. Authoritarian managers rely more often on assertiveness to influence subordinates, and personalized help to influence the boss in an unfavorable climate. In contrast, they report the more frequent use of exchange and challenge with subordinates and ingratiation and exchange with the boss in a favorable climate.

Organizational climate also affects the relationship between bases of power and the use of influence tactics. Managers with reward power make frequent use of rational tactics with both the targets in both favorable and unfavorable climates; however, they rely heavily on ingratiation and exchange tactics in a favorable climate. Coercive power gives rise to a combination of rational and non-rational tactics while influencing the boss as well as subordinates. Legitimate power relates to non-rational tactics in both the climates for influencing subordinates. Although it is unrelated to any upward influence tactics in an unfavorable climate, it is associated with non-rational tactics like blocking and defiance, and rational tactics like expertise and reasons in a favorable climate. Managers with referent power and expert power report a greater use of rational tactics with both the targets in both the climates. Information power appears to be unrelated to any downward influence tactics. But it gives rise to both rational and non-rational upward influence tactics. Connection power is generally positively related to devious means with both the targets in both the climates.

Organizational climate also appears to modify the relationship between leader behavior and influence strategies. Under a nurturant-task boss, managers frequently use such tactics as assertiveness and upward appeal to influence subordinates in an unfavorable climate, whereas nurturant-task behavior is completely unrelated to any downward influence tactics in a favorable climate. On the other hand, nurturant-task behavior encourages the use of upward influence tactics like ingratiation and exchange, and discourages the use of expertise, reasons, coalition, blocking, and defiance in an unfavorable climate. However, it also discourages the use of blocking and defiance in a favorable climate. Participative behavior encourages the use of such downward influence tactics as threat and upward appeal in an unfavorable climate, whereas it is unrelated to any tactics in a favorable climate. On the other hand, participative behavior encourages the use of upward influence tactics like ingratiation and exchange but discourages the use of expertise, reasons, and coalition in an unfavorable climate. However, it encourages and discourages, respectively, the use of coalition, and blocking and defiance in a favorable climate. Under a bureaucratic boss, managers report the frequent use of coalition and manipulation in an unfavorable climate, and upward appeal in a favorable climate to influence subordinates. On the other hand, the bureaucratic manager discourages the use of upward influence tactics like blocking, defiance, expertise, and reasons in an unfavorable climate, and encourages the use of ingratiation, exchange, and coalition, and discourages the use of blocking and defiance in a favorable climate. Under an authoritarian boss, managers report the frequent use of assertion, coalition and manipulation in an unfavorable climate, and exchange, challenge, and assertiveness in a favorable climate to influence subordinates. On the other hand, autocratic behavior in an unfavorable climate relates to a single upward strategy (i.e., coalition) while it is asociated with upward influence strategies (like blocking, defiance, ingratiation, and exchange) in a favorable climate.

Implications

Let us now translate the conclusions of this volume into recommendations for practical policy. This research has several implications for both individual managers and organizations that may be in order.

The survey has discovered that a manager's leadership style is a critical determinant of the exercise of power over the immediate subordinates and superior, as it is a critical determinant of organizational climate (Litwin and Stringer, 1968). This implies that managers should diagnose their leadership styles and power bases and then develop skills in order to change the climate in the desired direction. Accordingly, they should use effective tactics of influence which fit in with their style and the climate of their organization. The data show that the climate helps determine the kinds of influence tactics that are actually used by managers in order to get their way with their immediate subordinates and superior. In essence, climates tend to moderate the relationship between leadership styles and influence tactics, between bases of power and influence tactics, and between leader behavior and influence tactics. The implication is that climates can and do influence the motivational behavior of organization members. Therefore, changes in certain climate properties could have immediate and profound effects on the use of influence strategies. Evidence (such as, Rosenberg and Pearlin, 1962) exists that organizational norms governing decision-making processes may constrain leaders in the choice of influence tactics. Even a cursory look at the present data suggests that some organizational climates encourage the use of rational tactics (expertise and reasons), while others encourage non-rational tactics (like threat and manipulation).

If organizational climate has such an important impact on the relationship between leadership styles and influence strategies, then Indian organizations should be changed in such a way as to provide a favorable environment for leadership effectiveness. It should be noted at this point that the present survey concerns itself with only those influence strategies which are effectively used by managers in getting their way with people at work. The data show that, in order to be effective, even participative managers sometimes use non-rational tactics whereas autocratic ones use rational tactics. Similarly, a favorable climate sometimes gives rise to non-rational tactics. Even if an influence tactic is successful, we would not recommend its use unless it does not have any positive bearing on the mind of the target person(s) and does not have long-lasting effect. For example, a manager may successfully use negative sanctions or threat in order to get his or her way with subordinates, but the use of such tactics may also produce a negative effect (like disliking the boss) on the part of the subordinates. In view of this, a manager must be supportive and task-oriented (the participative or nurturant-task type); he or she must be aware of popular rational influence tactics and their consequences; and the organization must provide a supportive organizational climate (as expressed in terms of reward and participation, warmth and support, and clarity of the task demand). Only then can we have effective organizations. Such objectives can be met if certain guidelines be followed.

One, the chief executive officer or the top management must deliberately change the policy choices. Past research has shown that it is the top management which sets the climate (Likert, 1967), which is the most crucial for organizational effectiveness in Indian organizations (Ansari, forthcoming; Baumgartel, 1981; Sinha, 1980). Thus, the most important and dramatic determinant of organizational climate appears to be the leadership style utilized by top managers. The emphasis a manager puts on adherence to rules, the kinds of goals and standards he or she sets, and his or her communication with people at work, all have a tremendous impact on the climate (Litwin and Stringer, 1968). Another option, according to Baumgartel (1981, p. 8), is an 'organizational development program—a planned program for changing the character of an organization involving the use of behavioral science consultants and social scientific technologies of planned change.'

Second, which power tactic is most appropriate? It all depends on the circumstances in which a particluar tactic is being used. However, choosing the most important strategy can be improved by self-examination and a management development program (Kipnis and Schmidt, 1984). In such a training program, managers need to be made aware of a variety of influence tactics and their possible effects rather than rely on traditional methods like reward, coercion, and legitimate tactics.

In sum, the present survey has provided a contingency framework and, if it is understood by managers, it may provide the much needed perspective for the effective management of people at work. It suggests that managers must have influence (or power) over their subordinates and superiors, but such an influence cannot only be aimed at style. If managers are to become more effective in using their styles and influence strategies, they must learn to understand some of the critical contingencies. That is, managers must learn about the climate of the organization of which they are a part. The data provide enough evidence to suggest that Indian managers are flexible at using effective influence tactics and, thus, they must be trained in using the most appropriate strategy in a given organizational climate. Thus, action to enhance effectiveness should focus on both a manager's influence tactics and organizational climate.

Limitations

The study is not free from limitations. One major drawback relates to the self-report measures employed in the study. Although the present findings are not inconsistent with those in previous studies, more objective measures need to be developed so as to enhance the convergent validity. The second problem relates to the problem of method variance. It is possible that respondents might have tried to maintain consistency in terms of their responses. However, in order to overcome this problem, influence tactic items were properly randomized in the two influence strategy scales (downward and upward). Also, the two scales were placed far apart in the questionnaire. Finally, since the data were collected only from seven organizations, no claim can be made that the findings would stand validity across all types of organizations in India. Therefore, the results of the study should be viewed and interpreted with caution.

Looking into the Future

The overall results of this survey suggest several directions for future research.

Consequences of the use of influence tactics represent one obviously important area for exploration. It is hoped that the use of rational persuasion (which has its origin in information power), showing expertise (which has its origin in expert power), or personalized help (which has its origin in referent power) may have positive effects in the targets' mind as well as have a long lasting effect.

Future research should employ experimental methodology (perhaps field experiment would be the best choice) to investigate the causal connections between predictors and criterion variables. In correlational studies such as this, no direction of causality can be inferred. Although this study employed such sophisticated statistical techniques as factor analysis and multiple regression analysis, one cannot make tall claims about the presence of causality.

Research is needed to examine the causes of the success or failure of influence attempts. It may also be of interest to examine how managers attribute their success or failure to internal or external factors. Such future studies would lead to a more complete view of influence processes in organizations.

The survey has tried to explain the role of organizational climate as a moderator of the relationships between the key variables (i.e., predictors) and the use of influence tactics. It should be pointed out, however, that while the magnitude of relationships was not overly large, much criterion variance is still left unexplained. Attention should, therefore, be directed at investigating the role of other factors (such as characteristics of the target persons and those of influencing agents, tasks, and organizational cultures) in determining the relationship between managerial behavior and influence strategies. In other words, a thorough mapping of moderators is necessary before such knowledge can be used meaningfully in organizations with any strong probability of success.

Conclusion

This study has viewed leadership as a power phenomenon. It suggests that managers must exercise power (and influence) over their boss and subordinates. It recommends that power is not a dirty secret, but the secret of success (Salancik and Pfeffer, 1974). One should use the influence tactic most likely to be successful with the individual one is trying to influence. 'Different techniques are more effective with different people. It makes good sense to use the strategy that is most likely to be most effective' (Huber, 1981, pp. 70–71).

References

Adler, S. 1983. Subordinate imitation of supervisor behavior: The role of supervisor power and subordinate self-esteem. *Social behavior and personality*, 11, pp. 5–10.

Adorno, T.W., E. Frenkel-Brunswik, D.J. Levinson and R.N. Sanford. 1950. *The authoritarian personality*. New York: Harper.

Allen, R.W., D.L. Madison, L.W. Porter, P.A. Renwick and B.T. Mayes. 1979. Organizational politics: Tactics and characteristics of its actors. *California management review*, 22, pp. 77–83.

Andriessen, E.J.H. and P.J.D. Drenth. 1984. Leadership: Theories and models. In P.J.D. Drenth, H. Thierry, P.J. Willems, and C.J. de Wolff (eds.), *Handbook of work and organizational psychology*, Vol. I. New York: Wiley, pp. 481–520.

Ansari, M.A. 1980. Organizational climate: Homogeneity within and heterogeneity between organizations. *Journal of social and economic studies*, 8, pp. 89–96.

—————. 1981. Some of the determinants of success on executive positions. Unpublished doctoral dissertation, Patna: Patna University.

—————. 1986. Need for nurturant-task leaders in India: Some empirical evidence. *Management and labour studies*, 11, pp. 26–36.

—————. 1987. Effects of leader persistence and leader behavior on leadership perceptions. *Pakistan journal of psychological research*, 2, pp. 1–10.

—————. In press. Leader behavior and organizational effectiveness: Moderating effect of organizational climate. In A. Hassan and S. K. Singh (eds.), *Organizational behavior: An Indian perspective*. New Delhi: Mittal.

Ansari, M.A., H. Baumgartel and G. Sullivan. 1982. The personal orientation-organizational climate *fit* and managerial success. *Human relations*, 35, pp. 1159–78.

Ansari, M.A. and A. Kapoor. 1987. Organizational context and upward influence tactics. *Organizational behavior and human decision processes*, 40, pp. 29–39.

Ansari, M.A., A. Kapoor and **Rehana.** 1984. Social power in Indian organizations. *Indian journal of industrial relations*, 20, pp. 237–44.

Ansari, M.A. and **Rehana.** 1986. Upward influence tactics as a function of organizational climate and goals of influence attempt. *Indian journal of industrial relations*, 22, pp. 168–76.

Ansari, M.A. and **R. Shukla.** 1987. Effects of group performance and leader behavior on leadership perceptions. *Psychological studies*, 32, pp. 111–18.

Arnold, H.J. 1982. Moderator variables: A classification of conceptual, analytic and psychometric issues. *Organizational behavior and human performance*, 29, pp. 143–74.

Bacharach, S.B. and **M. Aiken.** 1976. Structural and process constraints: A level-specific analysis. *Administrative science quarterly*, 21, pp. 623–42.

Bacharach, S.B. and **E.J. Lawler.** 1980. *Power and politics in organizations.* San Francisco: Jossey-Bass.

Bachman, J.G., D.G. Bowers and **P.M. Marcus.** 1968. Bases of supervisory power: A comparative study in five organizational settings. In A. S. Tannenbaum (ed.), *Control in organizations*. New York: McGraw-Hill.

Bass, B.M. 1960. *Leadership, psychology and organizational behavior.* New York: Harper.

Baumgartel, H. 1974. *Some reflections on the process of participation in university settings.* Lawrence: University of Kansas (mimeo).

—————. 1981. Human factors in the transfer of technology in national development. *Human futures*, 4, pp. 1–9.

Baumgartel H., L.E. Dunn and **G. Sullivan.** 1976–77. Management education, company climate and innovation. *Journal of general management*, 4, pp. 17–26.

Baumgartel H., G. Sullivan and **L. E. Dunn.** 1978. How organizational climate and personality affect the pay-off from advanced management training sessions? *Kansas business review*, 5, pp. 1–10.

Bellingrath G.C. 1930. Qualities associated with leadership in extra-curricular activities of the high school. *Teach. Coll. Coutr. Educ.* No. 399.

Bennis, W.G. 1959. Leadership theory and administrative behavior: The problem of authority. *Administrative science quarterly*, 4, pp. 259–60.

Bierstedt, P. 1950. An analysis of social power. *American sociological review*, 15, pp. 730–38.

Blake, R.R. and **J.S. Mouton.** 1964. *The managerial grid.* Houston: Gulf Publishing.

Blau, P.M. 1964. *Exchange and power in social life.* New York: Wiley

Blau, P.M. and **R. A. Schoenherr.** 1971. *The structure of organizations.* New York: Basic.

Bowers, K.S. 1973. Situationism in psychology: an analysis and critique. *Psychological bulletin*, 80, pp. 307–36.

Bruner, J.S. 1950. Social psychology and group processes. *Annual review of psychology*, 1, pp. 119–50.

Byrd, C. 1940. *Social psychology.* New York: Appleton-Century-Crofts.

Cartwright, D. 1959a. Power: A neglected variable in social psychology. In D. Cartwright (ed.), *Studies in social power.* Ann Arbor: Institute for Social Research, pp. 1–14.

—————. 1959b. A field theoretical conception of power. In D. Cartwright (ed.), *Studies in social power.* Ann Arbor: Institute for Social Research, pp. 183–220.

Cartwright, D: 1965. Influence, leadership, control. In J.G. March (ed.), *Handbook of organizations*. Chicago: Rand McNally, pp. 1–47.

Cartwright, D. and **A. Zander** (eds.), 1968. *Group dynamics: Research and theory*. London: Tavistock.

Chattopadhyay, G.P. 1975. Dependence in Indian culture: From mud-huts to company board rooms. *Economic and political weekly*, 10, pp. 30–38.

Cheng, J.L.C. 1983. Organizational context and upward influence: An experimental study of the use of power tactics. *Group and organization studies*, 8, pp. 337–55.

Christie, R. and **F. Geis.** 1970. *Studies in Machiavellianism*. New York: Academic Press.

Cobb, A. 1980. Informal influence in the formal organization: Perceived sources of power among work unit peers. *Academy of management journal*, 23, pp. 155–61.

Collins, B.E. and **B.H. Raven.** 1969. Group structure: Attraction, coalitions, communication, and power. In G. Lindzey and E. Aronson (eds.), *The handbook of social psychology*, Reading: Addison-Wesley, Vol.4, pp. 102–204.

Daftuar, C.N. and **K.P. Krishna.** 1971. Perceived characteristics of good and bad supervisors by white collared bank employees. *Indian journal of psychology*, 46, pp. 45–53.

Dahl, R.A. 1957. The concept of power. *Behavioral science*, 2, pp. 201–18.

Dansereau, F., G. Graen and **W.J. Haga.** 1975. A vertical dyad linkage approach to leadership within formal organizations: A longitudinal investigation of the role making process. *Organizational behavior and human performance*, 13, pp. 46–78.

Datt, R., and **K. P. M. Sundharam.** 1985. *Indian economy*. New Delhi: S. Chand & Company.

Dayal, I. 1975. *Key variables in organizations study*. Ahmedabad: Indian Institute of Management.

De, N.R. 1974. Conditions for work culture. *Indian journal of industrial relations*, 9, pp. 587–98.

Drenth, P.J.D., H. Thierry, P.J. Willems and **C. J. de Wolff.** (eds.). 1984. *Handbook of work and organizational psychology*. New York: Wiley, Vol.1.

Dunnette, M.D. (ed.). 1976. *Handbook of industrial and organizational psychology*. Chicago: Rand McNally.

Emerson, R.M. 1962. Power-dependence relations. *American sociological review*, 27, pp. 31–41.

Etzioni, A. 1969. A basis for comparative analysis of complex organizations. In A. Etzioni (ed.), *Sociological reader on complex organizations*. New York: Holt, Rinehart, & Winston, pp. 59–76.

———. 1975. *A comparative analysis of complex organizations*. New York: Free Press.

Falbo, T. 1977. Multidimensional scaling of power strategies. *Journal of personality and social psychology*, 35, pp. 537–47.

———. 1982. PAQ styles and power strategies used in intimate relationships. *Psychology of women quarterly*, 6, pp. 399–405.

Falbo, T. and **L.A. Peplau.** 1980. Power strategies in intimate relationships. *Journal of personality and social psychology*, 38, pp. 618–28.

Farrell, D. and **J.C. Petersen.** 1982. Patterns of political behavior in organizations. *Academy of management review*, 7, pp. 403–12.

Festinger, L. 1950. Informal social communication. *Psychological review*, 57, pp. 271–82.

Festinger, L., S. Schachter and **K. Back.**1950. *Social pressures in informal groups.* New York: Harper & Row.

Fiedler, F.E. 1967. *A theory of leadership effectiveness.* New York: McGraw-Hill.

Filley, A. C. and **R. J. House.** 1969. *Managerial process and organizational behavior.* Glenview: Scott & Foresman.

Franklin, J.L. 1975. Down the organizations: Influence processes across levels of hierarchy. *Administrative science quarterly*, 20, pp. 153–64.

French R.L. 1956. Social psychology and group processes. *Annual review of psychology*, 7, pp. 63–94.

French, J.R.P. and **B. Raven.** 1959. The bases of social power. In D. Cartwright (ed.), *Studies in social power.* Ann Arbor: Institute for Social Research, pp. 118–49.

Gabarro, J.J. 1979. Socialization at the top: How CEOs and subordinates evolve interpersonal contacts. *Organizational dynamics*, 7, pp. 3–23.

Gamson, W.A. 1968. *Power and discontent.* Homewood: Dorsey.

Gandz, J. and **V.V. Murray.** 1980. The experience of workplace politics. *Academy of management journal*, 23, pp. 237–51.

Gibb, C.A. 1954. Leadership. In G. Lindzey (ed.), *Handbook of social psychology*, Vol. 2. Cambridge, Mass.: Addison -Wesley, pp. 877–920.

————. 1969. Leadership. In G. Lindzey and E. Aronson (eds.), *The handbook of social psychology*, Vol. 4. Reading: Addison-Wesley, pp. 205–82.

Goodchilds, J.D., C. Quadrado and **B.H. Raven.** 1975. Getting one's way: Self-reported influence strategies. Paper presented at the meeting of the Western Psychological Association, Sacramento, California, April.

Goodstein, L.D. 1981. Getting your way: A training activity in understanding power and influence. *Group and organization studies*, 6, pp. 283–90.

Gowin, E.B. 1915. *The executive and his control of men.* New York: Macmillan.

Graen, G., K. Alvares, J.B. Orris and **J.A. Martella.** 1970. Contingency model of leadership effectiveness: Antecedent and evidential results. *Psychological bulletin*, 74, pp. 286–96.

Halpin, A.W. and **B.J. Winer.** 1952. *The leadership behavior of the airplane commander.* Columbus: Ohio State University Research Foundation.

Hassan, A. 1986. Subordinate and task characteristics as moderators of leadership effectiveness. Unpublished doctoral dissertation. Patna: Patna University.

Heider, F. 1958. *The psychology of interpersonal relations.* New York: Wiley.

Heller, F. 1971. *Managerial decision making.* Assen: Van Gorcum.

Hersey, P. and **K.H. Blanchard.** 1977. *Management of organizational behaviour: Utilizing human resources.* Englewood Cliffs: Prentice-Hall.

Hersey, P., K.H. Blanchard and **W.E. Natemeyer.** 1979. *Situational leadership, perception, and the impact of power.* Escondido: Centre for Leadership Studies.

Hickson, D., C. Hinings, C. Lee, R. Schneck and **J. Pennings.** 1971. A strategic contingencies theory of intra-organizational power. *Administrative science quarterly*, 16, pp. 216–29.

Hill, W. 1973. Leadership style: Rigid or flexible. *Organizational behavior and human performance*, 8, pp. 35–47.

Hinings, C., D. Hickson, J. Pennings and **R. Schneck.** 1974. Structural conditions of intraorganizational power. *Administrative science quarterly*, 17, 22–44.

Hollander, E.P. and **J.W. Julian.** 1969. Contemporary trends in the analysis of leadership processes. *Psychological bulletin*, 71, pp. 387–97.

Homans, G.C. 1958. Social behavior as exchange. *American journal of sociology*, 63, pp. 597–606.

House, R.J. 1971. A path goal theory of leader effectiveness. *Administrative science quarterly*, 16, pp. 321–30.

House, R.J. and **M. L. Baetz.** 1979. Leadership: Some empirical generalizations and new research direction: In B. Staw (ed.), *Research in organizational behavior*, Vol. 1, Greenwich: JAI Press.

House, R.J. and **G. Dessler.** 1974. The path goal theory of leadership: Some *post hoc* and *a priori* tests. In J. Hunt and L. Larson (eds.), *Contingency approaches to leadership*. Carbondale: Southern Illinois University Press.

House, R.J. and **T.R. Mitchell.** 1974. Path-goal theory of leadership. *Contemporary business*, 3, pp. 81–98.

Howell, J.P., P.W. Dorfman and **S. Kerr.** 1986. Moderator variables in leadership research. *Academy of management review*, 11, pp. 88–102.

Huber, V.L. 1981. The sources, uses and conservation of managerial power. *Personnel*, 58, pp. 62–71.

Hunt, J.G., R.M. Osborn and **L.L. Larson.** 1975. Upper level technical orientation of first level leadership within a non-contingency and contingency framework. *Academy of management journal*, 18, pp. 475–88.

Jain, S.P. 1971. Leadership patterns in a north Indian community. *Sociology and social research*, 55, pp. 170–80.

Janda, K.F. 1960. Towards the explication of the concept of leadership in terms of the concept of power. *Human relations*, 13, pp. 345–63.

Jones, E.E. 1960. Review of D. Cartwright (ed.), *Studies in social power* (Ann Arbor: Institute for Social Research, 1959). *Contemporary psychology*, 5, pp. 130–31.

Kakar, S. 1971. Authority patterns of subordinate behavior in Indian organizations. *Administrative science quarterly*, 16, pp. 298–307.

Kanter, R.M. 1977. *Men and women of the corporation*. New York: Basic.

Kaplan, A. 1964. Power in perspective. In R.L. Kahn and E. Boulding (eds.), *Power and conflict in organizations*. New York: Basic Books, pp. 11–32.

Kapoor, A. 1986. Some of the determinants of intraorganizational influence strategies. Unpublished doctoral dissertation. Kanpur: Indian Institute of Technology.

Kapoor, A., M.A. Ansari and **R. Shukla.** 1986. Upward influence tactics as a function of locus of control and organizational context. *Psychological studies*, 31, pp. 190–99.

Katz, D. 1951. Social psychology and group processes. *Annual review of psychology*, 2, pp. 137–72.

Katz, D. and **R.L. Kahn.** 1966. *The social psychology of organizations*. New York: Wiley.

——. 1978. *The social psychology of organizations*. New York: Wiley.

Kelman, H.C. 1958. Compliance, identification and internalization: Three processes of attitude change. *Journal of conflict resolution*, 2, pp. 51–60.

Khandwalla, P.N. 1977. *The design of organizations*. New York: Harcourt, Brace, Jovanovich.

——————. 1988. Organizational effectiveness. In J. Pandey (ed.), *Psychology in India: The state-of-the-art*, Vol. 3. New Delhi: Sage, pp. 97–215.

Kipnis, D. 1958. The effects of leadership style and leadership power upon the inducement of an attitude change. *Journal of abnormal and social psychology*, 57, pp. 173–80.

——————. 1976. *The power holders*. Chicago: University of Chicago Press.

Kipnis, D., E. Cohn and **L. Schwarz.** 1976. The measurement of influence among dating couples. Paper presented at the meeting of the American Institute for Decision Sciences, San Francisco, November.

Kipnis, D. and **S. Schmidt.** 1983. An influence perspective on bargaining. In M. Bazerman and R. Lewicki (eds.), *Negotiating in organizations*. Beverly Hills: Sage.

——————. 1984. Patterns of managerial influence: Shotgun managers, tacticians and bystanders. *Organizational dynamics*, 12, pp. 58–67.

Kipnis, D., S. Schmidt, K. Price and **C. Stitt.** 1981. Why do I like thee: Is it your performance or my orders? *Journal of applied psychology*, 66, pp. 324–28.

Kipnis, D., S.M. Schmidt and **I. Wilkinson.** 1980. Intra-organizational influence tactics: Explorations in getting one's way. *Journal of applied psychology*, 65, pp. 440–52.

Kipnis, D. and **R. Vanderveer.** 1971. Ingratiation and the use of power. *Journal of personality and social psychology*, 17, pp. 280–86.

Kirk, R.E. 1968. *Experimental design: Procedures for the behavioral sciences*. Belmont: Brooks Cole.

Kochan, T.A. 1975. Determinants of the power of boundary units in an inter-organizational bargaining relation. *Administrative science quarterly*, 20, pp. 434–52.

Kochan, T.A., S.M. Schmidt and **T.A. DeCotiis.** 1976. Superior-subordinate relations: Leadership and headship. *Human relations*, 28, pp. 279–94.

Korman, A.K. 1966. 'Consideration', 'initiating structure', and organizational criteria: A review. *Personnel psychology*, 19, pp. 340–62.

——————. 1971. *Industrial and organizational psychology*. Englewood Cliffs: Prentice-Hall.

Kumar, P. 1986. Supervisor's authoritarianism and ingratiation among workers. *Psychological studies*, 31, pp. 165–68.

Lawler, E.E. 1976. Control systems in organizations. In M.D. Dunnette (ed.), *Handbook of industrial and organizational psychology*. Chicago: Rand McNally, pp. 1247–91.

Lewin, K., R. Lippitt and **R.K. White.** 1939. Patterns of aggressive behavior in experimentally created social climates. *The journal of social psychology*, 10, pp. 271–99.

Likert, R. 1961. *New patterns of management*. New York: McGraw-Hill.

——————. (1967). *The human organization*. New York: McGraw-Hill.

Lippitt, R., N. Polansky and **S. Rosen.** 1952. The dynamics of power. *Human relations*, 5, pp. 37–64.

Litwin, G.H. and **R.A. Stringer.** 1968. *Motivation and organizational climate.* Boston: Harvard University Press.

Locke, E.A. and **D.M. Schweiger.** 1979. Participation in decision making: One more look. In B. Staw (ed.), *Research in organizational behavior*, Vol. 1. Greenwich: JAI Press, pp, 265–339.

Lord, R.G. 1977. Functional leadership behavior: Measurement and relation to social power and leadership perceptions. *Administrative science quarterly*, 22, pp. 114–33.

Madison, D.L., R.W. Allen, L.W. Porter, P.A. Renwick and **B.T. Mayes.** 1980. Organizational politics: An exploration of managers' perceptions. *Human relations*, 33, pp. 79–100.

March, J.G. 1955. An introduction to the theory and measurement of influence. *American political science review*, 49, pp. 431–51.

————. (ed.): 1965. *Handbook of organizations.* Chicago: Rand McNally.

Martin, N.H. and **J.M. Sims.** 1956. Power tactics. *Harvard business review*, 34, pp. 25–29.

Martin, T.N. and **J.G. Hunt.** 1980. Social influence and intent to leave: A path-analytic process model. *Personnel psychology*, 33, pp. 505–28.

McClelland, D. C. 1975. *Power: The inner experience.* New York: Irvington.

Meade, R. D. 1967. An experimental study of leadership in India. *Journal of social psychology*, 72, pp. 35–43.

Meade, R. D. and **J. O. Wittaker.** 1967. A cross-cultural study of authoritarianism. *The journal of social psychology*, 72, pp. 3–7.

Mechanic, D. 1962. Sources of power of lower participants in complex organizations. *Administrative science quarterly*, 7, pp. 349–64.

Miner, J.B. 1980. *Theories of organizational behavior.* Hinsdale: Dryden.

Minton, H.L. 1967. Power as a personality construct. In B.A. Maher (ed.), *Progress in experimental personality research*, Vol. 4. New York: Academic Press, pp. 229–67.

Mintzberg, H. 1984. Power and organization life cycles. *Academy of management review*, 9, pp. 207–24.

Mowday, R.T. 1978. The exercise of upward influence in organizations. *Administrative science quarterly*, 23, pp. 137–56.

————. 1979. Leader characteristics, self-confidence and methods of upward influence in organizational decision situations. *Academy of management journal*, 22, pp. 709–25.

Mulder, M. 1971. Power equalization through participation? *Administrative science quarterly*, 16, pp. 31–38.

Mulder, M., D. Binkhorst and **T. van Oers.** 1983. Systematic appraisal of leadership effectiveness of consultants. *Human relations*, 36, pp. 1045–64.

Mulder, M., R. D. de Jong, L. Koppelaar and **J. Verhage.** 1977. *Power, situation and leaders' effectiveness – An organizational field study by means of the Influence Analysis questionnaire.* Inter-university Foundation for Business Administration at Delft, the Department of Clinical Psychology, Utrecht University, and the Department of Social Psychology, Free University, Amsterdam.

Murphy, L.B. 1953. Roots of tolerance and tension in Indian child development. In G. Murphy (ed.,) *In the minds of men.* New York: Basic, pp. 46–59.

Ng, S.H. 1980. *The social psychology of power*. New York: Academic Press.

Nie, N.H., C.H. Hull, J.G. Jenkins, K. Steinbrenner and D. Bent. 1975. *Statistical package for the social sciences*. New York: McGraw-Hill.

Nunnnally, J.C. 1978. Psychometric theory. New York: McGraw-Hill.

Pandey, J. 1976. Effect of leadership style, personality characteristics and method of leader selection on member's and leader's behavior. *European journal of social psychology*, 6, pp. 475–89.

———. 1978. Ingratiation: A review of literature and relevance of its study in organizational settings. *Indian journal of industrial relations*, 13, pp. 381–93.

———. 1981. A note about social power through ingratiation among workers. *Journal of occupational psychology*, 54, pp. 65–67.

———. 1988. Social influence processes. In J. Pandey (ed.), *Psychology in India: The state-of-the-art*, Vol. 2. New Delhi: Sage, pp. 55–93.

Pandey, J. and K. A. Bohra. 1984. Ingratiation as a function of organizational characteristics and supervisory styles. *International review of applied psychology*, 33, pp. 381–94.

Pandey, J. and R. Rastogi. 1979. Machiavellianism and ingratiation. *The journal of social psychology*, 108, pp. 221–25.

Patchen, M. 1974. The locus and basis of influence in organizational decisions. *Organizational behavior and human performance*, 11, pp. 195–221.

Patridge, E.D. 1934. Leadership among adolescent boys. *Teach. Coll. Coutr. Educ.*, No. 608.

Peabody, R.L. 1962. Perceptions of organizational authority: A comparative analysis. *Administrative science quarterly*, 6, pp. 463–82.

Pestonjee, D.M. 1973. *Organizational structure and job attitudes*. Calcutta: Minerva Associates.

Pfeffer, J. 1981. *Power in organizations*. Marchfield: Pitman.

Pfeffer, J. and A. Leong. 1977. Resource allocations in united funds: An examination of power and dependence. *Social forces*, 55, pp.775–90.

Porter, L.W., R.W. Allen and H. L. Angle. 1981. The politics of upward influence in organizations. In B. M. Staw and L.L. Cummings (eds.), *Research in organizational behavior*, Vol. 3. Greenwich: JAI Press, pp. 109–49.

Prakasam, R. 1980. Leader behavior and situational favorableness. *Indian journal of social work*, 40, pp.389–97.

Ralston, D.A. 1985. Employee ingratiation: The role of management. *Academy of management review*, 10, pp. 477–87.

Raven, B.H. 1965. Social influence and power. In I. D. Steiner and M. Fishbein (eds.), *Current studies in social psychology*. New York: Holt, Rinehart, & Winston, pp. 371–82.

———. 1974. The comparative analysis of power and power preference. In J. Tedeschi (ed.), *Perspectives on social power*. Chicago: Aldine, pp. 172–98.

Raven, B.H. and J.R.P. French, jr. 1958a. Group support, legitimate power, and social influence. *Journal of personality*, 26, pp. 400–9.

———. 1958b. Legitimate power, coercive power, and observability in social influence. *Sociometry*, 21, pp. 83–97.

Raven, B.H. and A. Kruglanski. 1970. Conflict and power. In P. Swingle (ed.), *The structure of conflict*. New York: Academic Press, pp. 69–109.

Raven, B. H. and **J.Z. Rubin.** 1983. *Social psychology.* New York: Wiley.

Ray, A. 1970. The Indian managers of the 1980s. *Economic and political weekly,* 5, pp. M105–M106.

Riecken, H.W. 1960. Social psychology. *Annual review of psychology,* 11, pp. 479–510.

Rosenberg, M. and **L. Pearlin.** 1962. Power-orientations in the mental hospital. *Human relations,* 15, pp. 335–49.

Rousseau, D.M. 1978. Characteristics of departments, positions and individuals: Context for attitudes and behavior. *Administrative science quarterly,* 23, pp. 521–37.

Russell, B. 1938. *Power: A new social analysis.* New York: Norton.

Saiyadain, M.S. 1974. Personality predisposition and satisfaction with supervisory style. *Indian journal of industrial relations,* 10, pp. 153–61.

Salancik, G.R. and **J. Pfeffer.** 1974. The bases and use of power in organizational decision making: The case of a university. *Administrative science quarterly,* 19, pp. 453–73.

———. 1977. Who gets power and how they hold on to it: A strategic-contingency model of power. *Organizational dynamics,* 5, pp. 3–21.

———. 1978. A social information processing approach to job attitudes and task design. *Administrative science quarterly,* 23, pp. 224–53.

Sarveswara Rao, G.V. 1973. Interpersonal trust and its correlates as perceived by superiors and subordinates. *Indian journal of industrial relations,* 10, pp. 359–69.

Sayeed, O. B. and **H.B. Mathur.** 1981. Least preferred coworker and four factor theory of leadership: Scales analysis and conceptual relationships. *Indian journal of industrial relations,* 17, pp. 55–63.

Schein, V.E. 1977. Individual power and political behavior in organizations: An inadequately explored reality. *Academy of management review,* 5, pp. 3–21.

Schilit, W.K. and **E.A. Locke.** 1982. A study of upward influence in organizations. *Administrative science quarterly,* 27, pp. 304–16.

Schlenker, B.R. and **J.T. Tedeschi.** 1973. Interpersonal attraction and the exercise of coercive and proper power. *Human relations,* 25, pp. 427–39.

Schnake, M.E. 1983. An empirical assessment of the effects of affective response in the measurement of organizational climate. *Personnel psychology,* 36, pp. 791–807.

Schneider, B. 1983. Interactional psychology and organizational behavior. In L. Cummings and B.M. Staw (eds.), *Research in organizational behavior,* Vol. 5. Greenwich: JAI Press, pp. 1–31.

Schopler, J. 1965. Social power. In L. Berkowitz (ed.), *Advances in experimental social psychology,* Vol. 2. New York: Academic Press, pp. 177–218.

Schriesheim, C.A. and **S. Kerr.** 1977. Theories and measures of leadership: A critical appraisal of current and functional directions. In J. G. Hunt and L.L. Larson (eds.), *Leadership: The cutting edge.* Carbondale: Southern Illinois University Press.

Schultz, D.P. 1982. *Psychology and industry today.* New York: Macmillan.

Sharma, M.L. 1973. Initiating structure behavior of the headmaster and school climate. *Indian journal of psychology,* 48, pp. 30–36.

Sherif, M. 1962. Intergroup relations and leadership: Introductory statement. In M. Sherif (ed.), *Intergroup relations and leadership*. New York: Wiley, pp. 3–21.

Sheth, N.P. 1972. Management of organizational status: A case study of the supervisor in a textile mill. *Indian journal of industrial relations*, 8, pp. 97–119.

Singh, A.P. and **D.M. Pestonjee.** 1974. Supervisory behavior and job satisfaction. *Indian journal of industrial relations*, 9, pp. 407–16.

Singh, C.B.P. 1985. Behavioral strategies in power relationships. Unpublished doctoral dissertation, Patna: Patna University.

Singh, M.P. and **R.P. Misra.** 1973. Scaling the determinants of the emerging leadership. *Interdiscipline*, 10, pp. 17–26.

Singh, R. 1983. Leadership style and reward allocation: Does LPC scale measure task and relation orientation? *Organizational behavior and human performance*, 32, pp. 178–97.

Sinha, D. 1972. Industrial psychology: A trend report. In S.K. Mitra (ed.), *A survey of research in psychology*. Bombay: Popular Prakashan, pp. 175–237.

Sinha, J.B.P. 1970. *Development through behavior modification*. Bombay: Allied.

——————. 1973. Organizational climate and problems of management in India. *International review of applied psychology*, 22, pp. 55–64.

——————. 1974. A case of reversal in participative management. *Indian journal of industrial relations*, 10, pp. 179–87.

——————. 1980. *The nurturant-task leader: A model of effective executive*. New Delhi: Concept.

——————. 1981. Organizational dynamics. In U. Pareek (ed.), *A survey of research in psychology, 1971–76*, Part 2. Bombay: Popular Prakashan, pp. 415–75.

——————. 1982. Power in Indian organizations. *Indian journal of industrial relations*, 17, pp. 339–52.

——————. 1983. Further testing of a model of leadership effectiveness. *Indian journal of industrial relations*, 19, pp. 143–60.

Sinha, J.B.P. and **M. Sinha.** 1974. Middle class values in organizational perspective. *Journal of social and economic studies*, 1, pp. 95–114.

Stinson, J.E. and **T.W. Johnson.** 1975. The path-goal theory of leadership: A partial test and suggested refinement. *Academy of management journal*, 18, pp. 242–52.

Stogdill, R.M. 1948. Personal factors associated with leadership: A survey of the literature. *Journal of psychology*, 25, pp. 35–71.

——————. 1974. *Handbook of leadership*. New York: Free Press.

Stone, E.F. and **J.R. Hollenbeck.** 1984. Some issues associated with the use of moderated regression. *Organizational behavior and human performance*, 34, pp. 195–213.

Student, K.R. 1968. Supervisory influence and work group performance. *Journal of applied psychology*, 52, pp. 188–94.

Szilagyi, A.D. and **M.C. Wallace.** 1980. *Organizational behavior and performance*. Glenview: Scott, Foresman.

Tannenbaum, A. 1962. Control in organizations: Individual adjustment and organizational performance. *Administrative science quarterly*, 7, pp. 236–57.

——————. 1968. Control in organizations: In A. Tannenbaum (ed.), *Control in organizations*. New York: McGraw-Hill, pp. 3–30.

Tannenbaum, R. and W.H. Schmidt. 1958. How to choose a leadership pattern. *Harvard business review*, 36, pp. 95–101.

Tannenbaum, R., I.R. Weschler and F. Massarik. 1961. *Leadership and organization: A behavioral science approach.* New York: McGraw-Hill.

Tedeschi, J.T., B.R. Schlenker and T.V. Bonoma. 1973. *Conflict, power and games.* New York: Aldine-Atherton.

Terborg, J.K. 1977. Validation and extension of an individual differences model of work performance. *Organizational behavior and human performance*, 18, pp. 188–216.

Thibaut, J.W. and H.H. Kelley. 1959. *The social psychology of groups.* New York: Wiley.

Venkoba Rao, A. 1970. Mental health and industrial executives. *Proceedings of the eleventh conference on human relations in industry*, SITRA, pp. 91–102.

Vroom, V.H. 1976. Leadership. In M.D. Dunnette (ed.), *Handbook of industrial and organizational psychology.* Chicago: Rand McNally, pp. 1527-52.

Vroom, V.H. and P.W. Yetton. 1973. *Leadership and decision-making.* Pittsburgh: University of Pittsburgh Press.

Warriner, C.K. 1955. Leadership in the small group. *American journal of sociology*, 60, pp. 361–69.

Weber, M. 1947. *The theory of social and economic organization.* New York: Free Press.

Weinstein, D. 1979. *Bureaucratic opposition: Challenging abuses of the workplace.* New York: Pergamon.

Wilke, H. and M. Mulder. 1971. Coalition formation of the game board. *European journal of social psychology*, 1, pp. 339–55.

Wilkinson, I. and D. Kipnis. 1978. Interfirm use of power. *Journal of applied psychology*, 63, pp. 315–20.

Winter, D.G. 1973. *The power motive.* New York: Free Press.

Wrong, D.H. 1968. Some problems in defining social power. *American journal of sociology*, 73, pp. 673–81.

Yukl, G. 1971. Toward a behavioral theory of leadership. *Organizational behavior and human performance*, 6, pp. 414–40.

————. 1981. *Leadership in organizations.* Englewood Cliffs: Prentice-Hall.

APPENDICES

APPENDIX I

Background Facts About Respondents: Organization-Wise
(Frequency-Count into Percentage)

	Organization							
	1	*2*	*3*	*4*	*5*	*6*	*7*	*Total Sample*
	(n=60)	*(n=40)*	*(n=28)*	*(n=77)*	*(n=71)*	*(n=99)*	*(n=65)*	*(N=440)*
Age (In Years)								
25 or less	1.7	7.5	42.9	11.7	2.8	5.1	9.2	8.6
26 to 30	8.3	37.5	35.7	9.1	5.6	17.2	23.1	16.6
31 to 35	6.7	20.0	0.0	16.9	28.2	28.3	16.9	19.1
36 to 40	26.7	10.0	0.0	22.1	22.5	26.3	16.9	20.5
41 to 45	25.0	2.5	7.1	10.4	15.5	12.1	13.8	13.2
46 to 50	11.7	5.0	7.1	15.6	15.5	8.1	7.7	10.7
51 to 55	13.3	5.0	3.6	11.7	8.5	3.0	7.7	7.7
56 to 60	5.0	2.5	0.0	2.6	1.4	0.0	4.6	2.3
60 or older	1.7	10.0	3.6	0.0	0.0	0.0	0.0	1.4
Formal Education Attained by Respondents								
High school	0.0	0.0	0.0	0.0	0.0	1.0	1.5	0.5
Some college	21.7	27.5	50.0	15.6	18.3	30.3	7.7	22.3
Bachelor's degree	55.0	25.0	28.6	53.2	67.6	52.5	50.8	51.1
Master's degree	11.7	27.5	10.7	20.8	12.7	16.2	26.2	18.0
Professional degree	11.7	20.0	10.7	10.4	1.4	0.0	13.8	8.2

(Appendix I contd...)

	1	2	3	4	5	6	7	Total Sample
	(n=60)	*(n=40)*	*(n=28)*	*(n=77)*	*(n=71)*	*(n=99)*	*(n=65)*	*(N=440)*
Tenure in Present Organization (In years)								
4 or less	0.0	52.5	60.7	16.9	7.0	17.1	24.6	20.2
5 to 9	19.9	22.5	28.5	16.9	16.9	40.4	20.1	24.3
10 to 14	23.3	15.0	23.7	36.4	28.1	42.4	15.4	28.0
15 to 19	20.1	5.0	20.1	23.4	22.4	0.0	23.1	14.3
20 to 24	20.1	5.0	6.7	6.5	23.9	0.0	15.4	10.5
25 to 29	6.7	0.0	0.0	0.0	1.4	0.0	0.0	1.1
30 to 34	8.3	0.0	0.0	0.0	0.0	0.0	1.5	1.4
35 to 39	1.7	0.0	0.0	0.0	0.0	0.0	0.0	0.2
Tenure in Present Position (In Years)								
4 or less	36.7	70.0	78.6	81.9	71.8	57.6	80.0	67.0
5 to 9	41.6	20.0	17.9	16.9	16.9	36.4	16.9	25.0
10 to 14	13.3	2.5	3.6	1.3	2.7	6.1	1.5	6.0
15 to 19	5.0	2.5	0.0	0.0	0.0	0.0	1.5	1.1
20 to 24	1.7	5.0	0.0	0.0	0.0	0.0	0.0	0.7
25 to 29	1.7	0.0	0.0	0.0	0.0	0.0	0.0	0.2
Number of Subordinates Reporting to Respondent								
1 to 4	18.3	37.5	50.7	19.5	62.0	44.4	50.8	40.7
5 to 9	11.7	40.0	28.6	26.0	25.4	25.3	26.2	25.2
10 to 14	13.3	12.5	3.6	29.9	5.6	10.1	4.6	12.3
15 to 19	10.0	2.5	7.1	5.2	1.4	6.1	6.2	5.5
20 to 24	6.7	0.0	0.0	6.5	0.0	2.0	1.5	2.7
25 to 29	3.3	5.0	0.0	1.3	0.0	3.0	1.5	2.0
30 to 34	3.3	0.0	0.0	3.9	0.0	1.0	0.0	1.4
35 to 39	3.3	0.0	0.0	3.9	0.0	1.0	1.5	1.6
40 or more	30.3	2.5	0.0	3.9	5.0	7.1	7.7	8.6
Present Monthly Income (Rs)								
Honorary	0.0	0.0	7.1	0.0	0.0	0.0	0.0	0.5
1,500 or less	11.7	65.0	57.1	0.0	5.6	7.1	9.2	15.0
1,501 to 1,800	11.7	15.0	10.7	11.7	2.8	17.2	3.1	10.5
1,801 to 2,100	5.0	15.0	7.1	13.0	14.1	19.2	33.8	16.4
2,101 to 2,400	5.0	2.5	7.1	18.2	14.1	17.2	12.3	12.5
2,401 to 2,700	21.7	0.0	0.0	19.5	25.4	15.2	9.2	15.2
2,701 to 3,000	11.7	2.5	0.0	10.4	14.1	8.1	7.7	8.9
3,001 to 3,300	20.0	0.0	3.6	10.4	8.5	4.0	4.6	7.7
3,301 to 3,600	5.0	0.0	0.0	9.1	7.0	7.1	10.8	6.6
3,601 to 3,900	3.3	0.0	0.0	5.2	5.6	0.0	0.0	2.3
3,901 to 4,200	18.2	0.0	3.6	2.6	2.8	3.0	1.5	2.5
4,201 or more	11.1	0.0	3.6	0.0	0.0	2.0	7.7	2.0

(Appendix I contd...)

	1 (n=60)	2 (n=40)	3 (n=28)	4 (n=77)	5 (n=71)	6 (n=99)	7 (n=65)	Total Sample (N=440)
Number of Times the Respondent was Promoted During His or Her Professional Career								
2 or less	80.0	70.0	85.8	61.1	26.5	77.8	49.2	65.7
3 to 4	18.3	20.0	7.1	35.1	45.1	18.2	40.0	28.2
5 to 6	1.7	10.0	0.0	2.6	8.4	4.0	9.2	5.2
7 or more	0.0	0.0	7.2	1.3	0.0	0.0	1.5	0.9
Level at which Respondent's Present Job Fits in Organizational Structure								
Top management	56.7	55.0	57.1	51.9	26.8	34.3	23.1	18.2
Middle management	36.7	15.0	25.0	35.1	47.9	47.5	56.9	40.9
Lower management	6.7	30.0	17.9	13.0	25.4	18.2	20.0	40.9
Number of Other Organizations Respondent Worked for in Adult Career								
None	66.7	32.5	46.4	49.4	32.4	24.2	55.4	42.5
1 to 2	23.3	42.5	36.7	41.6	53.6	53.5	32.3	42.0
3 to 4	10.0	17.5	14.2	7.8	12.6	18.2	7.7	12.5
5 to 6	0.0	5.0	3.6	1.3	1.4	3.0	4.6	2.5
7 or more	0.0	2.5	0.0	0.0	0.0	1.0	0.0	0.5

APPENDIX II

Background Facts About Respondents: Level-Wise
(Frequency-Count into Percentage)

	Level		
	Lower Management	*Middle Management*	*Top Management*
Age (In Years)			
25 to less	15.6	5.6	0.0
26 to 30	23.9	16.1	1.3
31 to 35	18.3	23.9	10.0
36 to 40	18.3	21.7	22.5
41 to 45	11.1	11.1	22.5
46 to 50	5.0	10.6	23.8
51 to 55	4.4	7.2	16.3
56 to 60	2.2	2.8	1.3
61 or older	1.1	1.1	2.5

(*Appendix II contd...*)

	Level		
	Lower Management	*Middle Management*	*Top Management*
Formal Education Attained by Respondents			
High school	0.6	0.6	0.0
Some college	42.2	10.0	5.0
Bachelor's degree	39.4	61.1	55.0
Master's degree	13.9	20.0	22.5
Professional degree	3.9	8.3	17.5
Tenure in Present Organization (In Years)			
4 or less	25.5	17.8	13.8
5 to 9	27.3	26.2	13.8
10 to 14	26.6	28.3	30.2
15 to 19	11.1	13.9	22.5
20 to 24	8.4	15.6	15.1
25 to 29	0.0	1.1	3.8
30 to 34	0.6	2.3	1.3
35 to 39	0.6	0.0	0.0
Tenure in Present Position (In Years)			
4 or less	64.4	71.7	62.6
5 to 9	25.5	22.8	28.9
10 to 14	7.8	4.0	6.3
15 to 19	2.3	0.0	1.3
20 to 24	0.0	1.2	1.3
25 to 29	0.0	0.6	0.0
Number of Subordinates Reporting to Respondent			
1 to 4	38.9	46.1	32.5
5 to 9	25.0	21.7	33.8
10 to 14	13.3	11.7	11.3
15 to 19	6.1	5.0	5.0
20 to 24	3.3	2.2	2.5
25 to 29	2.2	1.7	2.5
30 to 34	2.8	0.6	0.0
35 to 39	1.1	2.2	1.3
40 or more	7.2	8.9	11.3

(Appendix II contd...)

	Lower Management	Middle Management	Top Management
		Level	
Present Monthly Income (Rs)			
Honorary	0.0	0.0	2.5
1,500 or less	32.2	4.4	0.0
1,501 to 1,800	18.9	3.9	6.3
1,801 to 2,100	19.4	17.8	6.3
2,101 to 2,400	10.6	18.9	2.5
2,401 to 2,700	12.2	25.0	0.0
2,701 to 3,000	3.9	13.9	8.8
3,001 to 3,300	2.2	10.5	13.8
3,301 to 3,600	0.0	4.4	26.3
3,601 to 3,900	0.0	1.1	10.0
3,901 to 4,200	0.0	0.0	13.8
4,201 or more	0.6	0.0	10.0

Number of Times Respondent Promoted During His or Her Professional Career

2 or less	83.4	64.5	18.9
3 to 4	14.5	32.2	50.0
5 to 6	1.1	3.3	18.8
7 or more	1.2	0.0	2.5

Number of Other Organizations Respondent Worked for in Adult Career

None	50.0	41.7	27.5
1 to 2	37.3	42.2	52.6
3 to 4	10.0	12.8	17.5
5 to 6	2.8	2.8	1.3
7 or more	0.0	0.6	1.3

APPENDIX III

ICSSR Project on Getting One's Way

This project is supported by a grant from the Indian Council of Social Science Research, New Delhi. The fundamental aim of this study is to add to the scientific knowledge concerning the various influence styles being practised in the service as well as manufacturing organizations in India. Your *frank* and *sincere* replies will help us understand your organization and suggest some ways which might make it a better place wherein to work.

As with any professional social science research of this type, only general findings will be reported. Individual *anonymity* is completely guaranteed. No one other than the researchers will ever see any of your individual responses. **Do not write your name or sign anywhere on this booklet.**

You will find that it will not take long to complete the questionnaire. Thank you very much for your cooperation.

Project Director
MAHFOOZ A. ANSARI

Research Assistants
Reeta Kool
Rashmi Shukla

Department of Humanities and Social Sciences
Indian Institute of Technology
Kanpur

SECTION I

Your Subordinates

1 (BS–Behavioral Strategies).

Below are described various ways of obtaining information about how you go about changing the mind (or opinion) of your subordinates so that they agree with you. Please describe each statement on a 5-point scale given below, how *frequently* during the *past six months* you used it to influence your subordinates at work.

Very often	5
Often	4
Sometimes	3
Seldom	2
Never	1

Please select the number of your choice and write it on the small line to the left of each item. Answer each item in terms of *what you generally did, not what you would like to do.*

——— (01R) I convinced them by telling them the urgency and utility of the issue at hand.
——— (02S) I gave them an unsatisfactory performance evaluation.
——— (03C) I brought some friends along to back my request.
——— (04I) I asked them to do some task in a polite way.
——— (05S) I shouted at them in front of their co-workers.

202/Managing People at Work

—— (06P̃) I did personal favors for them.

—— (07I) I made them feel important.

—— (08A) I set a time deadline for them to do what I asked.

—— (09S) I gave them a satisfactory performance evaluation.

—— (10P) I repeatedly forced them to comply with my arguments as they were the need of the time.

—— (11U) I usually referred the matter to a higher authority if the situation so demanded.

—— (12S) I praised them verbally for their outstanding performance.

—— (13E) I promised to help them in getting further advancement if they helped me now.

—— (14S̃) I withheld their future advancements.

—— (15R) I told them the reasons why my plan was the best.

—— (16D) I showed that I was concerned about their welfare.

—— (17E) I offered an exchange of favor.

—— (18A) I repeatedly checked to see if my directions were followed.

—— (19T) I threatened to fire them if my request was not followed.

—— (20U) I obtained the informal support of higher-ups.

—— (21A) I demanded that they do what I requested.

—— (22U) I obtained my boss's approval before making the request.

—— (23T) I threatened to give them an unsatisfactory performance evaluation.

—— (24I) I praised them with superlatives.

—— (25Ẽ) At times I showed my knowledge of the specific issue.

—— (26U) I got the support of someone higher up to back my request.

—— (27S) I recommended (or gave) them extra benefits (e.g., overtime) for getting my work done.

—— (28D̲) I created the impression that I cannot really work without their help.

—— (29C) I got everyone else to agree with me before I made the request.

—— (30R) Sometimes I told them the reasons for making a request to them.

—— (31A) I repeatedly reminded them about what I wanted.

—— (32M) I gave them distorted information about the reasons to comply with me.

—— (33D) I showed that I sought their help.

—— (34P̃) I helped them even in personal matters.

—— (35Ẽ) I told them that I had a lot of experience with such matters.

—— (36S̃) I showed a feeling of dislike towards them.

—— (37C) I called a staff meeting to back my request.

—— (38T) I threatened to curtail further advancement.

—— (39Ẽ) I influenced them because of my competence.

—— (40E) I reminded them of some past favor that I did for them.

—— (41P) I got my way by convincing them that my way was the best way.

—— (42R) I argued my points logically.

—— (43D̲) I pretended that they had the responsibility to decide things for me.

—— (44S) I recommended (or offered) a salary increase.

—— (45Ẽ) My knowledge of the technical issues won their favor for me.

—— (46C) I obtained the support of co-workers to back my request.

—— (47D̲) I made them realize that I needed their help.

—— (48S̃) I challenged their ability (e.g., "I bet you can't do that.").

——— (49E) I asked them to cooperate to get the work done while promising extra benefits for it.

——— (50A) I simply ordered them to do what was asked.

——— (51I) I used words which made them feel good.

——— (52M) I kept a record of their mistakes.

——— (53P̂) I went out of my way to help them in the time of their need.

——— (54E) I offered some personal sacrifice in exchange (e.g., doing a part of his/her or another's job).

——— (55R) I told them exactly why I needed their help.

——— (56I) Even when I knew I would not use their advice, I consulted them.

——— (57P̂) I encouraged them to discuss even their personal problems.

——— (58D) I showed that I always supported them.

——— (59A) I pointed out that the rules required that they comply.

——— (60M) I usually got my way by making them feel that it was their idea.

2 (BP–Bases of Power).

What makes you influential? Please describe on a 5-point scale to what *extent* these statements are true regarding your subordinates.

To a very great extent	5
To a great extent	4
To some extent	3
To a small extent	2
Almost no extent	1

You change your subordinate (s)' mind because:

——— (1) You can administer sanctions and punishment to those who do not cooperate with you.

——— (2) You possess or have access to information that is valuable to others.

——— (3) You can give special help and benefits to those who cooperate with you.

——— (4) Your position in the organization provides you with the authority to direct their work activities.

——— (5) You have connections with influential and important persons.

——— (6) You have the knowledge required for the job.

——— (7) You are a likeable person.

SECTION II

Your Immediate Superior

1 (LB–Leader Behavior).

The following statements are about the behavior of *your immediate superior*.

Please read each of them carefully and decide whether it is true or false in his/her case. Select the number of your choice as given below and put it on the small line to the left of each item.

Quite true	5
True	4
Doubtful	3
False	2
Quite false	1

———— (01P) He/she maintains partnership in the group.

———— (02N) He/she helps his/her subordinates in their career planning.

———— (03F) He/she keeps crucial information to himself/herself.

———— (04N) He/she helps his/her subordinates to grow up and assume greater responsibility.

———— (05T) He/she explains to his/her subordinates what he/she expects from them and what they can expect from him/her.

———— (06P) He/she makes his/her subordinates feel free even to disagree with him/her.

———— (07B) He/she avoids taking decisions by forwarding the files above.

———— (08P) He/she provides all information to his/her subordinates and lets them jointly find the solution of a problem.

———— (09F) He/she behaves as if power and prestige are necessary for getting compliance from the subordinates.

———— (10N) He/she helps his/her subordinates even in family matters.

———— (11P) He/she interacts with his/her subordinates as if they are equal.

———— (12B) He/she maintains an impersonal relationship in the group.

———— (13P) He/she goes by the joint decisions of his/her group.

———— (14T) He/she takes special care that work gets top priority.

———— (15P) He/she treats all group members as his/her equal.

———— (16B) He/she believes that most of the interpersonal troubles start because people try to be over-friendly and informal on the job.

———— (17T) He/she maintains a high standard of performance.

———— (18N) He/she believes that subordinates acquire a sense of responsibility under the care and guidance of a good leader.

———— (19B) He/she thinks that clear job descriptions are necessary for the effective functioning of the employee.

———— (20T) He/she expects his/her subordinates to increase their knowledge on the job.

———— (21F) He/she does not think that his/her subordinates deserve to be officers.

———— (22N) He/she openly shows affection to those subordinates who work hard.

———— (23F) He/she thinks that he/she is always right.

———— (24N) He/she gives as much responsibility as his/her subordinates can handle.

———— (25T) He/she believes that one can really grow up by learning to do a job well.

———— (26B) He/she considers seniority as a time-tested criterion for promotion.

——— (27T) He/she sees to it that subordinates work to their capacity.

——— (28B) He/she always follows standard rules and regulations.

——— (29P) He/she grants full freedom and autonomy to his/her subordinates so that they can work best.

——— (30F) He/she rules with an iron hand in order to get the work done.

——— (31F) He/she wants to have full power and control over his/her subordinates.

——— (32P) He/she encourages free and frank interaction among members.

——— (33P) He/she believes that all of us have more or less equal potentialities.

——— (34T) He/she drives himself really hard.

——— (35F) He/she easily categorizes his/her subordinates as good and bad.

——— (36N) If the subordinates need help, he/she helps as much as he/she can.

——— (37T) As and when necessary, he/she gives specific directions to his/her subordinates.

——— (38B) He/she favors that the area of responsibility should be clearly demarcated according to ranks and positions.

——— (39T) He/she always keeps track of the progress of work.

——— (40B) He/she confines himself/herself to his/her own jurisdiction.

——— (41T) He/she tells his/her subordinates how well are they doing their job.

——— (42N) He/she feels responsible for the well-being of his/her subordinates.

——— (43F) He/she makes it clear that personal loyalty is an important virtue.

——— (44P) He/she is a friendly type.

——— (45B) He/she always goes by the rules and procedures.

——— (46B) He/she maintains a strict division of labor even in his/her own group.

——— (47N) He/she finds time to listen to the personal problems of the subordinates.

——— (48F) He/she does not tolerate any interference from his/her subordinates.

——— (49N) He/she has affection for his/her subordinates.

——— (50F) He/she believes that if he/she does not watch out, there are many people who may pull him/her down.

2 (BS–Behavior Strategies).

Below are described various ways of obtaining information about how you go about changing your immediate superior's mind (or opinion) so that he/she agrees with you. Please describe each statement on a 5-point scale given below, how *frequently* during the *past six months* you used it to influence your immediate superior at work.

Very often	5
Often	4
Sometimes	3
Seldom	2
Never	1

Please select the number of your choice and write it on the small line to the left of each item. Answer each item in terms of *what you generally did, not what you would like to do*.

———— (01R) At times I explained the reasons for my request.

———— (02U) I appealed formally to higher levels to back my request.

———— (03B) At times I withheld some crucial information from him/her.

———— (04P̃) I helped him/her even in personal matters.

———— (05E) I offered an exchange of favor (e.g., 'If you do this for me, I will do something for you.').

———— (06I) I praised him/her with superlatives.

———— (07D̲) I showed that I was dependent on him/her only.

———— (08R) I used logic to convince him/her.

———— (09P) I got my way by convincing him/her that my way was the best way.

———— (10D̲) I pretended that he/she has the responsibility to decide things for me.

———— (11C) I obtained the support of my subordinates to back my request.

———— (12Ŭ) I showed a feeling of dislike towards him/her.

———— (13R) I provided sufficient information in support of my view.

———— (14P̃) I helped him/her and went out of my way when he/she was in need of help.

———— (15B) I engaged in a work slow-down until he/she did what I wanted.

———— (16C) I brought some friends along to back my request.

———— (17R) I told him/her the reasons why my plan was the best.

———— (18Ŭ) I voiced my wishes loudly.

———— (19Ė) I influenced him/her because of my competence.

———— (20M) I usually got my way by making him/her feel that it was his/her idea.

———— (21R) I convinced him/her by explaining the importance of the issue.

———— (22D̃) At times I differed from him/her.

———— (23P) At times I tried to persuade him/her that my way was the best way.

———— (24U) I got the support of someone higher up to back my request.

———— (25I) I made him/her feel important.

———— (26P) I repeatedly persuaded him/her to comply with my arguments as they were the need of the time.

———— (27E) I offered to help if he/she would do what I wanted.

———— (28D) I showed that I always supported him/her.

———— (29D̃) I opposed him/her openly, if it was necessary.

———— (30Ė) At times I showed my knowledge of the specific issue.

———— (31I) I acted very humbly to him/her while requesting my point.

———— (32D̃) If necessary, I put a note of dissent on his/her proposal.

———— (33Ŭ) I paid friendly visits to him/her.

———— (34C) I obtained the support of co-workers to back my request.

———— (35D) I made a show that I had respect for him/her.

———— (36B) I acted unfriendly or did not cooperate with him/her.

———— (37D) I pretended that I cared for him/her.

———— (38Ė) I told him/her that I had a lot of experience with such matters.

———— (39I) I used words which made him/her feel good.

———— (40U) I usually referred the matter to a higher authority if the situation so demanded.

———— (41D̃) Sometimes I fought with him/her.

———— (42B) I stopped the work in-between if my demands were not met.

———— (43E) I reminded him/her how hard I had worked and that it would only be fair for him/her to help me now.

——— (44M) I distorted or lied about the reasons why he/she should do what I wanted.
——— (45<u>D</u>) I made him/her understand my need for his/her help.
——— (46C) I got everyone else (my colleagues) to agree with me before I made the request.
——— (47D) I showed that I sought his/her help.
——— (48E) I offered to work harder in the future.
——— (49M) I presented my ideas in a disguised way.
——— (50Ė) My expertise of the technical issues won his/her favor for me.
——— (51C) I called a staff meeting to back my request.
——— (52D̄) I challenged his/her ability.
——— (53M) I kept track of his/her omissions and commissions.
——— (54P̄) I did personal favors for him/her.
——— (55E) I offered some personal sacrifice in exchange (e.g., doing part of his/her/and another's job).

3 (BP–Bases of Power).

What makes you influential? Please describe on a 5-point scale to what *extent* these statements are true regarding your immediate superior.

To a very great extent	5
To a great extent	4
To some extent	3
To a small extent	2
Almost no extent	1

You change your immediate superior's mind because:

——— (1) You have the knowledge required for the job.
——— (2) You are a likeable person.
——— (3) You have connections with influential and important persons.
——— (4) You possess or have access to information that is valuable to others.
——— (5) You can make things difficult for those who do not cooperate with you.
——— (6) You are available to your immediate superior.
——— (7) You have your own personal authority.

SECTION III

Your Organization

1 (OC–Organizational Climate).

The following set of statements are concerned with your perceptions and observations about the organization in which you are now working. Please read each of them carefully and judge to what *extent* each item is true of your organization and put the number of your choice on the small line to the left of the statement.

To a very great extent	5
To a great extent	4
To some extent	3
To a small extent	2
Almost no extent	1

_____ (01) The assignments to this organization are clearly defined.
_____ (02) In this organization, we set very high standards for performance.
_____ (03) We don't rely too heavily on individual judgment; almost everything is double-checked.
_____ (04) If you make a mistake in this organization, you will definitely be criticized.
_____ (05) People are proud of belonging to this organization.
_____ (06) The policies and goals of this organization are clearly understood.
_____ (07) The goals I am supposed to achieve in my area are realistic.
_____ (08) There is a feeling of pressure to continually improve our personal and group performance.
_____ (09) Our philosophy emphasizes that people should solve problems by themselves.
_____ (10) There is not enough reward and recognition given in this organization for doing good work.
_____ (11) People in this organization don't really trust each other very much.
_____ (12) Things often seem to be pretty disorganized around here.
_____ (13) In this organization, I am given a chance to participate in setting the performance standards for my job.
_____ (14) In this organization, people don't seem to take much pride in the excellence of their performance.
_____ (15) Management frowns upon your checking everything with them; if you think you've got the right approach, you just go ahead.
_____ (16) We have a promotion system that helps the best person rise to the top.
_____ (17) People in this organization tend to be cool and aloof toward each other.
_____ (18) Our productivity sometimes suffers from lack of organization and planning.
_____ (19) I very seldom sit down with my manager to review my overall performance and effectiveness.
_____ (20) Management sets challenging goals.
_____ (21) In this organization, people are rewarded in proportion to the excellence of their job performance.
_____ (22) In this organization, performance is evaluated regularly against agreed-upon goals and standards.
_____ (23) The standards in this organization do not usually demand the maximum effort of every individual.

——— (24) There is not much encouragement to take on increased responsibility in this organization.

——— (25) The rewards and encouragements that you get usually outweigh the threats and criticism.

——— (26) There is a lot of warmth in the relationships between management and other personnel in this organization.

——— (27) I have had very little opportunity to say what I think about the goals and standards that are set for my work.

——— (28) In this organization, people are encouraged to initiate projects that they think are important.

——— (29) Good performance is recognized fairly quickly in this organization.

——— (30) I have a clear idea of what I am supposed to do in my job.

SECTION IV

Yourself

1 (LS–Leadership Style).

The following statements describe various things people do or try to do (or think) on their job. Please read each of them carefully and decide whether it is true or false in *your* case. Select the number of your choice as given below and put it on the small line to the left of each item.

Quite true	5
True	4
Doubtful	3
False	2
Quite false	1

——— (01T) I take special care that work gets top priority.

——— (02F) I do not tolerate any interference from my subordinates.

——— (03N) I go out of my way to help my subordinates.

——— (04B) I believe in strict division of labor even in a work group.

——— (05T) I expect my subordinates to increase their knowledge on the job.

——— (06T) I drive myself really hard.

——— (07N) I feel responsible for the well-being of my subordinates.

——— (08N) I spare time to listen to the personal problems of my subordinates.

——— (09F) I do not tolerate any loose talk from my subordinates.

——— (10F) I think that these days power and prestige are necessary so that subordinates will listen to me.

——— (11N) I help my subordinates in their career planning.

——— (12F) I can easily categorize my subordinates as good and bad.

——— (13T) I always keep track of the progress of work.

——— (14P) I create a climate where members respect each other's individuality.

———— (15B) If clear job descriptions are available, there will be less conflicts in an organization.

———— (16N) I try to help my subordinates even in family matters.

———— (17P) I am a friendly type.

———— (18T) I believe that one can really grow up by learning to do a job well.

———— (19F) I believe that personal loyalty is an important virtue.

———— (20P) I place high value in maintaining partnership in the group.

———— (21B) I believe that persons at the top are in the best position to make major decisions.

———— (22N) I give responsibilities to my subordinates only when they can handle them.

———— (23N) I do not discuss with my subordinates their personal problems.

———— (24F) I think that not all employees have the potential for being officers.

———— (25P) I treat all group members as my equal.

———— (26B) I do not like too much paper work at my job.

———— (27P) I believe that all of us have more or less equal potential.

———— (28P) I grant full freedom and autonomy to subordinates so that they can work best.

———— (29T) As and when necessary, I give specific directions to my subordinates.

———— (30F) A wise executive should keep crucial information to himself/herself.

———— (31B) I try to confine myself to my own jurisdiction.

———— (32F) I take decisions quickly and I am confident of being right.

———— (33P) I make my subordinates feel free even to disagree with me.

———— (34N) I openly favor those subordinates who work hard.

———— (35F) If I am not careful, there are people around who may pull me down.

———— (36T) I see that subordinates work to their capacity.

———— (37P) I go by the joint decisions of my group.

———— (38B) I believe that the area of responsibility should be clearly demarcated according to rank and position.

———— (39P) I provide all information to my subordinates and let them jointly find the solution to a problem.

———— (40B) I always follow standard rules and regulations.

———— (41N) I help my subordinates grow up and assume greater responsibility.

———— (42B) I maintain an impersonal relationship in the group.

———— (43T) I report against subordinates who are not doing their job well.

———— (44T) I explain to my subordinates what I expect from them and what they can expect from me.

———— (45B) I do not consider seniority as the best criterion for promotion.

2 (PD–Personal Data).

(1) Your age (please fill in): ———— years.

(2) Your education (degree, diploma, etc.): ————.

(3) Your job title or designation in this organization (optional): ————.

(4) Designation of your immediate superior: ————.

(5) How many years have you been with your present organization? ————

(6) How many years have you been working in your present position? ————

(7) How does your present job fit into your organization's structure? (check one)
——— (1) Top management.
——— (2) Middle management.
——— (3) Lower management.
——— (4) Others (please specify) ———.

(8) How many persons directly report to you? (no. of your immediate subordinates): ———.

(9) What is your earned monthly income (including salary, allowances, etc.)? (check one).
——— (1) Under Rs 1,500.
——— (2) Between Rs 1,501 and Rs 1,800.
——— (3) Between Rs 1,801 and Rs 2,100.
——— (4) Between Rs 2,101 and Rs 2,400.
——— (5) Between Rs 2,401 and Rs 2,700.
——— (6) Between Rs 2,701 and Rs 3,000.
——— (7) Between Rs 3,001 and Rs 3,300.
——— (8) Between Rs 3,301 and Rs 3,600.
——— (9) Between Rs 3,601 and Rs 3,900.
——— (10) Between Rs 3,901 and Rs 4,200.
——— (11) Over Rs 4,200.

(10) How many promotions have you received (since your first job)? ———.

(11) How many other organizations have you worked for in your adult career? ———.

Thank you once again for helping us making this a meaningful study.

APPENDIX IV

Interrelationships Among Bases of Power, Leadership Styles, Leadership Behavior and Organizational Climate

Variables	1	2	3	4	5	6	7	8	9	10	11	12	13	14	15	16	17	18	19	20	21	22	23	24	25
Downward Bases of Power																									
1. Coercion	X																								
2. Information	26	X																							
3. Reward	29	35	X																						
4. Legitimate	33	12	24	X																					
5. Connection	28	30	26	24	X																				
6. Expert	7	7	11	28	12	X																			
7. Referent	8	17	16	17	16	38	X																		
Upward Bases of Power																									
8. Expert	5	13	3	13	6	40	27	X																	
9. Referent	10	10	5	5	15	22	52	37	X																
10. Connection	18	23	14	1	61	3	8	8	22	X															
11. Information	27	51	23	9	40	13	20	16	22	47	X														
12. Coercion	26	18	17	6	29	4	1	4	8	39	34	X													
13. Reward	11	14	13	10	21	25	22	27	25	11	14	4	X												
14. Legitimate	5	13	7	13	25	5	12	16	17	22	22	27	26	X											
Leadership Style																									
15. Participative	-2	10	8	3	6	13	17	7	15	0	12	-5	23	2	X										
16. Task-oriented	12	9	8	15	11	25	19	26	21	0	10	-7	29	2	35	X									
17. Bureaucrat	17	13	9	10	20	10	5	14	14	13	11	16	26	4	10	49	X								
18. Authoritarian	21	18	16	14	17	7	7	15	10	16	17	24	17	8	-1	37	68	X							

(contd ...)

Variables	1	2	3	4	5	6	7	8	9	10	11	12	13	14	15	16	17	18	19	20	21	22	23	24	25
Leadership Behavior																									
19. Nurturant-task	24	7	14	20	11	7	2	0	7	4	8	1	16	6	14	18	19	1	X						
20. Participative	23	8	10	17	8	9	1	0	8	0	10	-1	15	2	14	6	20	16	85	X					
21. Bureaucrat	13	3	2	17	9	12	9	3	11	10	11	6	17	-2	13	5	24	30	46	36	X				
22. Authoritarian	10	3	13	6	8	7	17	12	18	11	16	23	9	8	0	6	17	38	-23	-37	11	X			
Organizational Climate																									
23. Reward and participation	15	14	9	20	25	-2	7	-4	10	17	16	8	6	14	3	1	-3	-10	29	21	19	-9	X		
24. Structure	10	4	10	29	9	15	8	11	9	1	-1	0	17	12	1	26	2	6	29	18	24	-3	47	X	
25. Warmth and support	-8	-10	0	6	9	5	-10	-9	-9	-21	-25	-13	-1	-6	-5	9	-6	-13	19	18	11	-24	11	28	X

Note: *Decimal points are omitted.*

$r(438) = 0.10$ at $p < 0.05$; $r(438) = 0.13$ at $p < 0.01$.

Index